The

Evolving

Human

ൠ

A TRUE STORY OF AWAKENED
KUNDALINI

PENNY KELLY

Other Books by Penny Kelly...

The Elves of Lily Hill Farm

Robes - A Book of Coming Changes

Getting Well Again, Naturally

Consciousness and Energy, Vol 1 - Multidimensionality and a Theory of Consciousness

Consciousness and Energy, Vol. 2 - New Worlds of Energy

Consciousness and Energy, Vol. 3 - History and Consciousness

THE EVOLVING HUMAN

A TRUE STORY OF AWAKENED KUNDALINI
BY
PENNY KELLY

Published by:
Lily Hill Publishing
32260 - 88th Avenue
Lawton, MI 49065
www.pennykelly.com

ISBN 978-0-9632934-7-3

Previously published in 1992 under the title:
The Evolving Human, subtitled *And The Development of The Body/Mind System;*
and from 1984-1991 under the titles:
Developing The Body/Mind System
and
Original Mind

Dedicated...

...to my very first students -
Donna, Esther, Cori,
Doug and Barb G.
Barb M.
Diane, Debra,
Helen, Sylvia, and Jack,
who taught me that
I *could* be what I never planned to be,
and
to the little men in brown robes,
who first insisted that I came here
to write and teach.

In Acknowledgment...

Many thanks belong to all those who
read and re-read this manuscript
throughout its many incarnations.
Grateful thanks go to:
Chuck Reinert, for his frequent reading
and unfaltering support...
Don Schuster and Dr. Guerin Montilus
for both reading and suggestions...
Norma Shifrin and Ron Aronson for
teaching me to get organized and stick to
my subject.
Very special thanks are due to my
daughter Penelope Wood for typing and
re-typing and re-typing...
to my daughter Kelly Wood for
proofreading again and again...
and especially to Jim Jenzen for his
patience, his belief, and the sense of
humor in his occasional question,
"Is it a book yet?"

Table of Contents

Preface
20th Anniversary Edition

ଔ

ALTHOUGH IT SEEMS LIKE YESTERDAY, NEARLY **38** YEARS HAVE PASSED since the first awakening of kundalini and the all-consuming struggle to figure out not only what happened to me, but how to manage the changes. Although it took seventeen years of serious work to integrate it into my life, I cannot imagine life without it and I'm entirely grateful for the gift it was and continues to be.

There are lots of people who have never heard the word *kundalini* and have no idea that such a thing can happen. When they hear it for the first time, many ask, "What is it?"

When I say, "It's the awakening of consciousness," they look puzzled. They think they are already conscious. They have no idea what a fully awakened consciousness is or what it can do. To help them grasp the bare minimum of what I'm talking about, I have begun saying, "Kundalini is an old Eastern term for the awakening of unlimited consciousness." With this, they pause, trying to take in what that might mean. However, until you have experienced it, you cannot even begin to imagine the raw power, the roar, the shaking, the Void, the *I Am*, or the orgasmic bliss of an awakening. Nor can you get your mind around the experience of an unlimited consciousness!

Lots of people assume that an awakened consciousness will just add a little power to their reason and logic, but it doesn't work that way.

Reason and logic are useless in the face of Truth, and the loss of these two mental anchors is confusing and very frightening. You eventually come back around to integrate them in a new way once many life-changing adjustments are in place, but never again will you string moments of reality together in the way you used to. Why limit yourself to sequential logic and reason when you can have access to all of creation and the multi-dimensional reality that exists all around us?

In many of my talks and interviews, I have tried to create a small realization, one that plants the awareness that we are like an acorn waiting for the right conditions to unfold into a great oak tree. We have a blueprint inside for unfolding our consciousness. Sadly, almost no one understands this and our culture does not support the unfolding. If it happens spontaneously, as it did for me, you are on your own to sink or swim.

A full kundalini awakening doesn't just dip you into a wider reality, it is a wholesale dive into unlimited, multi-dimensional consciousness and the nature of reality. Once in that river, you must swim for your life with everything you've got. Those who drown don't die, they end up in institutions labeled with schizophrenia, bi-polar disorder, or psychosis. No one ever teaches them how to reorganize the reality system they grew up in. The people who maintain such institutions know nothing about unlimited consciousness, or what you will find and experience there.

It was difficult to review this first book of mine. There were so many places I could have added information and explanations. I did break many of the longer chapters into two and I completely re-organized Chapters 14 and 15, breaking them into five separate chapters. I then re-wrote my original explanation of the stages we go through because they were too confusing and hard to follow in the original edition.

However, other than these organizational changes and the rewrite of chapters 14 and 15, I made very minor changes. I wanted the book to stand as it was for me back than...an unexpected journey, a beginner's struggle, the hundreds of uncertainties, the fear of insanity, the inability to manage perception, the beginner's shock at hearing voices and seeing lights, the intrusion of strange beings or great heat through the body, the inability to sleep or to read, and the constant *knowing*...knowing that just kept expanding and deepening with no regard as to whether I was ready and willing to deal with such knowledge. The knowing did not care whether I was able to organize the ongoing avalanche of knowledge into something useful or helpful. It didn't care how disruptive it was to my worldview, my life, my habits, or my comfort zone.

We humans have devolved down to our current level and are now beginning to round the corner to return to higher frequencies of consciousness. Stories of 'the gods' are not myths or fanciful imaginings. The gods were human beings who unfolded their consciousness and reached the full potential that is built into the human energy system. I have been in those higher states of consciousness and can state unequivocally that the power available to us is extraordinary. In today's lingo, it is mind-blowing. Re-entry into more expansive states of consciousness will end the world as we know it and introduce new ways of being, new rules, traditions, cultures, and kinds of civilization. The only parts of our current world that will remain are Mother Earth and all of Nature, and even these will be beautifully transformed as we relearn how to communicate with all things.

The Earth is our Mother as well as the setting for our reality system. The objects that appear here, from cats, cups, and beer, to cars, boats, birds, or computers are all part of the language of energy. Each object is an example of a particular use of energy. We will use this language to create as we evolve to greater consciousness and power. The language of energy learned here in Earth's reality system is unique and beautiful and is recognized across the cosmos as a particularly diverse and expressive language. Since all communication is telepathic at the higher frequencies of consciousness, the many and subtle shades of meaning that accompany the objects, sounds, and actions communicated using this language make for excellent and rich exchanges that foster deep understanding.

Abundance is not having a lot of money and physical stuff, it is a state of consciousness in which you have the ability to produce whatever is needed. In the higher states of consciousness this is the ability to manipulate fields of light and frequency to create matter at many levels of density, including physical. When abundance has been mastered, we will not need the carbon, copper, lead, oxygen, uranium, or other elements of the periodic table to make stuff. We will simply maneuver frequency fields into position to create whatever is needed. Eventually, we will let go of the need for a physical planet and will transition to being comfortable in much more fluid states of being. We will become space-based instead of land-based creatures, changing drastically as we do.

We will develop the ability to maneuver and manipulate the fields of the body, renewing ourselves endlessly and living to great age, moving to the next level whenever we are ready. Our current lack of responsibility toward the human body will end and we will embrace the steady process of turning the body into light, which is what enlightenment really is.

In the end, we will move onward and upward into reality systems that operate very differently. As we do, we will begin to understand that *Life* is a system that must keep itself going and that it does so via the 'reality system,' which is an incubator of various forms of life. Some forms die out, but others survive long enough to figure out the system of life and the nature of reality and begin to work with these, evolving to become creators of great power and wisdom. It is a process that evolves over millions of years. And for the forms of life within each reality system, there is always a turning point...a moment of awakening. First one awakens, then another...and another...and eventually the awakened ones begin to turn the tide for others. Eventually, the entire group realizes they are moving on and they 'put the house in order,' restoring, repairing, and renewing their home planet in order to leave it ready for the next group.

This book is about the turning point for just one individual, but it was always my hope that it be a guide for those who seek to know the truth about our path and our potential as human beings. Those of us who have already awakened recognize the clear signs and symptoms of others who are in the process of their own awakening. Thirty-eight years ago, it seemed like I was all alone in this process. Now there are lots of others. We are on our way. ∞

Penny Kelly
February 2, 2017

Original Preface
ೞ

THIS BOOK IS AN ATTEMPT TO DOCUMENT A JOURNEY THAT BEGAN IN February of 1979 when I experienced what is known as a 'full, spontaneous awakening of kundalini.'

If you have heard the term *kundalini* before, you may be curious about what it involves. If you have done some reading about it, you may have a whole set of ideas built around what you think it is and what it means.

If you've never heard the term before, what you read in these pages may shock or surprise you. It might even illuminate you a little bit. The thing to remember is that kundalini is vital to the full development of human potential.

The 'awakening' as it is called, refers to a great and sudden increase in the energy, activities, and capacities of consciousness. Back in 1979 I had never heard of kundalini or anything remotely like it, and was unaware of the possibility that a human being could have such a thunderous, life-transforming experience.

I was also ignorant of the after-effects that commonly followed such an awakening. After the initial experiences occurred, I struggled for years – first to figure out exactly what had happened to me, later to understand why it happened, still later to figure out what it all meant. It took me seventeen years to integrate and accept kundalini.

Kundalini is often spoken of as a spiritual phenomenon that brings high spiritual development. This is true, but such a description is extremely misleading because it leaves out a great deal of information. The complete and spontaneous awakening of kundalini can be a very frightening, physical, highly sexual experience that is followed only much, much later by something we might call the emergence of true spirituality.

This spirituality blossoms only *after* one has dealt with the physical pains, the possibility of bursting into flame and self-incinerating, the fears of insanity, the avalanche of psychic abilities, the raging sexual passions, and the slow disintegration of the singular reality that, once upon a time, was the only reality.

At first I thought I must be the only one in the whole world to have experienced such strange and frightening phenomena. Later I began to wonder if there were others and thus, one of my original reasons for writing this book was to find out if such a thing had ever happened to anyone else.

By writing the book, I hoped they might discover it, read it, and writes to me so we could share the difficulties and support one another. I also wrote this book partly because, in the beginning, I could find very little specific information for myself about the processes of this awakening. As my understanding grew, I wanted very much to help anyone else who might be experiencing kundalini. If my experiences could provide an explanation of what the signs and symptoms of a full awakening were, it might save others from much grief and terror, others who, like me, knew nothing about the evolutionary processes that were designed and built-in to the human being.

For these reasons the book has been written with as much personal detail as I could be comfortable sharing. Over my years of teaching and counseling for many people who wanted to develop intuition or were already struggling to manage the effects of kundalini, I have found that detailing my own experiences has been both helpful and reassuring to them.

In addition, sharing the personal circumstances that surround common pitfalls, which are amazingly similar in many cases, helps people to recognize where they are at in their own evolutionary processes and perhaps choose more wisely than I did.

Probably the biggest difficulty for me was the internal split in my own self that left me constantly struggling against what was happening to me. I just wanted everything to return to normal. The result was that for seventeen years I cycled from denial, to embarrassment, to waiting for everything to go back to ordinary reality, to mediocre acceptance, to curiosity, to experimentation, then back to embarrassment and denial.

The result of trying to ignore what was happening to me was that I was very slow and reluctant to seek out those who might have offered help or insight. Nor did I do the mental or emotional work that might have made things move faster or seem easier. The sense of being alone and lost was complicated by the fact that at the time of my awakening (1979) there were not nearly as many people, books, resources or open minds in the culture to whom I could turn for advice, support, or explanation.

In addition, my two best friends, one woman and one man, were psychologists and my carefully worded discussions with each led to their consistent statements that neither of them had ever experienced a single moment, spiritual or otherwise, similar to what I was trying to describe. Instead they were full of labels and diagnoses that 'explained away' my predicament and warned me about 'that kind of thinking,' so of course I did not tell them to what extent I was experiencing the frightening phenomena.

The good side of going through this experience on my own was that I did not have any ready-made answers and was forced to come up with my own. I had no concept of the possibilities, or even the limitations, inherent in the various phenomena, and was left to my own devices when it came to figuring out what was going on, and why, and what to do about it.

During this time, one part of me was cautiously curious while another was occasionally adventurous, frequently surprising myself with what I could do. After the initial panic of the early stages, I did settle into regular experimentation, often just to see what would happen, never really thinking of the results as spiritual discoveries or events. To my mind I was exploring as scientifically as the subject matter would allow.

Through the later stages I read, wrote, and taught but was seldom comfortable with what I considered to be my own outlandish psychic abilities. When students or circumstances pushed me to expose some of the extraordinary experimenting I had done in other realms, I shared, but always ended up high-tailing it back to my comfort zone where the ordinary woman in me just baked her bread, cleaned her house, and worked in her garden.

At this point it would perhaps be helpful to know that I was raised in a very ordinary middle-class household in a small town about 35 miles north of Detroit, Michigan. There were six children in our family; my mother was a housewife, my father worked for Consumers' Power Co.

I attended public school through the 3rd grade, after which my parents put me in the local Catholic school. I watched cartoons on Saturday mornings, ate Cheerios and Rice Krispies for breakfast and peanutbutter sandwiches for lunch. I read Nancy Drew mysteries, fought with my sisters and brothers, got mostly straight A's on my report card, went to Saturday night dances when I became a teen, and cried over various boys with my girlfriends.

I graduated from high school in June of 1966 and, already two months pregnant, got married the very next month, skipping any involvement in the counter-culture of the sixties that might have opened my mind a little bit. Indeed, my husband went on to become a Detroit cop, and the marriage produced four beautiful children but only lasted nine years until 1975 when we divorced. Up until that time my whole world was the world of the conventional, even the over-conventional, and I was quite comfortable there.

For several years after the divorce I was a welfare mother living in the city, struggling to get an education and take care of my children so that I could support myself and them. This was a very difficult period until, finally, I was ecstatic to get a career position with one of the Big Three car makers in March of 1978. I felt I was finally on my way to success and rebuilding my life. Little did I know that what I had gone through so far would eventually pale in comparison to what was waiting for me only a few months down the road.

The journey begins as I am working at Chrysler Corporation, a tool and process engineer, a career chosen strictly for the money, the possibility of advancement based on the fact that I was a woman, and the fact that I had four children to support.

After starting at Chrysler in the spring, it was only a few months later that I met and fell in love with one of the toolmakers at the plant. By autumn we were planning to be married and in December we bought our dream house on a small canal off Anchor Bay, just north of Mt. Clemens, Michigan, where we lived together. We had been in the house only two months when the first awakening of kundalini occurred.

Over the early chapters of the book it is clear that I am unnerved by the odd events that begin and then escalate. Like a lock of hair that keeps falling over your eyes and momentarily, even dangerously, obscures your vision, I brush these odd events away as if they are irritating distractions.

Nevertheless, they continue, and throughout the next few months I experience odd perceptual episodes that keep increasing in their ability to disturb me, that are longer in duration, less controllable, and less explainable in terms of the logical, linear, left-brain processing that we all take for granted. Gradually, it becomes more apparent that I am losing control of my perception and am struggling for my sanity. I am no longer able to just brush the events away and go back to what I was doing the moment before the illogical experience occurred.

With no background information and no prior knowledge that could have helped me form a reference point around which to organize and measure my experiences, I remained isolated and completely in the dark as far as what was happening to me. I had no concept or framework into which such experiences could be placed, and no idea that they could be understood, organized, or explained and worked with, so initially I didn't even try these approaches. My life was completely unraveling and I limped along at all levels, suffering terribly.

The next few chapters lead to a mental and emotional crisis, and then slowly to the beginning of some very tentative, shaky, yet deliberate explorations into the nature and possibilities of reality. This marks a turning point following which all of my ideas and concepts of what is possible with the mind, consciousness, and perception begin to expand.

Eventually, there comes a point when I am able to give a name to what I have experienced, but naming does not necessarily bring understanding or control. However, discovering that what I had experienced was an already recognized and documented phenomenon marked the beginning of a new phase in which I worked toward understanding what had happened, and was continuing to happen, in my physical body as well as with my mind.

The results of kundalini are often devastating to the way you have set up the structures and routines of your everyday life. This is especially true for careers, relationships, and finances, as well as priorities, values, ethics, and morals. Paths chosen for superficial or selfish reasons collapse and disappear, leaving you in apparent ruin, yet really clearing the way for you to do what you came here to do in the first place.

As the story unfolds, it covers my ongoing search for an in-depth explanation that would satisfy the scientific side of me, even as this side was more and more dwarfed by my growing ability to use non-linear methods to explore and explain reality.

Later chapters cover the climax of the search for a scientific explanation and the understanding of exactly what a kundalini experience is and how it occurs. I then go more deeply into what might be called a re-shuffling of my perspective in many areas involving changes in perception that occur naturally.

I cover my search for historical figures that might have experienced kundalini, and share the shift of my entire view of the basic institutions of religion, history, and even the physical universe.

The more I dug into the question of how our reality is created and sustained, the more I began to understand how physical reality emerges from the apparent nothingness that surrounds us and how material life is maintained by the activity of *thought*.

From this point, I begin the search for an answer to the question, "Why does kundalini happen at all? What's the point?"In the chapters that follow, I finally grasp that the point is that we humans are designed to pass through successive stages of development that move us forward into our full potential. From our entry into physical reality at birth, all the way to and through the death experience, we are meant to undergo a continuous evolution of our consciousness. Although we often get stuck along the way and fail to develop fully, consciousness is meant to evolve and change our very being and potential within reality – a potential that is seldom understood let alone reached and put into practice wisely.

As the book closes, I touch on my experiences within parallel realities, which I was told later by Maharishi Mahesh Yogi, were all about burning future karma. I also share the last dregs of the confusion and exhaustion of the ongoing processes of integrating kundalini within myself, processes I had been fighting for a long time. Finally, there is understanding and acceptance when an unexpected message brings peace.

At the back of the book are several appendices, one that lays out basic steps you can take to move your own evolution forward, and another that shows how to dissect and understand dream realities. There are two short sections that show the results of experiments with telepathy, and a chart that condenses the stages of human development set forth earlier. Finally, there is a glossary of old terms along with a few new ones that might be helpful in understanding how the languaging has changed over time in an attempt to communicate basic concepts about spirituality, consciousness, human development, and the dimensions beyond and yet interwoven with the physical.

ଔ

This book has been written and re-written again and again over the last several decades. At times, it has been a collection of personal stories, at times a textbook with important terms printed in boldface and italic followed by careful definitions and meant for use in the courses I teach.

At other times it has been a treatise on brain, mind, and consciousness that I thought might be useful to psychologists or psychiatrists. And at still other times, a mixture of all of the above in varying proportions with a few scientific odds and ends thrown in that I thought might help those who were interested in the more technical aspects of brain wave theory.

In earlier versions, I tried to keep myself as much to the background as possible. I believed that if people could just read and understand the experiences as they occurred, it would be easier for them to identify these kinds of experiences in their own life. It turned out that people needed to know that these things happened to a real flesh-and-blood person. I ended up putting myself back into the story, which made it easier to grasp because it wasn't just a collection of facts that seemed impossible to relate to.

The book as it is now eventually came down to simply getting tired of explaining my own story over and over to new groups of students, trying to satisfy their curiosity about what I had experienced and how I got to be the way I am. It seemed easier to just write it all down and let them read it outside of class, leaving me free to focus on them and their development during class time.

Over the years it has been my observation and experience that almost everyone has had at least a few of these types of experiences. Even if their own development is stalled somewhere along the line, sometimes just reading and recognizing the processes of ongoing human evolution and the development of consciousness can trigger a rekindling of movement toward one's more evolved self.

One of the criticisms of this book has been that it contains a fairly stark sequence of events written exactly as I experienced them and without any clues or hints as to what was going on. This has been intentional. One of my goals in writing it down this way has been to share the actual occurrences of my own kundalini awakening at the most intense level possible, carrying the reader along through the experiences in the same way I had them. I have wanted the reader to have to ask himself, "Now what was *that* about? Why did that happen?" or "What did that mean?" and then chew on those questions in the same way that I did, without any quick and easy answers. Like a mystery that was finally solved, eventually everything becomes clear and the answers appear. Instant gratification is not part and parcel of spiritual development and thus the reader is left to come up with his or her own answers, or wait until my own explanations appear as my understanding increases.

Wherever you are in your grasp of this subject, this book was written to increase your understanding of how you as a human being have been designed to evolve in terms of consciousness, perception, intelligence, behavior, and the purpose or meaning of your life (spirituality). Kundalini can be coaxed into a slow awakening, and as it becomes more active, your personal evolution moves forward in the way it was meant to. When it does, you unfold from a seemingly whole new core self that has deeply altered both the way you view reality, and the way you experience and participate in it.

When you do not understand how or why something could be possible, then you will discount it, the truth remains hidden, and you will remain subject to fears and manipulation, anger and insecurity.

I have hoped to demystify some of the areas surrounding the psyche, psychic experiences and abilities, intuition, and the occult, which basically means 'that which is hidden,' bringing it into the bright sunshine of ordinary, everyday living.

The path of human development is a long, personal trek into the center of your own spirit, which turns out to be the center of the universe, which turns out to be filled with peace, joy, and love. It is possible to live in that world if you are willing to make the journey. The path may be difficult, at times even dangerous, but it is more than worth the effort.

Penny L. Kelly
Nov. 11, 1997

1 ∽
The Awakening

*"You didn't think
when you got up this morning
that this would be the day
your life would change, did you?"*

Robert H. Schuler

IT WAS AN ORDINARY DAY WITH NOTHING MORE UNUSUAL THAN RUNNING errands, dealing with children, chores and meals. There were no special diets going on, I practiced no special rituals except for my exercises. I was not overly religious, in fact, I no longer went to church at all, and the concerns that occupied my time and energy were my children, my career, paying the bills, and especially, my relationship with Ben, the man who had asked me to marry him.

The night, however, was not an ordinary night. Ben and I had gone to bed early and, in the luxury of extra time, decided to make love. The lovemaking had only just begun when orgasm approached almost too quickly and without warning the most incredible series of events took place.

First there was a distinct rumbling sound, a shaking, then a roaring explosion, followed by a brilliant flash of light. I felt as though my body was turning inside out, ejecting me in the process. The explosion of light pulsed like a freight train up the center front of me, hit my brain and kept right on going, carrying me into what looked like the depths of outer space.

There was total silence and stillness, and I was peacefully afloat in an endless, timeless place of completeness. My ordinary sense of myself and the everyday world disappeared, and whatever was left of that self was floating like a brilliant point of light in a sky filled with other points of light.

I was not just a star in that sky, I was the whole universe of sky filled with uncountable points of light that spread out in every direction, flashing, twinkling and intermingling as points of myself. These points of light seemed to be a living continuation of my whole self or else I was an extension of them, seeing and feeling as one being, and somehow knowing all there ever was to know.

This oneness of light, love, and self sparkled and flowed in perfect union, riding on long, slow, pulsing waves of color, and in this state, if someone had asked me to explain all there was to know, I could have said it all in two words – I am.

There was no physical consciousness as I ordinarily knew it, but consciousness, rather than having been 'switched off' seemed to have been 'switched on.' I was no longer aware of the actual lovemaking going on, of the other human being involved, the bedroom we were in, or any of the other parts of my life as a woman or even a living being. As a matter of fact, the entire physical world had disappeared, yet I had no sense of shock or loss, nothing seemed to be missing.

In fact, just the opposite seemed true – somehow, I *knew* and *was* the completeness of the universe. Everything hung there in utter silence and peace. There was no sense of motion, and yet everything was undulating continuously in huge waves of light that pulsed slowly and evenly, with the ecstasy of pure pleasure through endless space. I was the empty space, I was the huge waves of light, I was the essence of pleasure and peace, and I felt as if I was one with everything that ever did or ever would exist. Then it was over.

I was back in an ordinary rectangular room with a small light burning and Ben, who was anxiously leaning over me.

"What happened? Are you all right?" he asked.

Not knowing what to say I mumbled something like, "Yeah...I don't know... I... don't really know... there was a roaring sound and a flash of light and then...then some more lights...and then...I was floating somewhere...I'm not really sure...like in space...everything was gone but... it seemed like nothing was missing... I don't know what happened..."

When no further explanations or insight into the extraordinary experience seemed forthcoming, the subject was dropped and eventually we rolled over and went to sleep.

Several times over the next few weeks the entire sequence of events happened again. There would be the sensation of rumbling and shaking, along with the feeling that some incredible force was roaring up through the center of my body. It would hit my brain with exquisite pleasure and culminate in an explosion of lights that disintegrated not only me, but all of physical reality, until all that existed was an ocean of stillness, blackness filled with tiny lights.

Those brilliant, sparkling points of light that seemed to spread out endlessly in every direction, the disappearance of the physical world, the undulating waves of light and color, the experience of blissful wholeness, and a sense of fulfillment that absolutely satisfied every wish, want, or desire of my entire existence – all went beyond any ordinary experience or sensation.

◌ૐ

This was the beginning. I did not know what happened to me or why, and beyond the initial shock of the experience, I didn't worry about it or even give it much thought. Ben and I had been in our new house for almost three months by this time and I was on the proverbial cloud nine. Our relationship had enjoyed an increasing closeness over the previous six months, so I assumed that we had reached some deep, new, and unusual dimension of love, and that this increased the power and pleasure of our lovemaking.

As I was to realize some years and much grief later, I had stepped into a new dimension of being, with totally new activities and capabilities of consciousness, perception, and intelligence.

This brief series of spectacular sexual events proved to be not only the awakening of kundalini, but like Joshua's horn in the battle of Jericho, they sounded the note that tumbled the walls separating me from many other realms and realities. Almost immediately, a series of experiences began that shook my life right to its foundations and it would be trite to say that life was never the same again.

These experiences began innocently enough one evening shortly afterward as Ben and I sat at the table eating dinner. We were having mashed potatoes, pork chops, applesauce, salad and a vegetable. While we ate, Ben talked about his day as a toolmaker at Chrysler. As he talked, I listened absentmindedly until I got to the point of wanting more applesauce. The bowl of applesauce was sitting across the four-foot round table right next to Ben, but I couldn't reach it and didn't want to interrupt him.

I listened to him chatter on until I found myself wondering if he was ever going to take a break long enough to let me ask him to pass the applesauce.

He seemed totally caught up in his story so I continued to eat and wait impatiently for a chance to make my request until, suddenly, in the middle of a sentence, without changing either his pace or his tone of voice, he asked briskly if I wanted some applesauce. Then he went right on with the account of his day, never stopping for breath, not bothering to hand me the applesauce, and seemingly unaware that he had even mentioned applesauce.

I stared at him for a moment, thinking that he must have somehow read my thoughts and feeling shocked at this idea. Then I decided I must have misheard him. When he finished his story, he silently handed me the bowl of applesauce. A few minutes later he finished eating and left the table, announcing that he was going out in the back yard.

I cleaned off the table after the meal wondering about the whole sequence of events. Had Ben picked up my thoughts about wanting more applesauce? He seemed to, but didn't appear to be aware that he *had* picked them up. His question, "Do you want more applesauce?" was sandwiched in among the details of his story about some incident that happened while he was at work. He spoke the words in a flat, descriptive tone, without the usual intonation people used when they were asking a question.

This struck me as unusual and I wondered if he really did ask me the question or if I just thought he had. Had he been aware in the back of his mind that I wanted more applesauce and had I then read *his* mind, thinking I actually heard him? Or had I somehow projected my thoughts strongly enough to interrupt his train of thought but not his actions? After all, he handed me the applesauce silently as soon as he was done with his story. Finally, I dismissed the entire episode as coincidence, deciding that mind reading was one of those ideas that existed somewhere between the ridiculous and the impossible.

ся

A few days later I was at work at the Chrysler trim plant where I had been employed for nearly a year. The manufacturing engineering of-fices were on the top floor of the plant and a door from our office opened directly onto the large flat roof of the plant.

I had discovered that during the summer it was blisteringly hot on the roof, but for warm and sunny days in fall or the late winter days of middle March it was the perfect place to spend a noon hour. Taking my lunch, I went out on the roof to eat, lie in the sun, relax, and get a bit of tan on my face and arms. After finishing my sandwich, I spread out a small afghan kept tucked in a desk drawer, then laid down and stretched out to enjoy the double warmth that seeped into my spine from the roof beneath me and into my face and abdomen from the sun above.

As I relaxed, my mind drifted here and there. I thought about the recently vacated position of Plant Engineer. Someone had suggested that, being a woman and an 'easy-in,' I should go for the job, but I felt that a single year of experience didn't give me anywhere near the experience needed to take on such a role.

Briefly I wondered who was going to be promoted into that position. Then I was wandering down the hallway that many of us at the plant referred to as Mahogany Row. This was where the executive offices with their expensive mahogany desks were located, and when I came to the vacant office of the Plant Engineer, I stopped and stared into the office in an idle way. Unexpectedly, someone brushed past from behind, startling me. It was Dan, a fellow engineer that I worked with, liked, and respected. As I watched, he walked into the empty engineering office, closing the door behind him as if it were his office. As if there was an obvious message in this I said aloud, "So! Dan is the one who will get that promotion!"

The sound of my own voice startled me, causing me to jump. This brought me back to the awareness that I was really lying on the factory roof in the sun and *not* walking down the cool hallway of Mahogany Row.

There was a moment of confused disorientation and something of a physical shock as I made what felt like a jerky transition back to the roof. I lay there for a moment thinking about the vividness of what I had just seen and experienced down on Mahogany Row, and the certainty of my conclusion that Dan was going to get the promotion. I wondered how I had thought I was walking along inside the plant when I was really dozing in the sun up on the roof. Still, I was sure Dan was going to get the promotion.

It was time to go back to work so I got up, folded the afghan, and headed back into the engineering offices. On the way past Dan's desk, I stopped.

"Hey, Dan, you're going to get that promotion to Plant Engineer," I said.

He laughed with a short, staccato ha-ha then asked, "Oh yeah? How do you know that? I'm not the only one going for the position, you know, and some of the others are pretty well-qualified."

"I just saw it," I told him.

He laughed again, an edge of derision in his voice, and said, "What do you mean by that?"

"Well... I was laying in the sun, out on the roof and then I was walking down Mahogany Row, looking at the empty plant manager's office there, when you walked into it and shut the door," I said in an explanatory fashion.

"So?" he replied, "What does that mean? What makes you think I'll get the job?"

"*Because*... " I said with extra emphasis, "I *saw* you... you went in the office and shut the door like it was your office."

"So?" he said, unconvinced.

"Well... it ... I just saw it...and was sure that you..." I started to stammer. The logic of his argument was causing me to ask myself the same questions he was asking. Why did I think that watching Dan walk into an office and shut the door during a moment of daydreaming meant that he would get a promotion? What had I really seen?

Dan interrupted my own thoughts as if he were some prosecuting attorney. "Yeah, sure...I thought you were laying on the roof?"

"I was!" I said.

"Well, how did you see what was going on down on Mahogany Row?" he inquired, amused.

By this time, the whole office was listening and I was embarrassed. It sounded irrational and crazy, even to me, and there was no real proof that I had seen anything. Maybe it had been a dream. Foolishly I tried once more to explain, then defend myself, but finally dropped it and everyone went back to work.

About three weeks later our boss came in one morning and announced that Dan had gotten the promotion. There was a moment of silence in the office and one of the men murmured, "Well, so you were right!" I *was* right, but no one was more surprised than I was.

This episode turned out to be the first of many episodes in which I saw little visions or scenes that showed me events of the future. In a slow but relentless way, other disturbing, unexplainable experiences began to appear in my life.

Still, I was blithely unaware that anything pivotal had occurred in my brain or mind. The applesauce incident had been dismissed as coincidence and my experience on the factory roof was buried in an avalanche of embarrassment over my inability to explain it in any logical fashion. Instead of being a signal that something was different, the experience on the factory roof remained in my memory as the first time that I encountered the question that would haunt me for a long time... "How did you know that?"

c&

Over the previous Christmas holiday my friends, Barry and Sherry, had given me a gift certificate for a massage at a small mental health clinic on the far west side of town. Barry was a psychologist who worked part-time at the clinic; Sherry was doing more and more personal growth seminars there, and both felt that bodywork was an important adjunct to personal growth. As friends, they had witnessed and supported the personal growth that eventually ended my very difficult marriage five years earlier and now they thought that the gift of a massage would be a way to nurture continued growth while providing a wonderful experience at the same time.

I scheduled the massage, not really knowing what to expect. When the experience turned out to be both healing and relaxing, I made a New Year resolution to take care of myself differently. Instead of spending money on 'repair-type healing,' I decided to use massage as a health maintenance step and, having the money, set up a standing appointment for every other week.

Now it was the end of what seemed like an unusually long week and I was headed across the city for that bi-weekly appointment. I arrived on time and after undressing and getting comfortable on the table, Ann, the masseuse, began by following the routine she used every time.

Starting with my face, then moving on to my neck and shoulders she worked silently and deeply. After this she would cover my eyes with cotton pads dampened with astringent, then wrap my entire head in a towel. Next, she would go on to do my stomach, legs, and feet. When she had finished the front half of my body, she always took a short break, telling me to 'relax now' and 'go to the center of your being, to the center of life which is breath and air and breathing...' Then she would leave the room and relax for five minutes before she came back in to turn me over and do my legs, buttocks and back.

This day, for some reason, I actually paid attention to what she said and found myself thinking about her words 'breath' and 'breathing.' Relaxed and with nothing else to think about, I ended up listening to my breathing. Without effort, I listened to the sound of the air moving into my nose under the towel wrapped around my head and holding two cotton pads over my eyes. I thought it sounded sort of like sighing.

I continued to listen in an absent-minded way and at first did not really notice that it seemed to be getting louder. Slowly and gradually it went from a quiet half-sighing, to a steady breeze, to a loud gale, to the sound of wind roaring in a wind tunnel. I was lost in the sound, surrounded by it, caught up in what I perceived to be the power of breath and breathing, and then the sound began to grow fainter as if moving into the distance.

Suddenly, I realized it was me who was moving into the distance, away from the sound. I was sliding up out of my body. My head and shoulders were already out. I could see my physical body lying there covered with towels. For a moment, it was as if the two bodies were lying parallel to one another, or maybe on top of one another.

Then I rose up toward the ceiling and looked around. I could see right through the walls of the clinic and gazed calmly at the beautiful sunny day outside, the traffic going by, and the large music store across the street! I thought about going outside to enjoy the sun when I saw that Ann was coming back down the hall, and I looked down hurriedly, thinking there really wasn't time to go anywhere… that I had to get back before Ann discovered I was gone.

Now the reality of what was happening started sinking in to my consciousness, terrifying me. My physical body tensed upward as if clutching at me, and then I was falling, almost as if I was being sucked back into the body on the table.

I had the silliest impression that I had not gotten my body on straight, a sensation akin to having your socks on crooked. There was great comfort in finding myself back where I belonged even though I was feeling a mixture of relief and shock.

Ann was already coming in the door and I had the distinct thought, "Phew, at least I got back in the body in time," even though I didn't seem to be back in quite right and was struggling to regain control of all my motor functions. The sense of being able to operate the physical body returned just as Ann was moving towels and telling me it was time to turn over, and in a sudden burst of words I blurted out, "Ann, I was just separated from my body!"

She did not seem to think this was unduly remarkable and continued to remove the towels from my head and the cotton pads from my eyes, murmuring things like, "It's okay... you're just fine now... maybe you're psychic..." and other comments meant to soothe me. Then she turned me over and went back to work.

The rest of the massage was quiet and uneventful, but I couldn't stop thinking about the incredible experience that had occurred during the break. On the way home I turned this impossible experience over and over in my mind. Had I died and quickly come back to life? What if I had floated away and gotten lost? Was there such a thing as accidental suicide?

These and other questions followed me for days and I began to feel a twinge of fear each time I remembered the experience because I did not want to die, intentionally or accidentally.

Two weeks later I was again on the massage table. I had worried all the way across town that the same experience would happen again, but once I was wrapped in Ann's towels and fully relaxed, I let the world and my problems fade into the background. The five-minute break with instructions to go to the 'center of life... which is breath and breathing' passed uneventfully, Ann returned, removed the towels, and rolled me onto my stomach so she could work on my back.

Quiet and with eyes closed, my mind wandered here and there daydreaming along with the music, letting it create an enjoyment so sweet that I could feel and almost taste it. It was classical music, something I had never been the least bit interested in, but now I began to wonder what the name of the piece of music was, and thinking I might buy it, roused myself from my reverie, intending to ask Ann to turn up the radio. I wanted to be sure to catch the name of the music and the orchestra when it was over. But when I returned my attention to the room, the music faded, there was nothing but the sound of Ann working on me, breathing evenly, steadily, and I found myself unable to hear any radio at all, whether in the room I was in, or elsewhere.

For one or two attentive moments I listened carefully, expecting the music to start up again, but heard nothing, not even static. Finally, I asked Ann if the radio was on. Intently working on my back she replied, "No, the radio isn't on, there's no radio in here."

Certain that there had been a radio playing I opened my eyes and lifted my head up to look around the room. To my shock the whole room was lit up with a glowing red light. I reasoned that Ann must have covered the lamp on the other side of the folding screen with a red shade or scarf or something while I continued to look for a radio. When I didn't see one or hear any more music I put my head down again, wondering if I was going crazy. I was sure I had just listened to the most beautiful music that had ever played, and now I was disappointed that I didn't know the name of the piece.

As I dressed to go home later I looked at the lamp on the other side of the screen. It had a cream-colored shade and was partially draped with a blue-green paisley print scarf. I wondered briefly about the red glow in the room but reasoned she must have had some other light on during the massage, or that I just imagined the room had been filled with a red glow. Then I left, feeling relaxed and well cared for but vaguely unsettled.

cs

Another long week went by with no recognition on my part of the subtle signs that something irreversible was in motion and working on me. The alarm went off at four-fifteen every morning, but lately I had been waking up before it sounded. When it happened again this particular morning, I got up, got ready for work and left early, feeling tired.

As I got in my truck and headed down Jefferson Avenue, dawn was breaking but the sun was not quite up yet. I drove along thinking how beautiful the world was at this time of day, so peaceful, soft, and dewy.

On the road that ran along Selfridge Air Force Base, a couple of geese on their way to the canal were crossing the road with a straggling line of newly hatched family behind them. I stopped to let them cross and sat there wondering how long it would be until the babies would fly. "What was it like to fly?" I wondered, and this triggered the whole memory of my experience on the massage table, which brought twinges of unease.

When the geese finished crossing, I took my foot off the brake and again headed west along the road, thinking nervously about my private experience of 'flying' without the physical body. Momentarily in a peculiar mood, I asked myself, "If I were a bird and could fly, what kind would I be?"

A cardinal was too flashy, an eagle too lonely, a hawk too warlike, a canary too often caged for its beauty, a crow too ordinary … and so on, until I hit on the red-winged blackbird. "That's it!" I thought to myself. "Plain and shiny, but with a little splash of color!"

At that instant I recoiled in shock and stomped on the brakes. About three feet in front of my windshield, gliding slowly past right at eye-level, was the most beautiful red-winged blackbird I had ever seen. It was much larger than I generally thought they were and the black feathers glistened in a silvery rainbow of colors reflecting the just-rising sun coming over the horizon from behind me. The wings were spread widely and along the bird's shoulders was a brilliant band of scarlet feathers, and then a thin band of yellow around the scarlet.

The whole bird seemed to glide past as if it were standing on the tip of one wing. It was an odd perspective, almost as if I was seeing it from above, during flight. This bird was truly beautiful and continued flying by in slow motion until it passed the windshield and disappeared through the line of trees at the side of the road, taking with it the unusual perception that I was seeing everything from a perspective located somewhere up in the sky far above.

The truck was nearly at a stop by this time and I was shaking, my heart pounding. The timing of the bird's appearance and the content of my thoughts just before it appeared made it a very unusual coincidence and I couldn't get the thought out of my mind that I had just seen myself in the form of a red-winged blackbird. That struck me as even crazier than the idea of flying around out of the body and for the first time I noticed that a lot of weird things seemed to be happening with my mind lately.

I drove on to work feeling some combination of apprehension and worry, completely unaware that for thousands of years, the bird had been a symbol of our hidden ability to fly, to travel out of the body. Birds and their flight implied the suggestion that it was possible to transport one's perception anywhere in space and time in order to study, observe, or learn from that place and time, but I did not know this at that time. Visions and symbols were part of a way of thinking and perceiving that I had never been introduced to, and in the family of farmers and workers that I grew up in, a bird was a bird was a bird. The idea that it could be anything else would have been considered preposterous.

However, there was to be no let up in the pressures on my perception. The very next day I was again on my way to work, traveling at a good clip down the expressway. I left early again and it was barely light out. The busy season was well underway at work and in my mind, I was already on the factory floor, organizing my day, deciding what I needed to do first, second, and so on when I noticed that something seemed to be at the side of the expressway up ahead.

Forgetting the engineering problems of the coming day, my attention swung back to the highway, and slowing down slightly, I stared at the structure, trying to figure out what it was.

It looked as if a gigantic archway resting on two portals had been built over the expressway. The closer I got, the more improbable the whole structure seemed and the more confused I became about where I was. For a few moments I felt lost. In my peripheral vision, even the landscape looked different, and I had the clear thought that the portals were markers at the border of some new country or new land that I was entering, unaware that at some very deep and inner levels, that was exactly what was happening.

Finally, almost even with the unusual structure, I stared in amazement at a pair of huge purple portals forming some kind of giant entryway over the expressway. Gaping in surprise out the driver's window, I drove through the portal opening, now going far less than minimum speed, with the car and my driving forgotten. The portals looked to be made of some heavy yet intricately carved material, they were a lovely shade of purple, and each column holding up the arch was approximately four feet square. They seemed to rise out of the earth rather than just be sitting on the ground and were easily twenty feet tall. They were connected at the top by a wide, curving arch made of the same purple material as the huge posts that held it up on each side of the expressway.

These portals had not been there yesterday. I immediately discarded the possibility that someone could have built them overnight, and it struck me as an unseemly place to put such a huge structure. There was nothing but open land around it, no town, no neighborhood, no expressway entrance or exit. Immediately after driving through the structure, I decided that a pair of purple portals was impossible and I must have seen a large billboard or something.

Quickly I looked in the rear view mirror, then both side mirrors, then turned bodily around and looked out the back window of my truck, trying to spot the billboard I was sure I had seen, but there was no sign of either billboards or purple portals.

A car in the next lane went zipping by and I could see the driver looking over at me as if to say, "What in God's name are you doing, lady?" I realized I had forgotten about the fact that I was driving, so I pressed jerkily on the gas pedal and hurried on to work.

For the rest of the day I tried over and over to put aside the surprising clarity of vision that had accompanied the appearance of the red-winged blackbird on the previous morning and the purple portals of that morning's drive. Surely my imagination was working overtime and the experiences meant nothing, I told myself. I was tired, spring brought the season of highest stress at the plant, and things would settle down soon. Fortunately, I was oblivious to the meaning of the symbolism in both the red-winged blackbird and the purple portals. ∞

2 ∞
Things Begin to Fall Apart

*"Sometimes things fall apart so that
better things can fall together"*

Marilyn Monroe

OVER THE NEXT WEEK, I FORCIBLY PUSHED THE ODD EVENTS AND COIN-
cidences to the back of my mind and concentrated intensely on my work.
We were approaching the point that our model year had to go into prepro-
duction test runs and I felt great pressure because I only had a four-day
work week. I was taking Friday off to go downtown for a child support
hearing.

At the time of my divorce several years earlier, I had taken physical custody of our four children. My ex-husband remarried almost immediately and about a year later he and his new wife purchased a house right
across the street from the children and me. Then he began asking regularly
if he could have at least two of the children, telling me that it was not fair
for me to have all four, or how simple it would be to share them for part of
the year because he was just across the street.

At first I absolutely refused to split the children, and for a while I
would not consider letting them move to his house for even part of each
year. I felt that we were just gaining some sense of peace and cohesive-
ness as a family. But I was a welfare mother at that time, struggling with
great difficulty to make ends meet. Getting four children off to school or
day care every morning, then getting myself and my rattling white station

wagon down to classes at Wayne State University for an education that would help me make a decent living took every bit of organization and determination I could muster.

By the time my childcare was cut off after two years of public aid, I had managed to earn three years' worth of college credits. I had one more year to go. I found myself searching for some way to stay in college long enough to finish that last year and get my degree in engineering.

Under pressure to make some unwanted decisions, I realized I would have to get a job and pay for that last year myself. I was more than willing to do this but found I was unable to get a job that would support myself and four children, as well as pay for childcare and college tuition. Feeling desperate and a little afraid, I became a bit more willing to compromise with John around custody.

Eventually we worked out a plan in which – without notifying either Friend of the Court or the circuit court – we decided that all four of the children would temporarily move across the street with him for one year so I could concentrate on finishing my degree as quickly as possible. During that time, he would stop paying child support, I would get the best full-time job I could, and when I finished my degree as early as one, and no more than two years later, the four children would come back to live with me. Then John and I would both go to court and ask to have his child support eliminated because I would no longer need it.

In the meantime, while the children were temporarily with him, we believed that as long as I did not press charges for child support, Friend of the Court would not bother him for the money. If they did, the stopgap plan was to let the courts know that he owed nothing because they were temporarily living with him. But the plan did not go as planned.

At the end of August 1977 the children moved across the street and I started a small business hanging wallpaper and painting. I worked from sun-up to sun-down five days a week, on the sixth day I picked up supplies and equipment, took care of paperwork, phone calls and accounting, and on the seventh I did laundry, cleaned house, and cooked. It made enough money to survive on, but there was no time or money left to pursue my college degree.

After six months of my own business, I decided to see if I could get a job as an engineer somewhere to find out if I liked the work and decide if I really wanted to go ahead and finish my degree in that field. I also reasoned that if I went to work for a big corporation, they might be willing to help finance my degree.

To my great surprise, I was hired by Chrysler and loved the job, but discovered that I had to work there for a year before I could apply for tuition reimbursement. By the time I had worked at Chrysler a year, my children had been gone for a year and nine months. I decided to apply for tuition from Chrysler and enroll in summer classes at the university to start moving toward my degree once more.

Just at that point, our assumptions regarding Friend of the Court's beneficence and lack of organizational capabilities turned out to be naïve. They issued a notice for a show-cause hearing and we were both called into court to explain why there was no child support being paid. We decided we would go to court and simply explain our agreement. Hopefully they would go along.

When the day of the hearing arrived, I took the day off from work and toward mid-morning left for the court building in downtown Detroit. I left about fifteen minutes later than I intended but did not hurry. John and I had talked briefly just the night before. He told me that I really didn't have to be there at all, this was really just a formality, and of course, we still had our agreement. I told him that I was going to be there anyway, just to back him up, and we again discussed everything we were going to tell the judge.

I drove along peacefully, enjoying the sunny day, and wondering how long I would have to sit in the courtroom, waiting for our case to be called. After a short while I forgot about the case and courtroom delays, my mind wandering off to think about other things.

I was only about ten minutes away from the courthouse when I began to feel an eerie electrical tingling at the top of my head. The sensation was almost like that of a snake curling around the top of my skull and I reached up to scratch my head, feeling somehow unnerved.

The tingling, growing much stronger, became an electrical current that moved all the way down the left side of my body to my feet and then began upward again.

As it traveled along me, I suddenly began seeing and hearing what was going on in the courtroom. At that very moment John and a strange attorney were standing in front of the judge, filing a petition that would give John permanent custody of all four children, with child support to be paid by me.

In horror I cried out, "No, no, no! There must be some mistake…" As I watched, I realized that there was no one there to speak for me or my side and that the judge was going to implement the order! I could hardly believe what John was doing. Too late I discovered he had broken his word and, as in the marriage, I had been foolish to make any agreements with him because he was not a man of his word.

The blast of a horn from a nearby vehicle brought my attention back to my driving. With my mind and full attention in the courthouse and my tension rising because of what I was seeing there, I had forgotten that I was driving a car along a busy expressway. In the rush of surprise, betrayal, and anger, my foot pressed hard on the gas pedal. My hands had a frozen grip on the steering wheel, and I had stopped responding to the conditions of the road. Worse, either traffic was moving much slower near downtown Detroit, or I had accelerated dangerously.

I was racing quickly toward a collision with the back end of a bread truck and instinctively I knew there wasn't even time to look at the speedometer. Experience told me not to stomp on the brakes at that rate of speed or I would go sliding out of control.

Glancing in the rear-view mirror and at the same time swerving sharply, I practically jumped into the middle lane. Miraculously I missed the back end of the bread truck by mere inches and the front corner of the semi-truck in the center lane which had been in my 'blind spot' and only visible once I made the move. I had accelerated as I swerved, then careened wildly about for a minute, but somehow regained control after scaring the other drivers in all three lanes as well as myself.

I was shaking so badly that I got off the expressway at the next exit and went racing along the surface streets the rest of the way downtown. I parked in the first available spot, ignored the parking meter, and ran all the way to the courthouse.

Once inside I rushed up the stairs and down the hallway toward the courtroom door. Just as I reached it, the door swung open…and there I stood, face to face with John and his attorney who were just leaving the courtroom. I backed up, letting them out and on their way past, the lawyer handed me the petition for modification of the original custody and child support order. Without even glancing at the papers I said angrily, "Why did you do this? We have an agreement!"

"Because I want the kids, that's why," was all he said, and he continued to walk, looking straight ahead, taking big, deliberate strides.

"You don't want those kids at all," I snapped. "You just want to avoid paying child support, that's what you've wanted all along, isn't it?"

He took a deep breath but said nothing and kept on walking.

"Look! You're not keeping those kids!" I said as I pursued him in cool fury, feeling like I was fighting underwater.

"Go ahead and fight me," he said. "I'll tell the judge you're not a fit mother, you're living with someone."

He walked away and I stood there in stunned silence. Then I ran after him, thinking I might be able to reason with him.

"John, we had an agreement...what happened to our agreement?" I pleaded.

"Give it up," he replied, continuing to walk at a brisk pace.

"How can you...?" I started to ask, but he cut me off.

"They're mine now," he said coldly.

Furious with him and struggling to keep pace, I realized it was too late to do anything to change the situation at that moment. Falling behind because of his fast pace, I snapped angrily at his receding back.

"Fine! You *have* their bodies...I'm going to have their hearts!"

ങ

For the rest of that day I was caught between rage and anguish over the loss of custody of my children. In addition to the shock over the custody issue, I was upset with the fact of the uncanny perceptual experience that had shown me the events of the courtroom before I even got there. Why had I seen this? Why had it even been possible to see it?

Weeks earlier when I blurted out to my massage therapist that I 'was separated from my body,' she had commented that perhaps I was psychic. The word disturbed me greatly, conjuring up pictures of gypsies, witches, and demons. I ignored her comment at the time, but after the clear vision of what happened in the courtroom that day, her words came back at me again and again.

Angry with John and his sneaky move to take custody of the children away from me, and frustrated with the unexplainable perceptions of the previous weeks, I cried hopelessly for the rest of that afternoon and far into the night. The next morning, gathering my guts together, I suggested to Ben that we marry right away so that I could begin the long process of getting my children back.

Ben and I met in the late spring of 1978 and by Christmas of that year, intending to marry, we bought a house together. It was my dream house on the water. Before I met Ben, he had applied for, and gotten, a Class C liquor license, then started the process of opening a small bar and restaurant in Pontiac, Michigan. Everything was settled except for the final approval of the location he had chosen, so when we got together, I joined him in his efforts to move the process along.

Originally, I expected our marriage to wait until the bar and restaurant was up and running, but now I wanted my children back. So I was devastated for a second time in one week when Ben said no, that he didn't want to get married right then, maybe in a year or so. The sense of devastation was followed by a numbness that sank all the way through me, body and soul, leaving me lost in some frozen landscape of emotion where I was too proud to cry any more, all I could do was ache. ☙

3 ⁊
Frightening Interludes in Consciousness

"When the light is green you go.
When the light is red you stop.
But what do you do
when the light turns blue
with orange and lavender spots?"

Shel Silverstein

ON THE FOLLOWING TUESDAY, IT WAS TIME FOR ANOTHER MASSAGE. Once on the table, I poured out my sorrows to Ann over loss of the children, Ben's refusal to marry me, and the upsetting vision of what had happened in the courtroom before I actually got there.

Ann, murmuring quiet words of empathy and support, continued to work on me without being judgmental about my stupidity, so I told her about some of the other strange experiences I'd had recently, and the fact that lately I couldn't seem to fall asleep. Between the stress, the weird experiences and the lack of sleep, I felt I was going crazy.

"Have you always had insomnia?" she asked.

"Insomnia! No, my problem has always been the opposite. I go to sleep two minutes after getting in bed and seem to need eight and a half hours of sleep, sometimes nine. I sleep like a dead woman," I told her.

"Is it the stress that's interfering with your sleep?" she said.

"I don't know, it doesn't seem like it. In the past, I've had nights when I just don't go to sleep but this is different. It's like I'm asleep, but even when I'm sure I am sleeping, I think I'm awake and that the things happening to me are really happening. Then later, I really do wake up and discover it's time to get up, but I'm dead tired because I was running around in these dreams all night thinking I'm awake. Lately there have been so many unexplainable things going on in my mind that I just feel I'm starting to go crazy. It's insane... or maybe I'm insane!"

"Look," she said, "I think it would be a good idea for you to keep a journal and write down all the things you're experiencing."

"I already do," I told her.

"No, these experiences should be kept in a separate log, not your daily journal," she replied.

"I don't know Ann," I said dubiously. "I'm working six days a week and there's barely enough hours in the day to take care of the daily necessities let alone keep track of all this craziness. Why would I want to keep track of it anyway?"

"To show yourself someday that you aren't going crazy," she responded.

Later, when I was dressed and ready to leave, she advised me to stay well grounded.

"Each time you find yourself tangled in fears that you're going crazy, turn the fears around by simply reaffirming to yourself that you're perfectly normal," she said.

I sighed. I didn't mention that I was already trying to do this and that it wasn't working very well. Still, I left the clinic feeling a bit cheered and a little more balanced. Back at home I tried to relax, and even went to bed early.

The next morning I arrived at work feeling rested and calm for the first time in a long while. The day was moving on quickly and I worked at my desk until shortly before lunch when I headed down to the tool room on the main floor of the factory.

To my surprise bright lights surrounded everything and everyone. The fabric cutters, the women sewing, the toolmakers, the repairmen, the lift trucks, even the beams holding up the plant itself, all looked as if they were encased in envelopes of light.

I stood in the aisle of the plant staring at people and things while a string of questions and answers ran through my mind.

"What's wrong with my eyes...? Is that some kind of light...? Why does it look like there's light everywhere...? I never noticed so much light before... Did they put new bulbs in the light fixtures over the week-end...? Am I imagining this...? It looks like everything has been dipped in light... It couldn't be..."

One of my bosses came along and asked me what I was staring at. I looked over at him but instead of a tall, good-looking man in a blue suit, there stood an old, wizened Chinese man in a white outfit with a black sash of some kind. Blinking rapidly and sucking in my breath, I wondered what I could possibly say in response to his question. To avoid answering I jumped into action and hurried off, telling him I would talk to him shortly but that I was in a hurry at the moment. I wondered if he thought I was acting strange as I walked hurriedly toward the tool room, wishing fervently for everything to return to normal, forgetting Ann's advice that I reassure myself that I was perfectly normal.

Upon reaching the tool room, Eddie was the first toolmaker I saw and he came up cheerfully asking what was new. I looked at him carefully because he really *was* Chinese and I couldn't stop wondering if I had somehow confused him with my boss. When I didn't answer his first question he tried again, asking, "How are you?" in a friendly way.

"I'm fine," I said, "I just think it's kind of bright in here."

"Oh yeah?" he said, looking around casually, "What do you mean?"

My mind was still making an effort to accommodate what I was seeing as I replied, "Well... everything is lit up like a Christmas tree."

Still looking around he said, "Yeah? Like how?"

He remained calm and continued looking about as I said, "Eddie, there are lights around everything... it's so bright in here I can hardly see. There are lights around the people, and the pipes, and the machines..."

"Really now...?" he replied, beginning to sound very interested about then.

Afraid that he was going to ask me what I thought it was, and feeling like I had already said too much, I told him I had to get going or the paperwork I was holding would never get delivered. Then I took off at a fast pace, leaving him in mid-sentence.

I told myself that I was tired, but I knew that wasn't the case. As I walked swiftly back along the main aisle I tried to reason with myself logically. Perhaps it was because I had cried for three days over the child custody mess, or because I hadn't cleaned my contact lenses well enough, or the sun coming in the high windows of the plant happened to be at some peculiar noontime angle that I had never noticed before.

Just then a man stepped in front of me. He was an old, gray-haired, black man, short and thin, and he waved a pencil and a scrap of paper at me. I had no idea who he was, but I stopped to see what he wanted.

"Please, kin I have yo' autograph?" he said.

Not believing what I was hearing I half-laughed and asked if he was joking. He brought the paper and pencil closer and said most seriously, "Please? You' gwan be famous some day an' I jes' wanna be able ta say I knew you an' workt wi' you."

The hair on the back of my neck was beginning to stand up and I had a familiar electrical feeling running down my left side. Embarrassed, I said to him, "Come on now! I can't sign your paper, this is silly."

"Please, jes' put yo' name on wi' you' own hand." By now he was hunched forward and down so that he looked like he was almost on his knees. "Please," he said again, "Jes' yo' name?"

By now thoughts were running through my head like wildfire. "This must be a joke... Somebody is after my signature... They put him up to this... But what if he's right... No, I'm being grandiose... This is crazy... It would be pompous to even think of signing it... Should I believe him... Why is this happening to me...?

In an attempt to be logical about the situation I asked, "What makes you think I'm going to be famous some day?"

"Please, I jes' know," he said in a quiet way, still holding the paper under my nose.

Afraid that any attempt to be logical would simply result in an argument, and with a sense of panic running through me, I put my hand over his hand – paper, pencil and all – moved it aside, and said "Please, I really don't think I should sign anything... I have to go..."

He backed away, disappointment running through his face and his entire body. Head down, he walked quickly away and I stood there, feeling like I had been ridiculously selfish. There was a sickening fear in the pit of my stomach and I turned and fled to the ladies' room in the manufacturing engineering offices.

I stood leaning against the sink for some time feeling exhausted. Something strange was happening. Something seemed out of control although I couldn't put my finger on exactly what or why.

I looked at my watch; it was past time for lunch. "Perhaps I should skip eating and take a nap," I told myself.

Down the hall from my office there was a room with a sofa that was occasionally used by various engineering staff for catnaps at lunch or during breaks so I went back there and lay down. Covering myself with an afghan, I finally relaxed and began drifting off. But, just like at night, I found myself fully awake in the middle of a dream. I knew that my body was really sleeping in the back of the engineering offices and that what I was experiencing was only a dream, but the dream was full of conflict and I could not slip back into the familiar mindlessness of sleep. I finally woke myself up and went back to work, feeling more exhausted than ever.

I slept poorly that night, and the next day I was still bothered by the bright lights. I was also becoming depressed at the constant consciousness. Whether my body was in the waking state or the sleep state, some strange part of myself was wide-awake and exquisitely conscious of everything. Hoping to perk myself up I decided to try another nap at lunchtime. Again, I found myself awake in my sleep, unable to forget who and where I was.

In frustration, I decided to do something useful while I 'slept.' In my waking life, Ben and I had been unable to find a place to put a second floor bath so that a plumbing wall could be constructed in a useful spot on the first floor. I tried designing the bathroom in every feasible place but nothing seemed to work.

Now, wide-awake in a dream, I proceeded to work out a location and a design that fit all of our criteria perfectly. When it was completed I woke up, took the idea to my drafting table and drew it up just as I had done in the dream.

This seemed like quite an accomplishment and I left for home that day tired but quiet, picking up a few groceries because we were having company that night. Ben, an excellent toolmaker, was now working at another Chrysler plant from the one where I worked. He discovered that one of his fellow toolmakers, a man named Rob, lived right across Jefferson Avenue from us, so we invited him to dinner.

When Rob arrived, there were introductions and we sat down to a simple meal. During dinner, the talk was 'shop' and I was enjoying myself for the first time in weeks when our guest began talking about his interest in the world of the mind and psychic phenomena. He needed no prodding to carry on and after a fascinating conversation he left, saying he thought I should do some reading on the subject and that he would be glad to lend me one of his books. I loved to read so I accepted the offer and he promised to bring the book over in a day or two. After Rob was gone, Ben went right to bed but I was too keyed up.

I sat alone, reviewing the strange events of the past few weeks and the things Rob mentioned in his obvious enthusiasm for the world of psychic phenomena. I told him about some of the strange things that were happening to me and he said I was 'probably psychic' but my discomfort with that word was extreme. When I got right down to thinking about everything that had happened, all I could do was wonder if I had imagined it all because it seemed so ephemeral.

Two days later Rob brought over the book he'd talked about and I began reading it that very evening. It was called *The Third Eye* by Lobsang Rampa, and was the story of a man who had been educated in a lamasery in Tibet, then made his way to the west.

The text was liberally sprinkled with references to reincarnation, astral bodies, and clairvoyance, and I had never read anything like it. It seemed overly simplistic and nowhere in the story had Rampa offered any proof, scientific explanations, logical arguments, or evidence to back up what he was saying. Yet because of the novelty of the story, I kept reading. I was sure it couldn't be more than just an incredible fantasy in someone's mind. Still, the newness of such a subject was interesting, and being a fast reader, I finished it quickly. When I was done, I didn't know what to think.

The following weekend I went to visit Barry and Sherry, and we began talking about books we were reading. I mentioned *The Third Eye* saying that it was 'almost unreal.'

Barry said he had recently begun a set of books by someone named Carlos Castaneda and that I should get them and read them if I was interested in that sort of thing. I wasn't sure just what he meant by 'that sort of thing' and he didn't go into detail, but the next day while browsing at the shopping mall with my daughters, I went into the bookstore and found myself trying to remember the name Barry had told me. I couldn't remember, but continued to look through various sections, hoping something would trigger my memory. Finally, I ended up in front of the occult books.

Feeling foolish, I looked through the various titles until I came across three or four books by someone named Castaneda. I was sure that was the name Barry had given me, but I was just as sure that Barry would not have been reading occult books. I rejected the idea of buying such books and left the bookstore empty-handed. However, when it was time to leave the shopping mall, I ended up hurrying back to the bookstore where I quickly bought three of the four books by Castaneda then headed home. Mysteriously excited, I began to read that very night and continued to read each evening after work.

For most of the first book, I thought I was reading about someone's adventure in trying to get research material for a college paper. It was interesting, but in my naiveté, I failed completely to pick up the deeper threads of what Castaneda meant by 'becoming a man of knowledge.' In my mind I pictured a wise professor at a college somewhere.

A week or two later and somewhere in the middle of the second book, my perception of what Castaneda was talking about began to shift. I sensed that the power he kept referring to was not the kind of power that I had recently been reading about in books by Michael Korda, John T. Molloy and Betty Harrigan. Castaneda was not describing a program for moving up the corporate ladder or getting ahead in life.

By now, I was curious even though I was not able to discern exactly what Don Juan was trying to get Carlos to do, and upon reaching the end of the second book, I felt a righteous sympathy for Carlos. He was not the only one caught up in fears and having trouble with perception, I was having troubles with mine, too.

I was halfway through the third book when a section about dreaming caught my attention. Because of my recent experiences of being awake in my dreams, especially during my naps at work, I felt I had some idea of what Don Juan was trying to get Carlos to do. He wanted Carlos to train himself to notice his hands when he was dreaming and then use this as a signal to become aware that he was dreaming.

I was already aware of my conscious self during most of my dreams and didn't really know what the point of this exercise was, but I got the idea that perhaps I could regain control of myself and stop the whole business by learning to look at my hands while I was dreaming.

For the next few nights, before going to sleep, I told myself to find my hands and wake up when I did so. Nothing happened for the first week, but I continued to give myself directions to find my hands and about ten days later I had an experience that terrified me.

I was asleep and dreaming that I was living back on Manistique Street on the lower east side of Detroit in the second-floor flat I had rented there long ago. In the dream, I was trying to climb the stairs to the upper flat and was having difficulty doing so. I was slowly inching my way up by hanging onto the walls that enclosed the stairway hall. My hands and arms were clutching at the walls, and it was at this point that I 'woke' in the dream, just as I had told myself to.

Instantly, the dream disappeared and, fully conscious, but not in the body, I found myself in my bedroom on Jefferson Avenue, floating above the bed. I looked down fearfully at Ben and I, sound asleep and thought, "This can't be happening! I'm not in my body again... oh no... this can't be..."

It occurred to me that details in dreams were never quite exactly like the reality of everyday life. "I know!" I thought, "I can prove I am just dreaming and not really floating here outside my body by looking around the house for exact details that will probably be slightly altered by the fact that I'm dreaming!"

With this thought and mounting fear pushing me, I floated toward the ceiling and right on through it, noticing the dust, dirt, nails, and general construction of the house as I passed between the ceiling and the floor above. Continuing upward through the floor, I found myself standing in the empty, unused, and unremodeled bedroom above the room that Ben and I shared.

Everything was exactly as I had left it back in December. A roll of Christmas wrapping paper was lying where it had fallen, and boxes of unpacked belongings with names and addresses of various companies stamped in black ink on their sides sat piled in disorder. I gazed at the poorly hung wallpaper on the steeply sloping walls along with their wide seams, torn spots, and crayon marks. Patiently, I waited for the scene to mutate or change like things do in dreams, but nothing happened. I just stood there and the room remained unchanged.

Gradually, the fears nibbling at the edges of my mind grew into horror as I realized that I could stand there as long as I wanted to, but the scene was not going to make one of those hazy, inexplicable changes so common in dreams. I really was wide-awake, standing up here in this unheated room while my physical body was curled up downstairs in bed.

Suddenly it was all too much. Refusing to return by merging back down through the floor into the bedroom below, I went screaming down the stairs, hysterically calling for my Grandma or someone to turn on the lights. I ran through the kitchen, half jumping, half floating right over the large round oak table and chairs, and into the bedroom where I rose over the bed and hung there for a moment.

My physical body was now tossing wildly about, mumbling and crying. Absurdly, I hesitated to get too close to the waving arms, fearing I might get hit, but the terror was too great and, fully conscious, I merged into it at a pace that seemed to take forever. As the merging took place, my body began to toss and cry more violently and as soon as I was fully back in it, my screams for help and cries for Grandma went echoing through the darkened house, waking Ben and, finally, my physical self.

Ben sat up in a fog and asked what was going on. Shaking and sobbing I told him what happened while he reassured me it was all over now and I could go back to sleep. Some time later I finally slept, but it was not to be a peaceful night. Again I dreamed, this time that I was in Alaska visiting my sister, Pam, and that when I returned home she followed me. In the dream, I was walking down a hallway and turned around to see her coming toward me. For a moment, I expected to see Pam smile in this surprise visit, but then quickly I realized it wasn't her.

Next, I thought it might be my daughter, but in an odd move she came right up to me and grabbed me by both arms, staring intently into my eyes. When she grabbed me, I experienced an electrical shock of such magnitude that I instantly woke up in the dream, which again became another powerful experience taking place out of the body.

The woman and I stared at each other eye-to-eye as it sunk in that, truly, she was not my sister or my daughter! She was a strange, fierce, feminine creature who seemed not only unknown but also dangerous. At that point, I had the thought, "Uh-oh, I'm going to become fully aware of my two selves again, the self that stays in the body and the one that moves around without it."

Rising fear began to course through me and with quick cunning I decided to trick the other creature. Calmly looking her square in the eyes, I told her I was going to fight her and that she should take off her glasses beforehand so they wouldn't get broken. When she let go of me to do so, I turned around and ran quickly back to my physical body, woke it up and stayed nervously inside it, watching for the other woman to appear. I was awake the rest of the night and could not get rid of the haunting feeling that the strange, unknown female creature I just met had been myself.

Soon it was time to get up. Once again, I was exhausted. As Ben and I were getting ready to go to work he mentioned his concerns about my state of mind and suggested we take a little vacation, driving over to Toronto for the Memorial Day weekend.

I was surprised because he had been so aloof since I asked him to marry me. Although it was only a week away, I wondered if I would last until the holiday, but finally the weekend arrived. We packed our bags Thursday night so we could leave early the next morning.

Friday morning dawned sunny and warm. We got up, ate breakfast, and Ben carried the bags out while I finished getting ready. When it was time to go, I headed for my truck. To my surprise, he had put our things in his car. I balked.

"We should take the truck," I said to him.

"Why?" he asked, sounding as if he thought that was a stupid idea.

"I don't know, I just think we should," I replied, staring doubtfully at his small green sports car, then at my big, ungainly pickup truck.

Nothing was said for a minute, and I still stood there, drawn to my truck.

"Well?" he asked, implying that it was time to go.

"Well…" I said uncertainly.

"Let's go then!" he said, moving toward his car and making a concerted effort to be cheerful, but still I balked.

"I…I think we should take the truck," I stammered. And then, trying to come up with a logical reason for my reluctance to get in his car, I added in a lame voice, "It's got more room…"

"I don't want to take that big, old gas pig all the way to Toronto," he said irritably, "and I don't want to be driving around the city in a truck either. Now let's go!"

I was insulted. My truck, nicknamed Harriet the Chariot, was comfortable and wonderful, but she definitely did not have the chic of Ben's little sports car. I said nothing and moved toward his car in an exasperated way, then stopped.

Suddenly conciliatory, he asked again, "*Why* do you want to take the truck?"

I didn't know what made it seem so important to take my truck but the inability to come up with a logical explanation now irritated me and I snapped, "I don't know! I just assumed we would go in my truck."

We stared wordlessly at one another for a few moments, each waiting for the other to change their mind, and finally I got in his car. After we had gone a couple of miles, I was still uncomfortable with the choice of vehicles and said so. Ben was angry by this time and barked that I was trying to ruin our trip. I replied in a very saucy tone that if the trip was ruined it would be his fault. After that we drove in silence.

About two hours later, somewhere between Chatham and Toronto, Ontario, we sat on an empty Highway 401 amidst thunder, lightning, black clouds, and a rain that seemed to come down almost viciously. We looked at each other, still silent. The car refused to move. He got out several times to look under the hood but nothing seemed to be wrong there and the intensity of the rain drove him back into the car. The roadside was muddy and Ben, already wet through, was not inclined to crawl under the car, but when twenty minutes had passed, it was time to do something besides sit there.

"What do you want to do, sit here and wait, or walk in the rain?" he asked.

"Flag someone down," I answered.

"Sure," he said sarcastically, glancing up and down the deserted highway.

It seemed ludicrous to me that we could be on such a major highway and not have seen a single car for twenty minutes. The day had started out sunny and beautiful but now the clouds were so dark it seemed like evening instead of mid-day. The rain poured with such intensity that for a moment I thought about the sunny morning, about my unwillingness to take the car, and wondered if we had blundered into the twilight zone.

"Well?" he asked impatiently.

"Someone will be coming," I said, trying to shake off the twilight zone feeling.

"Yeah? When? And what makes you think they'll stop?" he almost snarled as I sat there, again mute, not knowing what else to say. More minutes passed and finally he prepared to get out and start walking by himself. But just as he opened the car door and stepped out, an old man pulled up beside us, asking if we needed any help. He drove us to the next town where we called a wrecker and then called around among friends and family, trying to find someone to come and pick us up. Everyone was away for the holiday and we couldn't reach anyone so finally we rented a car and headed back home.

It was late in the day when we finally returned to our house by the bay. Neither of us was talking much, either about the ruined trip or the coming repair bill for a new transmission. ☙

4 ∝
Confusion Deepens

*"Wherever there is a reaching down into innermost
experience, into the nucleus of personality, most
people are overcome by fright, and many run away...
The risk of inner experience, the adventure
of the spirit, is ... alien to most human beings."*

Carl Jung

AS THE MONTH OF MAY CAME TO A CLOSE I WAS WRESTLING WITH MY
mind, my perception, and consciousness almost daily. It might have helped
if I had sat myself down and surveyed what was happening, but I didn't.
My most usual response to difficulties of any kind was to hope the problems would just go away and this situation was no different. Part of the
problem was that I either denied or failed to see the problem. Of course,
failure to recognize a problem almost always indicates a total absence of
strategy for dealing with it anyway, and that was the case with me.

My time and energy were committed in other directions. I lived
intensely, caught up in the daily dramas of big-time car production in the
car capital of the world, and whatever free time I had was spent planning
the remodeling of the home Ben and I had purchased the previous Christmas.

After overcoming years of abuse and agony in my first marriage,
and then the humiliations and enormous difficulties of being on welfare, I
was convinced that I could overcome any obstacle, that I could create my
life the way I wanted it to be. All I had to do was work at it. Slowly I was
putting my life back together the way I wanted it, and what I wanted was
a nice husband, a beautiful home on the water, my four children, a good
education, and career opportunities that offered excellent money.

I had most of the pieces for this perfect life already gathered and
in my mind, all I had to do was put them together right. This might take

some work, some time, some patience, and some love, but so strong was my determination, I had no doubt that I could make it happen. Thus, I continued to brush past the indications that something serious was brewing, something that would continue to change me and my life in ways I could not have imagined.

cs

Early the following week I had another massage and confided to Ann that things were getting worse. I was beginning to see ugly faces and tormented bodies when I went to bed at night. They floated in the air around me, picked or leered at me and would not go away. In an effort to be cheerful in front of her I called them 'my monsters and devils,' but their regular appearance every night added more fuel to the fear that I was going insane. When the massage was over and it was time for me to leave, Ann handed me a small scrap of paper with a woman's name and phone number on it.

"*Call* her," she urged me. "I think you might have some blossoming psychic abilities. This woman teaches classes in psychic development at the community college over on your side of town. She'll teach you how to use your abilities without being afraid."

I kept the number but it was a couple more weeks before I got up the courage to call. June was more than half over when I finally dialed the number on the scrap and heard a woman's calm, clear voice answer.

I was incredibly nervous about making the call and quite embarrassed that an educated, intelligent woman like myself would even think about giving credence to the idea of psychic abilities. The result was that I stammered and stuttered so badly, I half expected the woman to hang up in disgust. Patiently, she told me that she did teach through a local community college, but classes were over for the summer and I would have to wait until September. She suggested I practice meditating over the summer and call the college in the fall.

I hung up, almost relieved that there were no classes because I found it hard to believe that any normal, rational person would be teaching something like psychic development. But a tiny corner of me was disappointed. Things were more out of control every day and there was no telling what might happen by September.

I told myself that maybe the meditation would help and decided to try it, but the idea of meditating struck me as odd. Wasn't meditation something that monks might do? The truth was I really didn't have the slightest idea what meditating was, or when, why, or how to practice it.

ೞ

The weather was going from warm to hot and my problems with the unusual perceptions seemed to be heating up as well. It was as if my mind and conscious awareness were part of a radio that had accidentally been turned on and wouldn't turn off. I was less and less able to sleep, and the lights around people, animals, and things were getting brighter, more detailed. Dreams were so vividly real that I had a hard time remembering if something had happened in the real world or if I had dreamed it. There was a frequent buzzing or ringing in my head, along with a translucent, deep blue, cloud-like form that rotated slowly in front of my eyes constantly.

One warm afternoon I arrived home from work and laid down on the sofa, hoping to at least doze lightly. I was curled up on my side, almost asleep, with my back to the room when I heard a man's deep voice with a southern twang say, "It is time for you to develop a legal self and an aloof self."

Jumping in surprise I turned quickly, nearly rolling off the sofa. No one was there. I sat up, now wide-awake, and then walked over to the open front door, thinking maybe someone was on the porch talking. No one was there either, and neither was there anyone on the deck or the dock in our back yard or any of the neighbors' yards.

I sat back down and thought about what I'd heard. What was an 'aloof self?' For that matter, what was a 'legal self?' And what was the difference between the two? It made no sense to me, but I could not put it out of my mind. The thought that I was now hearing voices frightened me intensely and I felt panicky at the thought that this was truly a sign of my increasing mental deterioration. They locked people away in padded cells for claiming to hear voices. Anxiously I told myself not to pay attention to such voices and certainly not to answer them.

ೞ

The summer and I hung in suspended animation. I was awake and in a state of conscious awareness around the clock. Even when I could hear myself breathing the slow, deep breaths of someone whose body was supposedly sound asleep, some ineffable part of me was wide awake, full of energy, and engaged in one reality or another, realities that were as vivid and intense as everyday living.

Sometimes when morning came and the alarm clock went off, I got up, took my shower, brushed my teeth, then went back in the bedroom to get dressed – only to find my body still in bed. To my dismay, I would have to repeat the whole business of getting ready for work, often leaving late, and feeling scattered and uncertain about whether I was in the right time and space reality.

The spring rush to get the new car interiors ready for full production had passed and things slowed down at work, but we were still on overtime, working six days a week. Each day it was getting more and more difficult to go through the motions of my job. No matter who I had to deal with each day, I ended up knowing, seeing, and feeling everything they were going through in their private lives. Embarrassed about this and uncertain as to what had triggered such painful knowledge, I struggled to get through each week, carefully assessing what I was supposed to know and not supposed to know. Always, I counted the hours, even the minutes, until Sunday came and I could have some solitude and peace of mind.

Late one Saturday afternoon, I came home from work feeling more tense and exhausted than usual. I took a large beach towel and went out to lie on the dock beside the canal in the sun. The sound of lapping water was comforting, and lying on my belly with the sun warming my back, I relaxed for the first time in weeks. My arms were folded in front of me, my chin rested on my forearms, and my eyes were closed when I felt something crawling on my arm.

Normally, if I thought any kind of bug or insect was about to land or crawl on me, I would get panicky, swinging and swatting in a frenzy. This day I was so relaxed that I just picked my head up and looked casually down at my arm. A little black and white jumping spider was making his way along my forearm toward my elbow. In an easy manner, I tapped a forefinger right in his path and said, "Hey! Who do you think you are, walking on me?"

Instantly the little spider jumped off of my arm in fright and scrambled quickly toward the edge of the towel. Calm but curious, I watched him run, realizing he was terrified.

He jumped off the towel onto the dock and was about to disappear between two planks when I called to him, "Hey, don't run. I'm really more afraid of you than you are of me!"

To my surprise, he stopped in his tracks, turned part way around and looked at me. Pleased at his response and wanting to reassure him, I said, "Honest!"

At this, he turned all the way around and we simply looked at one another for a moment. Then he came trotting back across the towel, stopped right in front of my nose, and stood up on some of his hind legs. I set my chin back down on my arm and said, "I just don't like you walking on me, that's all!"

"Well, I won't walk on you, but just don't squash me!" he replied.

"OK," I said, "I promise."

The two of us stared into each other's eyes for a long time. I didn't know what to say but finally, amazed at the details of his tiny body I said, "I can see all your eyes!"

"I can see yours, too," he said. "They're big!"

There was more silence as we continued to look closely into one another's eyes. A feeling of great love welled up in me and I wondered why I had been so afraid of spiders and insects before. Suddenly I felt I needed to make him understand that I didn't hate him and probably other people didn't either. It was all fear.

"I…just don't want you walking on me," I told him apologetically, making another effort to explain myself and share my thoughts. "I guess I'm always afraid I'll get bitten. And it never occurred to me that you might be just as afraid as me."

"I'll go around you," he assured me, "just don't squash me."

"I won't," I said.

"Okay," he replied.

At this point he returned all his legs to the ground, walked right up to the edge of my arm, then turned and walked along it all the way to my elbow. He turned the corner at my elbow, walked alongside my upper arm for a moment, then turned again and continued on toward the edge of the towel and the dock, going over the edge and out of sight. A few seconds later he reappeared and followed almost the same path back around my arm and across the towel.

He made several trips, always going carefully around my arm, and I laid there thinking how clear his eyes had been, and how wonderful it was that we understood one another. Then, no longer feeling the need to be watchful of the little spider or other crawling things, I closed my eyes to doze, enjoy the sun, and relax.

Some time later, my oldest daughter who had come to visit me for the weekend, came out to the dock and sat down, dangling her legs over the edge in the water. She asked a few questions, and I answered her with eyes closed in peaceful relaxation. Suddenly I heard a tiny scream of horror and fear just as there was the loud smack of a hand on the dock. Before I could even get my eyes open, I knew what had happened. Jumping up in furious anger and guilt over my lack of watchfulness, I screamed at my daughter.

"What have you done? Why did you have to kill that little spider? Why? He was my *friend*! What is wrong with you that you have to just kill other things so automatically? How would you feel if some giant came along and smashed you just because you're smaller?" I cried hysterically.

She tried to defend herself saying "Mom…Mom! It was only a spider!" but I continued to yell at her, accusing her of murder, telling her to get in the house and stay there, and not to come out until she had learned not to be killing things for no reason.

In dumbfounded surprise, she retreated to the house and I sobbed brokenheartedly at the death of the little spider. Even though he was dead I could hear his voice calling, asking me "Why? Why? I thought you weren't going to squash me?"

"I'm sorry…I'm so sorry I didn't keep watching…I didn't know… I didn't do it… I'm sorry," I tried to tell him. Carefully I scraped his remains off the dock and buried him, terribly upset at my lack of vigilance after promising not to squash him.

By this time, some part of my mind was observing my own behavior and starting to question the rationality of the entire episode. Just then I was interrupted by two hoarse chirps. Turning to look, I found the brilliant, shining, red-winged blackbird sitting on the stub of a sawed-off tree limb staring at me. Goosebumps were rising as we looked at one another long and deep, and after what seemed like eons, she flew slowly off.

Standing there, watching the bird disappear in the distance, I experienced a feeling of total helplessness. At that moment, I knew somewhere inside of me that something beyond my understanding was happening to my mind and that I was not going to be able to stop it. I was sure that it was only a matter of time until I would be totally insane and incapable of negotiating the ordinary world I had once so easily taken for granted.

ᘏ

As August wore on, the unexplained perceptions increased dramatically. I began to hear conversations going on in the cars around me on the expressway, or across the restaurant in private booths. Sometimes I would find myself in two places at once, listening and watching the activities at home while at the same time experiencing what was happening on a local beach, at a friend's house, or in a grocery store.

"How could I do that?" I argued with myself. "Did one event happen first and the other event happen second? Were they both happening at the same time? How did I get from one place to the other… especially without being aware of the trip or the travel time? What happened to the time in between? Was I switching my attention back and forth very quickly, alternating between the two events? But they were in two different places! How could I be having experiences in two different places at the same time?"

I learned in high school science that two pieces of matter were unable to occupy the same space at the same time, but no one had ever said anything about one piece of matter occupying two spaces at the same time, especially when the two spaces were miles apart!

Sleep just did not happen any more, and worse, it was getting to the point where I did not expect it to. It was impossible to relax because all too often, when I did relax, I ended up out of the body and in some strange place that I knew I shouldn't or couldn't possibly be in – but was. Other times, relaxation brought on all kinds of unwanted visions and voices. Some of these visions had to do with family, some with friends, and some with people in places that were completely unfamiliar. The visions and voices were not as frightening as they were confusing, and their ability to disrupt my sense of continuity and complacency was overwhelming.

To complicate matters, I found it nearly impossible to read. For most of my life, the majority of my reading was novels, but at the time of my divorce I had taken to reading self-help books. After reading *The Third Eye* and the Castaneda series, I briefly looked for books that might help me understand and correct what was happening in my mind. But now I either could not concentrate, or found myself inside the author's mind experiencing all sorts of personal and private thoughts, as well as the feelings that had driven him to write a particular book, chapter, or paragraph. Other times I became caught up in the narrative to the point that my ordinary reality disappeared; I entered the book's reality and found myself actually living it.

Every time I got hold of a book that I thought might offer some possible explanation or helpful information, the book usually discussed or described other perceptual phenomena that I had never heard of – but immediately began to experience!

Embarrassed at my suggestibility, and afraid that I was going to end up in a situation that might cause me to disintegrate at either the body or the mind level, I clamped down on my roving mind and soon was forced to quit reading altogether.

In the last half of August, I was barely able to tolerate the factory, its noises, smells, and the ever-present sense of human agony emanating from the men and women who spent themselves among its machines each day. Overshadowing every moment of their hours inside the plant walls was a terrible sense of being trapped, of being engaged in meaningless activity.

As each week came and went, I felt a growing awareness of a dark despair in the minds and hearts of the people who worked there and hated it; people who felt they were pawns in countless little power games, but who had to have the money. To quiet my mind and get relief from the overwhelming stream of sensory experiences, I started going to a nearby park at lunchtime. The park was not in a very good section of Detroit, and I worried about the possibility of being mugged or raped.

One day, I stood leaning against a small tree near the tennis courts staring absentmindedly at the tennis players. I had completely forgotten about being careful to watch for dubious-looking characters when I felt a pair of arms slide around me. Nearly jumping out of my skin I spun around. There was no one there, which brought some relief, but over the pounding of my heart I heard someone say "Sorry to frighten you… Hello!" then "Hello!" again.

"It couldn't be…" I thought, when I realized it was the tree that was talking. Extraordinary experiences of this sort had become almost everyday affairs, but I still felt a combination of fright and irritation at the appearance of another variety of phenomena in the park where I had gone to get away from such things. In an effort to allay my fright, the small tree quickly explained that it was just trying to make me feel better.

"Fat chance!" I replied, then realized I was breaking my own rule in which I had forbidden myself to respond to disembodied voices.

The little tree invited me to lean against it and with an effort to appear casual, I did. Then it began talking about the importance of some kind of balance, and something about the power of male and female. I tried to listen yet did not understand much of what it said. Much of it was simply too foreign in concept for me to grasp. Besides, I was too busy trying to act as if I was just out enjoying a sunny day in the park. Yet while leaning against the tree, I began to experience something extraordinary. It was a warm, wonderful feeling, sensuous, yet healing, and when it was time for me to return to work, I was quiet and calm inside, something that was becoming extremely rare.

After that, I found myself going back to lean against the tree every day. It was almost as if I were going to meet a secret lover or to experience secret pleasures that left me calm yet energized, able to return to work and maintain an air of being normal for a few more hours.

Each time I went back to the park, the tree talked of keeping things in balance, and it was while in the park trying to grasp the little tree's concept of balance between male and female forces, that I devised my first mental measuring stick of sorts.

I was certain I was slowly going crazy…but there *were* areas of my life where things seemed to be organized and working smoothly. I did have some areas, like my job, the housework, and taking personal care of myself, under some semblance of control. Just looking at me briefly, other people would never guess that something was terribly wrong. So, I decided to watch myself. If I continued to function well in these areas, I would know that all was not lost yet. It would buy me some time, give me something to hold onto, and perhaps my mind would settle down. The perceptions seemed to have happened naturally enough, even though I had never heard anyone talk about such experiences.

Thus began my first period of intense observation and learning. During this period, I spent most of my time in what I came to think of as my 'twin' state. The normal, ordinary me would go through the motions of everyday life, while another, separate me would watch myself and others carefully, noting every single detail of what was said or done, what order these words and actions came in, and whether or not visions or voices interrupted or overlaid what was actually happening. I paid close attention to whatever feelings were expressed by other people, as well as their words and actions. Meanwhile, I carefully maintained the casual, detached perspective of an outside observer.

What I first hoped might be true about myself seemed to hold up under scrutiny – other people seemed to think I was normal. Eventually I decided that, for now, things were enough under control that I could at least keep up a normal-looking front while I figured out what to do next.

ꙮ

At the end of August, Ben reminded me that it was time to register for the classes in psychic development, but every day I put it off. Willing or not, he had witnessed some of my unusual experiences and he seemed more anxious for the classes to begin than I was. Still I put off the registration. He asked me several more times if I had gone to register yet and when I told him I couldn't afford the time or the money, he said I was being ridiculous, took the money out of his wallet, handed it to me and said "Go register!"

I made the trip over to the college and signed up for the class with an air of studied calm, but I was carefully noting the hidden attitudes and responses of everyone I had to deal with, defensively watching for signs and indications that they thought I might be wacky.

The first night of class I was extremely nervous yet very curious. As I walked from the parking lot into the building, I wondered what kind of people went to classes like this. To my relief, I found that there were no weirdos or obvious witches in the group. They seemed like average men and women, parents and grandparents, all with either curiosity or unexplained events like mine.

During the first few weeks of class, I was amazed and somewhat comforted to discover that there were names for many of the perceptual experiences I'd been having. I was even more startled to find that some people in the class had unsuccessfully used all sorts of approaches to try to *create* some of the very experiences I was having regularly and effortlessly. They were trying to make the odd perceptual stuff happen!

I also discovered that I had experienced an unusually wide variety of these experiences, more than anyone else in the class, except perhaps the teacher, and even with her I wasn't sure what she had read about and what she had experienced. As a whole, the class had something of an organizing effect on my approach to the strange perceptions and it was at this time I began applying my engineer's curiosity about how and why things worked to the events and experiences that went on in my mind.

"Maybe I can learn to function well in this area," I told myself. "There must be some logical explanation or reason for what is happening. Afterall, it's happening to others as well...maybe not as often or as drastically as it is with me, but still, it happens to them, and they even seem pleased."

In spite of the help offered by these classes, my mind continued to spiral open at an ever-faster rate. As the summer faded into fall, I was awake all day and aware all night. Information and strange perceptions continued to bombard me, and I was increasingly unable to sort out what was part of the physical, material world and what was not.

Complicating the avalanche of psychic phenomena was the recurring ache over the loss of my children and the desire to finish that last year of college. The time to enroll at Wayne State for fall classes had run out, classes had already started, and I had to make a decision quickly or it would be too late to get in and then catch up. More and more, I was aware that I had lost my interest in engineering, that I could barely get through each week at the plant, and yet I needed to keep going so I could apply for tuition assistance.

As my inner conflict grew over what I felt I should be doing to continue my engineering career, what I needed to do to get my children back, and to finish that last year of college, I began to balk at going to work. For reasons I could not clearly discern, there arose a vague but definite resistance to continuing along the corporate path I once calculated and mapped so carefully and efficiently.

"How can I afford my children if I don't keep going?" I asked myself. "How can I finish school if I don't stay on at Chrysler? How can I stay on at Chrysler when I can't stand it any more? And how can I follow a career in engineering when I no longer have any interest in it?"

Confusion seemed to grow daily, complicated by my wanderings in and out of everyday reality, multiple perceptual phenomena, and a host of odd physical difficulties that had plagued me increasingly over the summer.

Soon visits to the little tree were no longer enough to carry me through the afternoon. Driven by a rising inability to cope with the overwhelming sensory input coming at me from everyone and everywhere, and feeling that I was drowning in the anguish I experienced from those in the factory each day, I resigned from Chrysler in mid-October and left immediately. In doing so, I forfeited both the executive dreams of going through the glass ceiling, and the hope that Chrysler would pay for that last year of college. I decided that money was of small concern to me because I had a small amount in the bank, and I was certain that Ben and I were going to be able to open our bar and restaurant by Christmas.

Pressing me more than anything was the need to hide the fact that I was barely managing the conflicting perceptions and the resulting thoughts, feelings, and responses. Suddenly I had a driving need to get my mind under control, to understand what was happening to me and somehow get my sanity back to some semblance of normal. With sanity, self-control, and understanding as goals, I decided to abandon engineering, yet return to school to study and research everything that was known about the far reaches of the mind, the brain, and consciousness. I didn't know what kind of degree I would end up with or what kind of career I could make with such knowledge, I only knew I had to follow that path. ❧

5 ∾
Into the Fire

"We must reinstate the notion
that the body is an instrument of exploration
and counter the idea that its primary use
is for competition and combat."

Bob Samples

LEAVING MY POSITION AT CHRYSLER LEFT ME LOTS OF TIME TO EX-plore meditation and the mind, to renew my work toward a degree, and to help push forward the process of getting approval for our bar and restaurant, but I greatly underestimated the impact of such a move.

The job provided a necessary structure to my life and by leaving, I inadvertently created a gaping hole in my day-to-day routine. Worse, although Ben knew of my many perceptual difficulties and I had told him several times that I was thinking of leaving my job, his dismay and irritation was ill-concealed. Even after I announced that I had gotten our bar and restaurant approval onto the next agenda of Pontiac's city council meeting, he seemed to avoid me.

If I had not registered for five courses totaling twenty credit hours at Wayne State University, I would probably have fallen apart entirely. At first the classes seemed to be my salvation, providing an answer to the question of how to structure my life and time so as to be productive, but they quickly turned into a monumental challenge. The decision to return to school meant reading and study, which was an impossible task due to my inability to read, to concentrate, or to manage what I was now calling my '8-track mind.'

Just as I began to think that the semester was going to be a total loss, a small but important piece of information prompted me to experiment, thus saving the semester and initiating the very first, if isolated, step toward using my abilities.

Along with my classes at WSU, I was also continuing the classes in psychic development and it was in one of these classes that someone introduced the subject of Edgar Cayce and his healing abilities. Since I was taking a course in biomedical issues at WSU, I picked up a book about Cayce to see if there was anything in it that might be useful for both class-es. While browsing through the book, I ran across a line or a paragraph that described Cayce's ability to put a book under his pillow and after a night or two, absorb the contents of the entire book. We were several weeks into the semester and, since I had started late, I was already far behind in all of my classes. Given my predicament of being unable to read, yet needing to do so in order to study, do homework, and produce written papers, I decided this method of reading was at least worth a try.

At the very next class, I noted the reading assignment and that night put the book under my pillow. But all night I rolled and tossed, trying to get more comfortable. The book proved to be too bulky to put under my pillow, so the next night I tried it again, this time setting it on the floor beside the bed. I gave myself directions to 'read' the assigned chapters, and went to sleep. As had been the case for months, I slept poorly, if at all. However, that was such a common event that I took the fact of poor sleep for granted.

The next day, since I didn't know what to expect, I had no remark-able thoughts or ideas about the material. I decided to try it a third night, hoping that this would be my lucky night. When there were no special results after the third night, I decided I was doing something wrong, or I needed much more practice, or perhaps the whole idea was baloney. I worried about whether I should physically try to read the assignments but couldn't begin to force myself to sit still and concentrate. Me, who used to read by the hour!

Finally, it was the day of the next class. Because of my unconven-tional attempt to absorb its contents, I still had not even opened the book. We were now four weeks into class, and I knew either a paper or a mid-term was coming up. It was an hour before the class. Something in me told me I should at least open the book and put some yellow highlighting in it so it would at least look like I was reading. I took the highlighter, opened to the assigned chapters and randomly highlighted lines and paragraphs. Then I closed it, grabbed my bookbag and took off on the 30-minute drive to campus.

Once in class, I sat near the door, painfully aware of being behind and of my non-performance in the class so far. But I opened my book conspicuously, planning to listen carefully and take good notes. The class began, and as the professor led into his lecture, I found my head rapidly filling with ideas, arguments, and questions, a few of which I brought up. The professor seemed glad to have any response and began to direct many of his remarks in my direction.

Gradually, I became aware that the lecture was turning into a discussion and that I was spouting questions and statements that had never entered my head before. When the professor commented at one point that I 'must have gotten that argument from the paragraph on page 158,' I turned to that page and found I had highlighted the exact opinion I had just stated. An eerie feeling began to creep over me and I dropped out of the discussion briefly to pay closer attention to what the professor was saying and compare it to what I had highlighted. Gooseflesh rolled over me as I listened and realized I had highlighted most of the ideas and arguments the professor was emphasizing as important. By the time I walked out of class that night I knew that I had just conducted my first successful experiment with the possibilities of the mind. Needless to say I was pleased with the results.

I spent the rest of that quarter devising what I called 'a method of homework shorthand.' One by one I worked my way through each of the books, tracts, or papers that were assigned, using the following method each time. When the assignment was given, I would take the book to my bedroom that night, open it and look through the table of contents. Then I would put the book on the floor beside the bed and give myself instructions to absorb all of the author's ideas in the assigned chapters during the night.

The next night was similar, except that the instructions were to absorb all of the arguments to the author's premise, and to develop a response or conclusion of my own. Following this I put the book back in my book bag and left it there until the day before class. At this point I would get out my yellow highlighter and have myself a quick 'review' during which I would randomly highlight here and there, trusting that I would somehow hit exactly what I needed to know.

Finally, on the day of class, I would scan briefly through the things I had highlighted and after that I would go on to class, feeling ready and prepared...and each week the class was filled with fascinating lectures and engrossing discussions that the whole class often became involved in.

For papers that were due, I stacked all the books I had 'read' beside my bed, or that I thought were pertinent to the paper, then gave myself instructions to synthesize what I had learned. The next night the instruction would be to choose a theme for my paper and outline its major arguments. During the night, I would suddenly wake up with the theme and an outline in my head, write it down, and the next morning I was ready to begin my paper.

At first footnotes and references were quite a challenge since I had not physically read any of the material, but I soon learned to ask and then make notes in class of 'who had said what' in case I especially liked or disliked the idea we were discussing. Later, I could look in the index of the book and find the pages needed for quotes or footnotes. I also found I could, with a little determination, scan the material underlined, and come up with a quote supporting an idea that had occurred to me. When I couldn't, I simply treated the idea as my own.

For tests and midterms, I reviewed my notes and gave myself instructions to synthesize all of the material I had learned over the past term. When I got to class on test day and picked up my pencil, I would remind myself that I 'knew everything I needed to know and would recall it easily,' then settle in to take the test. Essay tests were especially easy and I found I could do them by the dozen. Multiple choice was a little more difficult, but I discovered that what I had always heard from teachers was correct – your first instinctive answer was usually the right one. I would read a question, glance at each possible answer, and immediately be drawn to one of them. If I understood the question at all, then I would usually 'have a feeling' about one of the answers. So, trusting – because I had no other option *but* to trust, I marked down the answer, went on to the next question, and when the test was done, I handed it in and went on my way.

In grade school, I had been a good student because I seriously worked at it. Throughout high school I carefully read the assigned materials, sometimes two or three times. I always completed my workbooks, handed in all homework assignments, and did the extra-credit work if it was offered. I took volumes of notes in class, studied regularly, and reviewed thoroughly before tests. By comparison, this new method seemed like cheating, but I reasoned that whether the ideas got into my head because I read them or because they just seemed to appear there, made no difference.

What did make a big difference was the qualitative change in my learning. There was a new dimension that I couldn't describe at the time. I was in an interdisciplinary program and perhaps it was just the synergistic effect of the ideas from five different classes that were meant to reinforce one another. Perhaps it was something happening inside me, but the fact was that I was no longer learning separate subjects, each with their own terminology and facts to be memorized. Instead, I was absorbing ideas and concepts and assessing them from many different perspectives.

In addition, my curiosity about how and why things worked was expanding. Now I was deeply curious, not just about who discovered this, wrote that, or invented a whirligig, but *how* the scientist, writer, or inventor got his ideas in the first place. I wanted to know exactly what he was doing at the time his bright idea, discovery, or brainstorm occurred. How had he arrived at his conclusion? What sorts of related projects had he been tinkering with when the structure of his theory, his invention, or his new book came to him? This kind of curiosity led me to search out information about the dawning of new ideas and to experiment with ways I might apply the same principles to my own goal – the drive to understand the mind and consciousness. From every angle, the semester was the most wonderful learning experience I ever had.

As I moved through the weeks at school, I was pleased with the new dimensions that learning had taken on and secretly ecstatic about the method of 'reading' I had devised. Excited about the next term, I asked several of my fellow students one day what they were going to take next semester, and one of them answered, "I'm taking whatever class *you're* gonna be in. I've never gotten so much out of school in my life as the two classes I've had with you!" I was pleased at this thought and it helped give me the feeling of being normal in spite of all the craziness still going on inside me.

🖎

As the semester progressed and the weather turned continuously colder, the perceptual experiences increased in intensity and length, and often accompanying these were frightening bodily experiences of great heat. One night, Ben and I were lying next to each other in bed, nearly asleep. I was extremely relaxed and a variety of daydreams were passing through my head when I was startled out of my reverie by a feeling of great sensuousness and what I thought was the sound of thunder.

I listened quietly while it continued, and then noticed that I seemed to be breathing in an odd, backward kind of way. My stomach sort of expanded when I exhaled rather than the other way around. I felt suddenly very sexual, and my heart started to beat quickly and then began to pound. Heat began to spread through me and I was certain I was on fire. I felt like a pressure cooker about to explode, and all the while the roar of thunder increased exponentially. In stark terror, I laid there pleading with my mind to stop doing this to me. When it continued, I got fierce, "STOP! Stop NOW!" I commanded.

The pounding heart was making me dizzy and the heat was unbearable when Ben suddenly sat up in bed snapping, "Jesus Christ, get away from me, you're like a goddamn oven!" This startled me and broke the chain of bodily events, but it provided the surprising affirmation that I was not imagining the events going on in my physical self.

Each time I went through one of these physical experiences of enormous heat and pressure, the perceptual theater would open further, staging new acts for my consciousness to deal with. Often, I found myself feeling incredibly sensuous and caught in the most demanding sexual desires I had ever known. The sensuousness was so overwhelming that at times I was embarrassed. Naturally, I attributed these sexual feelings to having somehow fallen even more deeply in love with Ben, even though he seemed to be growing cool and distant.

One evening right before Christmas, we went to bed early. I had experienced a growing passion all day and by evening it was a torrent of desire that no amount of logical reasoning or distraction would relieve. Ben was too tired for any kind of lovemaking and within minutes he drifted off to sleep.

After looking forward all day to going to bed and making love, I now lay on my back, fidgeting and trying to relax. I rolled this way and that, trying to get more comfortable but my body was like an electrical wire that wouldn't stop sizzling. I dozed, then woke up, still bothered by the intense sexual craving.

Again I dozed and woke, frustrated beyond belief. I thought about getting up to make a cup of tea, wished I had something to study, then decided I needed to stay in bed and get whatever rest I could get. Finally, I rolled over onto my right side, my arm dangling over the edge of the bed, and dozed again.

Suddenly I was wide-awake, out of the body, and hovering in mid-air, directly over Ben. Out of the corner of my eye I could see my own body curled over on its right side on the far edge of the bed, arm dangling over the edge. Ben's face was directly under me and as I gazed at him all the passion and feelings of intense desire gathered somewhere in the center of my abdomen. Then, as if some kind of union was taking place, I experienced a powerful electrical jolt. This was followed by an electrical current beginning to run through me with a feeling far more pleasurable than ordinary orgasm, far more gripping and more long-lasting. At the same instant, sparkling rays of beautiful, multi-colored lights began flashing and emanating from the center of my body. They were brilliant and spread out in every direction, going right through Ben and the bed. It looked as though we were being struck by colored lightning that was moving back and forth between us, but it would be more accurate to say that I had become the lightning itself.

As soon as the rays of light struck Ben, he began to move around. As they continued, he started to thrash about and I realized he was going to wake up. Foolishly afraid he would waken and see me hanging over him in mid-air with rays of brilliant light shooting out of me and an orgasmic kind of pleasure all over my face, I moved quickly over to my body, lined up with it and merged back into it.

Once back in the body, I sat up, in shock at what had happened. Ben settled down and went back to sleep, but I lay sleepless, stunned and silent. It took me two days to get up the courage to write the event down and weeks before I could think about the experience with even a hint of calm contemplation. I was now completely frightened at the power of my own mind and terrified at the loss of self-control. I was terrified that such unremitting sensuousness could create a sexual experience without mine or Ben's participation or consent. I couldn't just float around having sex with anyone I wanted!

Between the increasing episodes of thunderous roaring, shaking, intense electrical heat and pressure, the uncontrolled perceptions, and a demanding sensuousness, I remained caught in a slowly but steadily deepening fear of what was happening to me. I could not even begin to think about where it was all going, so I spent my time fighting off visions of an insane asylum. ઝ

6 ∞
Lost in the Land of Perception

*"Every experience
is not listed in the guidebook."*

Lois Wyse

CHRISTMAS CAME AND SO DID MY GRADES. I WAS PLEASED TO FIND I had earned twenty credits and five A's. I celebrated the success of having moved closer to the goal of earning my degree. I had absolutely no regrets about having abandoned the pursuit of a degree in engineering although I was still not at all sure where I was going with my study of the brain, mind and consciousness.

Occasionally, when I thought back over the fantastic semester, I felt guilty about not having physically read my homework, but I tried not to let it bother me. My unusual methods for reading and studying were almost the only activities in the realm of my growing psychic abilities that I had been able to bring even partially under some kind of useful control.

However, struggling with guilt over my homework methods was nothing compared to my struggles with perception or the strange physical experiences that regularly plagued me. During these, my heart began pounding, my body heated up, and there was occasionally a sense of being stabbed in the feet, back, or legs with an electrical prod which caused me to jump and cry out in pain. The terror I felt during these episodes was now surpassing every fear I had ever known. The fact that they were also sexual experiences added greatly to my difficulty in trying to figure out what was happening.

Over and over I tracked the beginning of the whole series of alarming events back to those first episodes of lovemaking in which the physical world had disappeared and I floated like a star in a sky of luminous waves moving through an eternity of blissful awareness.

Then, one day, I recalled that even before those first explosive experiences in February of 1979, our lovemaking had taken on an unusual dimension. For several months before those roaring excursions into the nothingness that was so complete, there were a number of times while making love that we had stopped being just two separate people and had become one giant, fluid body.

The first time this happened was in October or November of 1978. I remembered stopping in shock because my physical boundaries had dissolved and I was momentarily confused about just where I was and which body was mine. The next few times it occurred, I again experienced confusion, suddenly unable to tell where the 'other' body was. It was as if my individual self had dissolved or I was lost in the perception that I had expanded to become both of us. The fact was, I was no longer making love; I had *become* love. Gradually, this became a regular enough experience until even Ben was aware that something unusual was taking place.

Once he remarked humorously, "I *knew* I was waiting for something special..." Another time he emerged from the sense of oneness just long enough to note, "it's happening again..." but even talking did not disturb the sense of being just one body.

Although neither of us ever had such experiences before, we quickly accepted the feeling of oneness as if it were some heretofore undiscovered benefit of sex. I came to think of the whole thing as a sort of melting process in which I became this huge, fluid ocean of love without boundaries, flowing over, around, and through everything in the world.

As the months passed, each succeeding occurrence of this fluid oneness was stronger, more intense, lasted longer, and was more difficult to break. Finally, the fateful night in February arrived when ordinary love-making climaxed in the very extraordinary roar of thunder, the spectacular explosion of lights, the waves of color, the disappearance of physical reality, and the ocean of eternal awareness.

It had been difficult enough to put these experiences in perspective when they occurred at night while making love. But now they were happening spontaneously in the middle of the day and I was truly afraid. The sense of fluidity, the rumbling activity in my low back and groin, the pounding heart, the feeling that something was moving up through the center of me, the exquisite pleasure, the roaring explosion of light, and the sense of eternal peace and oneness – all began to happen in the middle of the morning, perhaps the afternoon or early evening, for no apparent reason and with no lovemaking to prompt it. Sometimes it happened during my meditation, but just as often I was sitting quietly, or standing at the window looking out at the water, or trying to take a nap.

For months, I had been watching myself for signs of worsening insanity and now, instead of focusing only on the frightening bodily experiences, I concentrated on watching the events *surrounding* them. I tried to note the conditions that preceded or perhaps triggered the experience. For a while, I thought the sexual craving for Ben was the trigger. Later, I came to suspect that this craving was more of a result of whatever was happening inside me, rather than something caused by Ben.

I noticed that my emotional state was often one of intense desire but not necessarily sexual desire, even though I felt the desire in my body as literally liquid streams of powerful feeling and sensuousness. Instead the desire was almost more of a 'reaching out' for something, perhaps to help someone, maybe to understand something, to brighten a stranger's day, or to resolve some sort of problem. The kind of desire or need or reaching out didn't matter; neither did the kind of problem make much difference. Whether it was something bothering one of my children, a decision regarding the small restaurant business Ben and I were trying to start, or any of the daily problems of living, I could see and feel these things with fierce intensity, and thus I could not simply overlook them. The act of focusing on the problem brought on the desire for a solution, and the desire for a solution brought on the sensuousness, and then the spontaneous physical experiences would begin again.

Now, like a cat crouched watchfully at a mouse-hole, I scanned the problems of both body and mind endlessly, wishing, hoping for a solution. I didn't know exactly when this sudden and deep caring about everything had begun, but I felt it constantly and it often added to my fatigue.

In an attempt to balance these cares and problems and find a moment of peace, I had gotten into the habit of concentrating on any little source of peace and pleasure I could find. I began to take exquisite pleasure in the simple act of 'seeing' and to notice the hundreds of small details found in any setting. The play of light across the water at sunset, the sensuous curve of a potato on my plate during a delicious dinner, an endearing look on someone's face, the shape, crackle, and movement of fire in the fireplace, the sound of children, or the rain and the traffic driving through it, all were sources of hypnotic pleasure. It seemed that lately I spent more and more time in the practice of focusing all my attention on any handy source of beauty or pleasure, no matter how small or how obscure, in order to provide some relief from the intense observation and desire. Doing so would create a little corner of quiet joy that would give me a break from the constant uproar and the intense vigilance I kept over myself.

After weeks of observation, I realized that my vigilance led me to focus deeply on resolving obstacles and problems…which then led to the search for pleasure, and it was my intense concentration on some small detail of pleasure that seemed to trigger the automatic change to 'backward' breathing. During the moment of concentration on peace, pleasure, and relaxation, the muscles of my abdomen would begin to move in their strange but now familiar pattern, then my heartbeat would join in the rhythm until both were moving synchronously.

If this continued for any length of time there would be a rumbling sound in the background, followed by a rocking sensation, sometimes a snakelike sense of movement, and frequently intense heat. The rumbling, along with the feeling that I was going to explode from both ends of my body, was followed by the feeling that something was moving up through the center of me, sometimes stopping at my navel or my chest, sometimes moving all the way up to the brain. My heart would begin beating like mad, faster than I ever experienced it or even thought it could go, and I would forget about everything around me and be lost in the experience of a world of light that had no name and no way to describe it because it was so completely empty except for the twinkling lights, the bliss, and the very singular knowing that amounted to – *I Am!*

Later, when the experience was over and I struggled to deal with this other world's lack of material form or activity, all I could say about the place that I went to and the experience I had there was that it was a place of utter fulfillment in which the only experience offered was the knowledge that I existed. In my imagination, I tried to explain to various people what this state of existence was like, and I always ended up with, "Well, all I can say is that when I'm in it, I am." To me this was a very lame description, so I never told anyone, not even my teacher in psychic development. And thus, I never learned that the things I was experiencing were classic symptoms of psychic development and the entry into mystical experience.

଄

About this same time there was another variety of perceptual phenomena that began to occur. The first experience happened at the end of an afternoon nap. I wakened but had not moved and was dozing on and off when I heard a sound and looked up. To my complete amazement a large, brilliantly colored, geometric form was moving through my bedroom. What was even more astonishing was that I recognized the form as my second daughter!

"Melissa?!" I called out to her in pleasant surprise, intending to ask what she was doing there like that. But the form kept right on going and disappeared, taking a sense of incredible sweetness with it and leaving the room suddenly darkened and drab. I put my head back down and burst into tears. For no apparent reason, I cried almost without stopping for two days. When the tears were finally over, I took out my journal, intending to write about the unusual geometric form and the fact that I had thought it was Melissa. But I ended up putting the journal aside, getting a blank piece of paper, and pouring out my experience in the form of a poem. This heralded an avalanche of poetry that poured out of me for several years, yet even now the poem *To Recognize Melissa* remains one of my favorites.

My dreams were increasing in vividness, length, and coherence, and many were lucid. Upon beginning the classes in psychic development, the teacher asked us to write down and study our dreams. She said this was an essential step in learning to plan and direct our sleep consciousness.

It wasn't at all clear just what you were supposed to do with your sleep consciousness, but I began giving myself directions to remember my dreams. I was nervous about doing so after the experience the previous spring in which I had given myself instructions to 'find my hands' but I made the effort anyway.

At first I had difficulty recalling anything let alone their details, even though I was awake in many of them. I always thought they were meaningless and paid little attention except for the nightmares. It took more than a month before I developed enough discipline to rouse myself as soon as a dream was over and jot down the basic events so that I could fill in the details in the morning.

At first it was a simple affair to jot down the remnants of whatever dream I had captured. But by December I was spending over an hour a day typing what I had written in the middle of the night and was also taking time to draw some of the unusual objects and scenes that appeared in them. Sometimes each dream would be two and a half, single-spaced, type-written pages. I always wrote them down, but I never got around to studying them for their meaning. I was too frazzled and distraught over the events of each day to fuss with the events of the night.

There were many nights when I did not sleep or dream at all. These were nights I would be in what I called 'suspended animation.' After going to bed for the night, I would get caught up in watching the colored lights around my body or Ben's and without realizing it, would drop into an altered state of awareness. In such a state, the perception of time was drastically changed and the whole night would be over before I knew it. I would greet the dawn suddenly aware that I had never gotten to sleep and now feeling tired and ragged.

Unable to sleep, I practiced detaching my consciousness from my body, traveling up through the roof, perhaps to sit on the peak, the edge of the chimney, or in a tree and watch what was happening on Jefferson Avenue. I didn't know what to do or where to go beyond that, and so the most important discovery I made at that time was that the night belongs to the animals! Other times I would travel in what seemed to be other realms of reality and existence, the most unusual and amazing being the realms of the 'light people,' or a place where everything was pink.

One night, feeling that I simply had to get more rest, I went to bed early and after some time, finally went to sleep. I dreamed I was in a castle in Scotland and that 'Sir Henry's ghost' kept appearing in the dead of night to play the organ in the sanctuary. I was secretly watching this ghost one evening when it collapsed over the keyboard and began to fall from the organ bench. I came out of hiding to lean over the altar railing and see what was going to happen next, but I tripped and lost my balance, nearly falling into the sanctuary right behind Sir Henry and the bench. As I hung over the railing, struggling quickly to regain my footing, Sir Henry's ghost grabbed a large machete and in sudden, horrified awareness I knew it was going to hurt someone.

I woke in terror and immediately upon awakening was cast into what seemed like still another world. There were wondrous, vibrant colors and shapes in motion all around me. I glanced at the clock and saw that it was 12:55 a.m., then looked around the room at the door, the antique sewing machine, the curtains, the bed, and Ben. Everything was in its usual place and yet everything seemed to be suspended within, or perhaps emanating from, a world of beautiful geometric shapes and colors, all undulating slowly.

Ben, awakened by the thrashing of my nightmare, asked me if I was all right and all I could say was "Ben! I see something...I can see something, Ben!" This was too vague for him and he rolled over and went back to sleep, but I continued to watch. It seemed like the colors and shapes went right through everything and yet gave the appearance of being some kind of transparent 3-D net that held all of physical reality. I wondered if I was seeing the molecular structure of things, but these undulating forms and colors didn't look like anything I had studied in chemistry or physics. Propped up on my elbows, I gazed at the beautiful forms for quite some time until gradually they faded and I was left in a dull, dark room. After laying back down, I was awake for a long time, wondering what I had just seen. Eventually I went back to sleep and to dream twice more before the night was through.

By early January, 1980, I was recording at least two and sometimes, three, four, or five dreams every night, typing them the next day. The dreams were lucid – meaning I thought I was awake – and I almost always got up each morning feeling like I had been up all night. Worse, nothing seemed to reduce the intense sexual desire that occurred and was accompanied by the spontaneous physical experiences of pain, heat, and pressure. All of this added to my fatigue, and I had a growing sense of depression over what was happening in my mind.

I was aware at one level that some unusual things were happening to me and that I had suddenly developed a considerable number of 'psychic talents,' but I remained unable to put together an explanation of how or why it was all happening. Nor was I very good at using them in any sort of organized way. It was all just miscellaneous craziness that didn't fit into any kind of framework yet filled my life and absorbed all my time and energy.

Infrequently, and more tenuously, I believed something important, even worthwhile, was happening but I couldn't explain exactly what. No one, not even Ben, knew the extent to which the perceptual phenomena were occurring, and I found it impossible to bring up the issue of the increasingly powerful sexual/physical experiences.

༼ ༽

By January I was in the poorest physical and mental condition of my entire life, often awake until Ben got up at 5:00 a.m. when I would get up briefly to help him get out the door to work. Sometimes I would return to bed, trying to sleep a couple of hours only to be involved in lucid dreams, and then forcing myself to get up despite feeling more tired than ever.

One cold, January morning I went back to bed at 5:15 a.m., right after Ben had left for work. When I couldn't sleep, I tried instead to meditate. Finally, I relaxed and was just dozing off, reaching for that blessed

sleep state when I heard the front door open and the jingle of keys. I figured Ben had come back for something he had forgotten so I lifted my
head and listened. He made a phone call and told someone he wouldn't be
in to work today because he had been 'stopped by the police.' I laid my
head back down thinking, "Uh-oh, now what's happened?" He had been
uncommunicative lately and I wondered if he would talk to me about what
just happened. I heard his keys jingle again and heard him coming up the
stairs.

I was lying on my right side with my back to the bedroom door
when he came in the room. I turned over to ask him what had happened
and there was no one there. I sat up, surprised. I listened to hear if he had
stepped back out of the room to go into the room across the hall, or maybe
back down the stairs. But after a few moments I realized I could not sense
his presence at all.

Now I got up and went downstairs to see where he had gone. I
couldn't find him anywhere in the house and when I looked in the driveway there was no car parked there. I was stumped, then frightened. I felt
that I could no longer tell the difference between reality and the strange
perceptions. ∽

7 ❧
Murdered

*"And when reality goes,
sanity has no reason."*

A.G. Smith

FEAR OF A DEEPER AND MORE PERVASIVE KIND OF INSANITY BEGAN TO grow, haunting every moment. A couple days later I came home from a trip to the grocery store to find my living room full of small, monkish-looking men wearing long brown robes. At first I tried to ignore the perception. I was at the kitchen sink trying to peel potatoes when they gathered in a circle behind me, asking if I would look at their pictures and trying to tell me I had something important to do here. When ignoring them didn't work, I tried to cover my eyes, then my ears, but they seemed to be communicating telepathically and I found I couldn't block them out.

Finally, I dropped to the floor and tried to cover my head, screaming hysterically at them to get out. When they started some kind of soft apologetic chant, I crawled into the bedroom, which was right off the kitchen. I climbed onto the bed and under the covers, berating myself for such irrational behavior and trying desperately to construct a white light around me as my psychic teacher had said. Eventually they left, telling me they would be back later when I was 'more open to conversation.'

At various times over the next two weeks I saw pink elephants, giant rabbits, and tropical jungles all within the four walls of my bedroom. One night in a long, lucid dream I met a tall, striking, blond woman who introduced herself as Pietra Pierello. She gave me some advice for dealing with my children, and invited me to call on her if there was a problem with them in the future.

Another night, I met a young, dark-skinned boy named Raoul who offered me help, but I didn't know what kind of help to ask for. And another night, I played cards until dawn with Uncle Lawrence, who had recently died and was living on the other side, looking extraordinarily healthy and with all his hair back. He asked me to tell his wife that he was doing wonderfully well and that he would wait around for her. I thought over the possibility of telling Aunt Beulah everything, but ended up sending only half the message, telling her simply that I had dreamed of her husband and he had asked me to tell her he was fine. I was still so terribly embarrassed about my psychic abilities that, even though the classes in psychic development made my experiences seem more normal, the less people knew about the troubles I was having with my mind, the better off I felt I would be.

It was now early February. The odd perceptions, my dreams, and my ordinary reality had become nearly indistinguishable from one another, and all took on an intensity and drama that gave them a nearly cinematic luster. I could barely tell what was real at all any more.

On the morning of February 5, I had an intense dream. In it, I was a small brown bear, and the experience was as lucid, as clear and as vivid as my life in the everyday world. Barely able to write about the experience of being an animal, I wrote about it in third-person English, as if I were describing someone else.

"There were two small bears, brown ones, living near Grandma's house in a large game preserve. One was dressed as a male. He wore blue jeans and a checked shirt. The other was a female. She wore a cotton print shirtwaist dress. They could talk and think and acted just like people. He, the male, got outside the game preserve one day. I'm not sure if he was lost or just really unwilling to find the way back in. Then he met or found the little female bear who was also outside the preserve.

"He complained a lot about everything. He was hungry and he was frightened and needed help, or protection, or to be taken home and taken care of, and a list of various other things. The little female bear just listened and smoked her cigarettes, was cool, calm, and unmoved by his inactivity or efforts to take care of himself. But she never left him. Once he begged her for something, either a cigarette or a cinnamon stick and she was about to share it when he said something wrong. She slowly and deliberately, without taking her eyes off him, put it back in the pocket of her dress and continued to watch him silently.

"He continued to complain and whine. Occasionally a tall, dark-haired man named Ahab would go hunting with a gun and one day he and a shorter companion saw the two small bears outside the preserve. The tall man aimed his gun at them but I don't think he ever pulled the trigger. It seems like the shorter companion intervened, or somehow the small bears were transported safely back into the game preserve.

"The sense of this place was fantastic – miles and miles of green forests and fields, rivers and mists, bushes and many vines, all like virgin land, protected and surrounded by a high fence. Once back inside, the female bear stayed near the male but refused to listen to his complaints, and he got weaker and weaker.

"One day she looked inside a tent-like covering that he was sleeping in and he was nothing but bones. All that was left was his skeleton. Yet she was not upset or sad; she knew he had chosen and also that he was really still alive.

"Then the little female bear was in a house, now as a person, with her sister, Pam, and her daughter, Nell. I'm not sure, but either they were coloring or doing some art activity. I vaguely recall they took something out of a box, and then later cut a round hole in the ceiling. Some copper, either a pole, or a pipe or something, was being worked with or used to pipe new water through the hole in the ceiling."

The alarm went off just as the dream was coming to an end and I was surprised to find that this was a dream as I had been sure I was a bear and was actually living the whole thing. Fighting a few moments of disorientation at discovering that I had been asleep, I immediately wrote the dream down. But then, too tired to think about it any further I put it away, tragically ignoring the message it contained.[1]

 C3

The next morning was the morning of February 6th and I was so mentally, physically, and emotionally exhausted that I stayed in bed when Ben got up to get ready for work at 4:30 a.m. After he left I cried, feeling helpless over the sorry condition of my life and the frustrating relationship with him. Adding to my misery was the fact that, now four months after leaving Chrysler and well past our Christmas target date, we still had not

---

1   See pg. 278 in Appendix B for a detailed analysis of this dream and for further information on dreams in general.

been able to get approval for the location of our bar and restaurant. The city of Pontiac kept asking for more and more information, paperwork, surveys, and meetings.

Then I dozed, dreamed a little, and woke up again shortly after 6 a.m. Still too tired and miserable to get up, I simply laid there on my left side, knees drawn up, hand tucked under my chin, going over the contents of the dream I'd just had when I thought I heard someone downstairs.

I wasn't sure I had really heard anything and recalled the morning three weeks earlier when I thought I'd heard Ben come in, keys jingling, and make a phone call to say he wouldn't be in to work that day because he'd been stopped by the police. So I listened carefully, trying to decide if I was really hearing something or if it was just another strange experience.

At that point, whoever it was started up the stairs. A bit frightened, I tried to pick up my head so I could hear better, but my hand seemed glued to my chin and my whole body was paralyzed and refused to move.

It was still dark out and whoever had come up the stairs was quietly coming into the room with me. Still, paralyzed, I was aware of the most terrible helplessness I had ever felt in my life. Suddenly, someone was dragging the covers over my head, trying to suffocate me.

In terror, I began struggling to pull them off but he – or it – was very intent and very powerful and my efforts seemed to accomplish nothing. I began to fight, but whoever it was crawled onto the bed, pressing upon me with great weight and holding both pillows and covers so firmly over my face that I could not breathe.

Bits of thought came in quick succession. "I have to be strong… He's bigger than me… I don't have enough strength… He's too strong… I'm not ready for this… not ready to die… I should have run…!"

The lack of air made my chest feel it was on fire. I tried to think of a white light. I screamed for Ben, for Jesus, for anyone who could help me get the covers off my face and breathe again. For an instant, I lay very still in an effort to marshal what little power I had left. At that moment, the living face of Jesus appeared right in front of me with eyes that seemed intensely alive yet calm. I heard the sound of loud humming, or the powerful buzzing that comes from high-powered electrical wires and then Jesus disappeared.

Again, I tried to move or roll over in any direction, but couldn't because of the great weight of whoever had me pinned down. Now I began to fight wildly, screaming, kicking, and clawing, trying to get some air. For a moment I was surprised at my own spunk, but then my efforts began to weaken when it crossed my mind that such insane wildness might cause a heart attack or I might die in a fit of apoplexy rather than by smothering.

By this time, I was aware that there was a sexual threat coming from whoever was on top of me and that I was going to be raped. I made one last superhuman effort to push my way into a sitting position but I was forced back down. Now the entire house seemed to be shaking and rumbling, and it struck me as odd that I was going to be raped and murdered during an earthquake, but I couldn't really dwell on anything anymore. Instead, I was aware that all was lost and I was going to die.

My body began to choke convulsively and I lost both the strength and the will to fight. My lungs were sizzling, I couldn't hold on any longer, and after a series of convulsive jerks, I melted into stillness. Then I found myself drifting out of the body, which was now dead and very still. I floated over to the window and right through it where I paused and looked back into the room.

This room was much bigger than mine and seemed to be on the third floor, while my bedroom was a second floor room, yet it had a slanted ceiling just like mine; and it seemed to be under the eaves, also just like mine. This room had some kind of flowered wallpaper on the walls rather than the rich, dark paneling of my own bedroom, and there was a large, oval, room-sized rag rug on the floor instead of the plush burgundy carpeting of the room I shared with Ben. Furniture was sparse in the strange room, and the sun seemed to be shining in from somewhere at the far end of the room. Near the door there was a dresser made of light-colored wood with six drawers. The top drawer on each side had a rectangular design carved in it and from where my body lay, the dresser would have been directly within reach.

I was looking at the room through waves of heat as everything shimmered and vibrated. I knew my life was over and tried again to think about Jesus and white lights but couldn't seem to focus on anything. One last time I thought of Ben… and suddenly the strange room, the dead body, and the oppressive force that had suffocated it were gone.

I was gasping for breath and shaking. The room was still quite dark and the clock sitting on the antique sewing machine registered 7:14 a.m. It took several shocking minutes for me to realize that I was really alive. I tried to calm down and relax by doing some deep breathing but as I did so I returned to another lucid dream in which I floated out of my body again and was suddenly outside, hanging in mid-air, looking through an attic window into the room I had just had the terrifying death experience in.

But now, instead of a body lying on the bed, I saw the body of a young woman dangling, swinging gently from the ceiling where a rope had been tied to one of the rafter braces. A man and a woman were staring at the body of a young slave girl. I had the inner knowing that this man was the one who murdered and raped the girl, then hung her body from the rafters to make it look like she committed suicide. The man, who looked terribly guilty, was telling the woman that the young girl had done it to herself. Suddenly, ignoring my first knowing about his guilt, I believed him and my thought shifted to, "My God, she did it to herself!"

Then, again without any sense of transition or shift of location, I was staring at the dark-paneled wall of my own bedroom, exhausted and fearful. Slowly I rolled over and stared across the room. I was alive and breathing, but fresh in my mind was the experience of having just been murdered.

I tried to think clearly about what just happened...Ben left for work...I had cried...then dozed...then wakened. Once awake, I heard someone come in the room and that's when the attack occurred. I thought I was awake and that the suffocation and death had really happened to me. I would have sworn I was awake, I could recount every vivid, terrifying detail. But here I was, lying safely in my own bedroom which was, in some ways, quite similar to the bedroom I had just been murdered in. I breathed deeply, conscious in a whole new way of how pleasurable breathing was.

In the end, unable to make sense of the whole series of events, I fell asleep but found myself in a long, lucid nightmare that ended with a stunning chase from rooftop to rooftop through a thoroughly modern South American city, pursued by International Agents from the central intelligence agency who were after me with machine guns. Giving up on the idea of rest, I got up and went downstairs to make a cup of tea, thankful that the last dream had been more of an ordinary nightmare, less real and without as much of the 'I-am-awake-and-this-is-really-happening' aspect.

For the next several days I was deeply unsettled and afraid. Was some malicious force trying to kill me? Was it still lurking in the house? And why? What had I done to attract such a force to my house or to experience such a fate?

For the first time I broke through the self-imposed taboo of keeping my experiences to myself and called a friend. I was truly frightened and needed the support. She didn't have a clue about the psychic world or the rest of what I was going through so I tried to be logical about what had happened to me. But it was difficult to tell a story like that and sound logical. I tried to be philosophical, but in the end I realized that I had just admitted to her that I could no longer tell which experiences were real anymore.

I hit a low point, caught between two worlds with no way of returning to the ordinary life I had once known and no way of moving ahead into a future that looked utterly insane.

The perceptual and physical experiences were now as regular and as constant as the ordinary world of doing laundry, raking the yard, washing my hair, or opening the mail.

To make things worse, I was running out of money, Ben was now openly angry that I had left engineering. He seemed to have forgotten that when I left Chrysler the previous October, we both expected the bar and restaurant to open by Christmas.

When he wasn't snipping at me to go back to work, he kept repeating over and over, "Just a couple more weeks and we'll have this show on the road. All we need is the okay on our location."

As much as I wanted to reassure him that we would be okay financially, I wasn't sure of anything. I knew I simply could not return to any job at that moment or I would crack and come apart completely. As much as I tried to join him in the enthusiasm that the bar and restaurant would all be happening in just a few more weeks, I was beginning to have serious doubts.

Over the rest of February, on through March, and into April, the uncontrolled experiences increased in intensity. I spent most of my time and energy trying to use my newfound psychic abilities to do some healing on myself, but there was little effect and I remained tired and drained, anxious about my waning relationship with Ben, and making a desperate effort to hide my fear about losing my mind. ✃

8 ❧
A Turning Point

> *"Strength is a matter*
> *of the made-up mind."*
>
> John Beecher

IT WAS NOW **A**PRIL OF **1980** AND **R**OB, OUR NEIGHBOR AND CO-WORKER from across the highway, invited Ben, myself, and several others to a lecture titled *Using The Other 90% of Your Brain.* The speaker was a woman who supposedly had many psychic abilities. In spite of my own experiences, I was still seriously prejudiced against people who claimed they were psychic or even interested in things of that nature.

As I considered whether to go or not, I bumped up against the same kinds of fears that came up around the classes in psychic development. I assumed that the only people interested in such things would be witches or social misfits. A few days later I decided to go anyway. More than anything I needed to get my life back on an even keel and I was desperate for any kind of help or insight into how to do this. Maybe this woman would have some helpful ideas.

The lecture hall was packed and the moderator and host for the evening began with a statement of what the guest speaker was going to talk about. He introduced her, said she would do a short demonstration of her abilities at the end of her talk, and then the speaker, a tall, dark-haired, soft-spoken woman with several university degrees in the hard sciences, launched into a talk about money and health. Her position was that health was the natural state of man and it was man's mind that made him ill physically, mentally, emotionally or otherwise. I couldn't have agreed more, especially given the physical, mental and emotional state I was in at the moment!

When the talk was over and it looked like things were going to end without a demonstration, I raised my hand to ask for one. I wanted to see for myself what a 'psychic demonstration' consisted of. She asked me to come up to the podium and said she was going to 'become a medium.' She instructed me to ask a question and then closed her eyes, looking strained. I didn't know what to ask so finally blurted out, "Where will I be a year from now?"

"Here," she said, "You are not going anywhere."

This seemed like an overly simplistic answer and I was trying to think of something else to say when she said she could sense a very great fear in me.

I answered evasively, "Well, I'm nervous about being up here in the first place."

She repeated that she could sense a terrible fear, then told me to ask something else.

"Is there anything that will get in the way of getting my degree?" I asked.

"No," she said, easily and spontaneously.

Then she rubbed the side of her head, said she was getting a throbbing pain on the right side of her head and asked me if the right side of my head hurt. I told her it did, and she went on to say again that I seemed to be consumed with fear, terribly afraid of life, and in conflict with authority. She suggested that perhaps I'd had a confrontation with my mother that I should review, then she told me to go on and ask something else because she didn't want to say any more in public.

I was casting around in my mind for a third question but the moderator of the lecture jumped up and, waving me to my seat, said, "...and the third question is 'Why have none of these been *mediumship* questions?'" He went on to say a few other things that closed the lecture and after standing there for several uncertain moments, I went to sit down, totally disgusted with myself for no apparent reason.

All the way home I berated myself because I didn't have any questions prepared, couldn't think of anything when I had the chance, didn't know enough to shut my mouth, and didn't know there were certain kinds of questions called 'mediumship questions.'

I was disappointed because I really hadn't learned anything useful about how to deal with my own mind and I felt foolish at having been told something so general as 'you have a problem with your mother.' I told myself there had been no confrontation with my mother, and I felt that anyone could walk up to a stranger and say they sensed fear. Angrily, I decided I had paid good money to attend only to be ripped off. I felt cheated. I wanted to be told something good, something fantastic and romantic and exciting. I didn't want to hear about my fear.

What I didn't realize at the time was that she had hit the nail on the head. My strict Catholic parents were refusing to come and visit me because I was living with a man and was not married to him. Worse, I was *consumed* by fear of what was happening to my mind and I wanted to be the authority in control again. I should have realized it was only normal for her to tune in to that because I was doing the same thing with other people – knowing and feeling what they were experiencing in their private lives! Instead I became enraged with her, turning her words over and over in my mind, arguing with her in my imagination, defending myself and demanding that she prove her psychic abilities by doing something real, or pertinent. When I went to bed I was still so angry I was completely unable to sleep or even rest.

In the morning I was even more upset to realize that I spent the entire night in suspended animation and it was once again time to get up without feeling the benefits of the badly needed sleep. I was still infuriated over the events of the night before and as I lay in bed stewing about it, it suddenly came to me that it was time to deal with the fear. Never before had I admitted being so consciously aware of fear until the terrible perceptions and physical experiences had begun, but suddenly there it was – overwhelming fear – and I was tired of fighting it.

As this realization swept over me, it was like a breath of fresh air, an idea both novel and astonishing. After a moment I decided to relax and let ideas come to me about how to deal with it. I began to wonder what fear itself was and decided to go exploring in my mind to see what I could learn.

This was followed by what seemed like another brilliant insight – that learning about fear might itself be a fearful experience, and that I should give myself special instructions to remain in control in case it got to be too much to deal with. Glancing at the clock, I also gave myself instructions not to fall asleep, and to rouse myself at 8:00 a.m. unless doing so would interrupt the information I was seeking.

Then I began to breathe slowly, relaxing each part of my body, and presently I became aware of the familiar sound of thunder in the background. For the first time I did not panic at the sound. Instead I concentrated on it and told myself this was a normal and regular part of my experiences. I reinforced the idea that I was doing well so far, and directed my attention toward achieving complete relaxation.

My physical eyes were closed and for a while I simply peered into the blackness all around me, wondering if I would see or learn anything in this experiment. Presently I saw what appeared to be a hand wearing a white glove. It reached in front of me and pulled a single sheet of newspaper off a tall, cone-shaped pyramid that suddenly appeared out of the darkness. I heard the crackling or rustling noise that paper makes when it is handled and I wondered why I was seeing and hearing those particular things. I waited, and when nothing else happened, it occurred to me to reach for the paper and crumple it up in a ball just to see if I could hear the crackling noise again. I did so, and heard the noise just as I had expected.

Again things seemed to come to a halt. At this point, I thought of Milton Erickson for some reason. I had just purchased a book about him, read the first couple of chapters, and now a line from the book came to me. It went something like 'it is easier to induce and maintain trance if a set of familiar sights, sounds, and feelings is systematically recalled.'

I was not exactly sure just what a trance was and wondered if I was in one, but I decided to acknowledge again that the sound of thunder was quite familiar, as was the feeling of complete relaxation. Still, I could distinguish nothing visually, there was only blackness.

After staring into the dark for a few minutes it occurred to me that the newspaper might qualify as a 'familiar sight' for at least this experiment, so I acknowledged the newspaper again.

Then I got the idea that maybe I could throw the crumpled ball of newspaper out into the darkness in front of me and follow it to see where it would lead. Just before doing so, I reaffirmed my instructions to stay in control, as this venture was to learn about fear and might be scary in itself.

The next thing I knew, I was out of the body, standing on the floor, facing the window at the north end of the bedroom. I could see everything, including myself laying on the bed with my eyes closed. It was so clear that for a minute I thought my physical eyes must be open. I got back in the body and concentrated on feeling my eyes to make sure they really were closed. I had the exquisite, momentary pleasure of feeling exactly where the two edges of my eyes – eyelid and lower rim – came together. I could also feel the feathery touch of my eyelashes resting on the skin just under my eyes. Everything seemed safe so I left the body and again stood in the middle of the room.

I looked around at the room itself, the sloping ceiling, the *Pinnoe* painting on the wall, and the archway to the dressing room. I knew I was in a state of full awareness outside my physical body, and reassured myself that my body was lying safely on the bed. This realization sent a small thrill of both excitement and fear through me, and just for good measure, I again reminded myself to stay in control. Then I turned around, opened the bedroom door, and walked into another world on the other side.

I found myself in a very large, elegant bedroom suite with an unfamiliar layout and dark, imposing furniture. I felt some shock but hung onto my sense of purpose and self-control. The room was English Tudor in decor with a very high ceiling, and I had on a long-sleeved, floor-length dress made of a dark, velvety, and very heavy fabric. The bodice was brocaded, the skirt smooth, and as I ran my hand across the fabric I was surprised and pleased at how rich and elegant the fabric felt.

There was a large four-poster bed in the middle of the room with curtains and lace around it, and there were matching velvet draperies at the huge windows that ran from the floor almost to the ceiling. I touched the bed and for a moment wondered how everything could look and feel so real.

If someone had asked me right then where I was, I would have had to swear that I was in a large English country home wearing a beautiful gown that looked like it came straight out of the eighteenth century. This critical assessment of the reality where I now found myself caused me to lose some of my self-control. I reminded myself that I was really lying safely on the bed in my house on Jefferson Avenue, but fingers of fear poked at me in spite of myself.

As I struggled to maintain control of the experiment, I sensed that someone dangerous was in the bedroom with me, and suddenly frightened, I ran over to the bed and buried my head under the pillow, trying to hide. This did not help the growing panic as the awareness of something frightening – terrifying – came closer and seemed more real.

"Get away from me!" I cried out, head still in the pillows, but my voice seemed to croak and make almost no sound at all. I had the clear thought that I was so tense I couldn't even talk or scream. In spite of the tension and the paralyzing fear, I continued to wave my arm crazily as if warding off something while crying, "Get away from me...get away!"

After a minute, I looked up and there were vague forms of several people in the room so I buried my head in the pillows again, aware that I didn't want to see them. As a matter of fact, it seemed that I was deliberately blocking my own vision, thinking that by doing so I would have nothing to be afraid of. But I could still feel and hear them around me, and by looking up, I saw that their white, ghost-like shapes were drifting toward the bed. Terror took full hold and I began screaming again, "Get away! Leave me alone," over and over again.

At this point, something distracted me from my terror. The cool, practical side of me that was determined to learn about fear noticed that when I screamed there seemed to be a roaring or pounding going on in the background as if a whole group of natives were beating or pounding on wooden drums with their hands and feet. I deliberately screamed several more times just to see if the same roaring or pounding could be heard, and noted that it could. I looked up and around me again, objectively wondering where the sound could possibly be coming from and, as if noticing my surroundings for the first time, it struck me at a very deep level that I was in a truly strange room in an unknown reality.

Suddenly, out of the corner of my eye, I saw a couple of ghost-like cats coming through the air toward the bed. I covered my head with one hand as if to protect myself and screamed again, waving the other arm crazily in front of me trying to ward off the ghosts. The fact that this was to be an experiment with fear was now forgotten and my self-control was slipping away.

Then a human-like ghost shape was right beside me. I scrambled onto the bed and kept on screaming, the terror mounting to unbearable proportions as the ghost got onto the bed with me and started to slide over toward me. The ghostlike shape reached out and touched me, and screaming in mindless, nearly convulsive horror, I went scrambling out of reach across the bed, jumped to the floor where I stood between the bed and the wall, shrieking and crying hysterically. From there I could see even more shapes and forms around me. I began to lose touch with the whole scene because of the extreme terror, but just then, the part of me that was conducting the experiment popped into my mind with the cool observation, "This is insane."

Remembering that I was tying to conduct an experiment on fear, I had several conscious thoughts in quick succession, "Yes, part of my fear is that I will go insane, be crazy." It occurred to me to return to my physical body, open my eyes, and just reassure myself that I was still in control of what was happening, still safe.

For a split second and with tremendous effort I went back to my body, blinked my eyes once, and managed, in that one difficult blink, to see the dark paneled wall, the red satin quilt, and the *Pinnoe* painting. Everything appeared to be upside down and out of context with what was happening in the English Tudor room, but in that instant I was satisfied that I was still safe as well as still intent on learning about fear.

Immediately I went back to the strange 18th century room, but by now I had stopped screaming. Everything was quiet, yet there was still a great deal of fear that the ghost-like things were going to come after me again. For the moment, though, I was in control and they had disappeared.

I walked to the heavy carved door, opened it and entered a hallway with a railing on one side that looked down over a spacious entryway and huge, elegant living room. As if I knew exactly where I was going, I went down the hall to a wide, curving staircase and walked down the stairs, noticing with pleasure the feel of the thick balustrade under my hand.

At the bottom of the stairs, I turned and walked through a short hall from which I entered a formal dining room with a long, polished, very beautiful table. Sliding my hand along the table I experienced a renewed amazement at how physically real everything felt in this other world.

Still exploring, I walked through the dining room to a set of tall French doors, which I opened, then stepped out onto a stone terrace edged by a low stone wall. I noticed several children playing in the courtyard nearby but I didn't look at them directly or even wonder who they were. I was beginning to be aware that I was almost afraid to see anything too clearly. I wanted to turn around and look at the entire structure I had just walked out of, but I resisted and instead kept walking. I went through a gate in the stone wall and headed down a long, sloping driveway toward the road. Finally, I could not resist turning around to look at the house. When I did I saw a very large, very lovely manor house with many tall, leaded glass windows.

My room had been on the second floor and looked out over the courtyard below. As I gazed at the window that had been in my room, I could see a light-haired man and recognized him as someone I loved. He was moving about the room, acting very sneaky. I was aware that he and others in the family thought I was crazy and often kept me confined to my room. From where I stood watching, it appeared that he went into a closet where he was looked for something he had hidden among the boxes and shelves in there. As he disappeared out of the range of my vision I had a gripping thought, "You can't trust anyone, not even those you love."

Immediately following that thought, the part of me conducting the experiment said, "Yes, that's another thing that may be connected to my fear, the fact that I don't trust."

With that observation I started to lose control, and the great fear returned. I reminded myself that I was to stay in control, and so again, with great effort, I returned to my physical body, and briefly blinked my eyes to make sure I was still in my bed, safe and sound. Again, the glance at the ceiling, the dark wall, and the painting was disorienting and out of sequence with what was happening in the English reality, but I knew everything was still all right with my physical body.

I returned one last time to the English countryside where I continued my walk, but now I was beginning to feel exhausted. I walked about for a bit longer, getting as far as a dusty road, but then decided that I had learned some very valuable things about myself and my fear and that was enough for now. I decided to end the experiment for the time being and return to the body. Once back in the body I opened my eyes and looked with unusual peace at the room around me. Then for the first time in more than a year and a half I rolled over and drifted into a quiet, restful sleep.

CB

And that was the turning point. Taking myself in hand, I began a journey with my conscious mind that took me one step backwards for each two steps forward. Gingerly I began to experiment here and there, no longer agonizing so much over experiences that others would have said were crazy. My earlier fears about the appearance of psychic abilities in my life were still there, but now there was a fascination with the system I had come to think of as the body/mind system, and I could think of nothing else but discovering more and more about how this magnificent system worked. I started by deciding first to learn something about the physical body that I had always thought I *was,* and now thought I was merely inhabiting. Not long after this I was able to begin reading again and went through books like *Introduction To Physiology* and *Gray's Anatomy* as if they were as juicy and dramatic as *Sweet And Savage Love.*

Following this, I began to study systems and patterns of all kinds from families, to educational systems, to religions, to technological systems. I didn't know exactly what I was searching for, but I was definitely curious about discovering the basic elements of any system that existed in our reality. Anything that even resembled an organized way of doing things, or that had become one of the common patterns of everyday life fascinated me. A number of my psychic experiences had been accompanied by a repeating set of circumstances and perceptions and I was certain there was a pattern to it all. Above all, I was determined to find out what had happened to me and why.

For now, it seemed most important to put myself back together in some kind of functioning mode that took into account everything that had happened and to begin redefining the reality I once thought was all figured out. Who was I... and what was I doing here in this place called Earth? What was possible for the human being... and which rules of reality did I need to rethink?

Gradually, I began to increase experimentation with telepathy and forms of communication considered to be 'other than normal.' I began to move forward and backward and around in time just to see what I could see, making notes of the events and the people observed. I watched to see if what I observed through other than normal channels came to happen in the 'real' world, or were otherwise verified or backed up.

Carefully, I observed how people and their behaviors fit together into patterns, whether the patterns were productive or not, as well as how, when, and why change happened in their lives.

I continued my Dream Record, which helped me begin planning, organizing and directing from one to five dreams every night, and made my first feeble efforts to decipher the dreams as they occurred.

Caught up in the discovery that I could play with the sparkling, swirling clouds of light that moved and changed color around every body, I decided to learn massage therapy and experiment, finding out what kinds of changes I could create in other body/mind systems.

The result of all this led to a singular observation that became critical to my own evolution and understanding. In my experimentation, each time a deliberate, specific direction was given or question was asked, my mind immediately set to work to present the answer to conscious awareness. So I formed a preliminary hypothesis. The hypothesis was that the mind would retrieve any information we needed or wanted to know and that all we had to do was ask the right question or give the proper directions.

This hypothesis also provided a solution to the problem of what I once described as my inability to control my perception. The source of all the strange, untimely, and conflicting perceptions was my own natural curiosity! This seemingly built-in need of mine to understand how and why things happened in the world around me had created dozens of unconscious, half-formed questions about everything – people, places and events – and my mind was simply trying to present me with all the answers to my own questions. The result was an avalanche of information coming at me in every form – visual, auditory, or kinesthetic – and from every direction.

Whatever had previously filtered out all of this competing information was no longer working, and the result was analogous to filling your plate with meat, salad, vegetables, a dinner roll, mashed potatoes, gravy, and dessert then trying to swallow food, plate, tablecloth, and table all at once!

My mind was an undisciplined child that flitted about, going in twenty directions at one time, wondering about this, curious about that, questioning everybody and everything. All of this questioning pulled in tremendous amounts of information, disrupted the continuity of my consciousness, and left me confused about what to pay attention to. Suddenly, with no order or priority to my thoughts or perceptions, no real interest in much of the information dredged up, and no basis for responding or even using the information, I found I had succeeded only in overwhelming my conscious mind. As tons of useless data gathered from all sorts of places in time and space poured in, my usual orderly perception and processing had been constantly interrupted. Now I discovered I needed to rein in my mind.

To help me with this, I practiced staying completely open and attentive to the present moment without making any decisions or judgments about anything that was happening. "Just watch!" I told myself again and again.

Gradually, this practice of just watching taught me that I had been trying to control the world so I could have a sense of security, a feeling of power in and over my life.

One of my biggest problems turned out to be the unconscious fear that something would happen and I would not know how to respond or how to behave. What if I didn't know what to say or what to do? I might end up feeling helpless, looking stupid, missing a juicy opportunity, being manipulated, or otherwise taken advantage of. Thus, I tried to control things. I didn't know where this fear of not knowing the right answer came from, but to help me balance the fear of inadequacy, I kept telling myself that I would know whatever I needed to know whenever I needed to know it. Again and again I took a deep breath and tried to let go of wondering, worrying, and trying to control everything so I would be safe.

In addition to watching myself, I began to spend more and more of my time just watching the world in general. I learned to observe without getting involved, without prejudice or bias, without applying my usual set of assumptions, and without jumping to conclusions or useless judgments.

It seemed like forever since my troubles had begun. Somehow I was surviving. As I mused on how lucky I felt to have made it so far, I made what turned out to be the first clear decision regarding my mind. The decision was simply to be more conscious of what I was conscious of, and that turned out to be the first in a long series of steps that would move me toward integrating my old self and my new abilities. ෆ

9 ❧

The Shifting Sands of Personal Reality

*"Reality is not an exhibit
for man's inspection,
labeled 'Do Not Touch'."*

J. Bronowski

THROUGHOUT THE SUMMER OF 1980, I CONTINUED TO EXPLORE AND experiment with consciousness. Although still tired and on edge, there was a gradual calming effect all through me and slowly I began to feel a sense of direction and power in my life and with my psychic abilities.

At deeper and deeper levels I was aware of people as both a body and a mind, the two of which worked together as a single, integrated, functioning self.

Previously, if I had thought about the mind at all, I had lumped it in as some part of the body. Now in a one-hundred-eighty degree reversal, I thought of the body as some part of the mind. A general reverence and awe for the mind filled me and I came to think of the individual mind as a personal collection of moving pictures, sounds, feelings, meanings, patterns, memories, colors and perceptual habits.

Embarking on another period of intense observation, I began watching people and was amazed at the ways individual minds could think, observe, express, interpret, know, synthesize, analyze, guess and worry! It was the mind and its perceptions that were used to create a personal reality, and it was the body/mind acting as a singular unit that made an effort to share or communicate that reality to others.

The most powerful and important communications came from parents! Everywhere I looked I saw mothers holding their children, feeding them, coaxing them to smile, to walk and talk while the children glowed expansively, took happy risks, learned, and enjoyed the reality they found themselves in. Many of these mothers did not really understand that they were teaching their child how to create a personal reality, they just wanted the child to feel loved and accepted. Thus, they tended to minimize time spent in situations that placed unnatural demands on their children, and to focus on creating a reality the child could learn to manage.

Other mothers pulled their children roughly by the arm down sidewalks and across shopping malls. They yelled at them, slapping them in public for their natural curiosity, insisting that they sit or stand still and shut up, while the children looked miserable. For these children, every move or unusual noise became a source of possible reprimand or abuse. They ended up living in fear. Their minds and hearts shriveled as they suffered the reality they found themselves in and learned how to create only misery. It never occurred to these mothers that an endless string of stores, banks, and offices was not a natural environment for children to be in, and expecting them to 'behave,' to be quiet and hold still was unrealistic and damaging to the brain's great need for constant movement and sensory input. These mothers did not seem to know they were expecting unnatural behavior and programming the child to expect misery.

I watched people of all ages walk, talk, their postures and positions, the quality of their movements, the sounds of their voices and thought how clear it was that we shape one another's existence by the messages we send and the responses we receive. To this day, I still watch the world struggling to communicate experiences in an effort to share those that are common because this is what allows the construction of a group reality system. When individual experience gets too far out of line with the group, we look for help in the form of teachers, therapists, and guides. This highly disciplined sharing makes us all feel a little less lonely and separate in our experiences as individuals – unless we start trying to dictate to one another what a reality is supposed to be like.

By the end of the summer I was feeling somewhat better about what was happening in my mind, and much worse about my finances and the relationship with Ben. Surprisingly, after a year of fighting with my ex-husband over custody of our children, I had talked him into doing the one thing I thought I would never do – splitting them up and allowing my two oldest daughters to come and live with me.

I awakened early on a Saturday morning and lay in bed daydreaming and letting various thoughts flow through my head. All of a sudden I heard a voice say, "Call John and ask him to let two of the girls come and live with you. He will say yes."

Without analyzing or hesitating, I got up and made the call. John was obviously still in bed and half asleep, but I didn't apologize. I just put it right out there in plain and simple language, "John, how about letting Kelly and Melissa come and live with me. I can take them now, so they'll be all settled by the time school starts. We don't have to change the child support either. I will continue to pay you the same amount, and you won't have as many mouths to feed so maybe it will be a little easier for you. What do you say?" There was only a moment of quiet at the other end of the line, and then he agreed. I hung up and started planning.

The girls arrived in August and I found they had a very good effect on my mind, giving my life more structure with less time to worry about my perceptual difficulties. Their arrival did nothing to help the relationship with Ben. Even though he encouraged me to bring the girls to live with us, he seemed disapproving of them once they arrived.

Approval of a location for the bar and restaurant continued to run into a multitude of snags, and even though we still had no clear idea of when it would open, I again asked Ben to marry me.

This time he did not answer. Instead he seemed to withdraw further and further from me. When I finally asked him point blank if he was ever going to marry me, he said he didn't know and suggested I go back to work. I was deeply committed to him and the relationship, I had been so from the beginning, and even more so since we bought the house. So when the girls started school at the end of August, I took a part-time job at a lumberyard, working six hours a day. This eased my growing financial pressures somewhat and provided an entry back into the world outside after nearly a year of seclusion at home.

Yet after starting back to work, I was alternately pleased and appalled; pleased at the feeling that things were coming back together for me, and appalled at the people I found myself working with. They were caught in the same meaningless, angry, half-lived lives that the people at Chrysler had been trapped in. I listened to their stories, their complaints, their dramas, and was heartsick. They seemed to think their lives were normal and that frustration, disappointment, misery, and misunderstanding were to be expected.

For the first time I saw that during my year of isolation at home in which I struggled to return to some semblance of normal perception, something deep within me had changed. Now I recognized the abysmal condition of most people as the same one I had recently come out of, a condition of constant fear and anger. I hadn't known I was in that abyss when I was in it, and I didn't quite know just where I was at present, but I knew I wasn't where I had been and they still were.

I could still see, hear, and know far too much of people's private lives, but found I had made some progress in disciplining my mind. Meanwhile, the lumberyard became a good place to practice this discipline further by not knowing and not becoming involved in their anguished, troubled lives.

I had only been at the lumberyard for a few weeks when it looked like Ben and I finally made enough progress with the approval of our bar and restaurant location to begin taking active steps toward opening day. We were pretty certain that we would be able to open before the end of the year and since I knew almost nothing about liquor, I decided to attend bartender's school.

In October, before I finished the bartender course, I left the part-time job at the lumberyard for a full time job as bartender in a large bowling alley and restaurant. I didn't mind having to work nights and was excited to be getting some real experience, but it turned out to be awful. I hated the smoke, the loud bands and the drunks, but kept at it, pleased that I could maintain normal perception even under great pressure.

CB

About this time, the voice with the soft, hillbilly twang, the same voice that had first told me it was time to develop a 'legal self and an aloof self,' spoke up again, giving me a message that felt very important. I was so surprised to hear that same voice after such a long interval of time that I forgot to pay attention to the message and couldn't remember what he'd said once I got past the shock of hearing him again. It had been over a year since I'd heard him, but I recognized the voice instantly. Since I was currently reading Edgar Cayce's *Story of Attitudes and Emotions,* I dubbed him 'Edgar' and tried to send a message that apologized for not catching his message.

In late October he returned, telling me that my Grandpa Kelly was with him and had a message for me. The message was that my father's lost brother, Bill, had died and I should tell my Dad.

When I did not do so, he returned a week later and again urged me to 'tell your Dad that his brother, Bill, is dead.' I sat quietly, wondering if I should say anything to my parents. They lived several hours north of me and knew nothing of what I was going through. I was sure they would think I did not know what I was talking about if I called them with such a message. Uncle Bill had disappeared more than forty years earlier and no one had seen him since. Absently I wondered where he was when he died and to my surprise the voice with the southern accent said, "Look!" Before my eyes appeared scenes of the desert and a pinkish-gold city with the sign 'Phoenix.'

"So! Uncle Bill was in Phoenix all this time!" I thought, and for the first time since the experience on the roof of the factory, my reaction was one of certainty rather than doubt. But the certainty was short-lived.

"I can't tell my dad such a thing," I decided. "What if it's wrong? What if he wants to know how I know or who told me? He already thinks I'm a wild, unruly radical for moving to the city and living with some man in the first place!"

For a while I did nothing, but the message about Uncle Bill got me to wondering if my parents had ever heard of psychic phenomena. I could not recall the subject ever even being mentioned let alone discussed in all the years I was growing up at home. Nor had there been such people as tarot card readers, dream interpreters, or the like in my childhood environment.

Since the Christmas season was not far off, I decided to buy a set of Carlos Castaneda's first three books and wrap them up as a gift for my father. He loved to read, and I hoped he just might read between the lines of the gift and perhaps guess what I was going through. If he didn't read between the lines, I figured he would at least have a little background on the subject if we ever got a chance to talk about it in the future.

I had just purchased the books and taken them home when my mother called one night to say hello and find out what was new since they hadn't heard from me in a long time. The conversation was going along as most mother-daughter talks do when she casually mentioned that they had just found out that Dad's long-lost brother, Bill, had died.

I was speechless for a minute, and then blurted out the story of the message to tell Dad that very thing. I told her I had first been told to tell him in October and asked if she knew when he had died.

"Yes," she said, "he died in October... I guess he was living in Arizona."

She seemed quite curious and interested that I had known, and when we finally hung up the phone I realized several important things. One was that I had just had some very real validation of something that I first thought would be impossible to prove or explain how I knew such a fact.

The second was that by not telling my father when I first got the message, I had missed an opportunity to share what was happening to me and then have it validated within my family.

The third was a comforting feeling that I had shared a hint of what was happening to me with my mother and she hadn't fainted away in shock nor had she laughed or made fun of me. Her attitude surprised me, her curiosity steadied me and made me feel almost normal. And for the hundredth time in the course of my adulthood I again discovered that my parents were not in the boxes I had imagined. They were simply on the canvas of my mind as only I had painted them and only I could revise them.

CB

Shortly after the messages about Uncle Bill came to a conclusion, Edgar began speaking to me again.

"Buy a year's worth of food and a wood-burning stove," he urged. I listened to this same advice over and over but did nothing about it at the time because I was too caught up in trying to decide how to handle such messages. I was also too busy trying to push the settlement of our bar's location, and too distraught about my relationship with Ben. With him working days and me working nights, we had seen very little of each other lately. When we did get together, we often wasted our time in a cool sparring match.

On Thanksgiving Eve, I was not feeling well at all, and since several days had passed without seeing or talking to him, I called in sick and stayed home, thinking I would spend the evening with him. My daughters had gone to visit their father for the holiday, so around 5:00 p.m. I fixed a tasty dinner for two, then sat down to write letters while I waited for Ben to come home.

Time passed unnoticed at first and before I knew it, seven o'clock came and went. For the first time I realized that Ben had no idea I did not go to work, or that I was at home waiting dinner for the two of us. He often stopped at the bar after work and I figured he probably did so again, celebrating the coming holidays with his buddies.

By nine o'clock I was getting tired. I put my letter-writing aside and built a fire in the fireplace. Then feeling very hungry, I decided to eat alone, reasoning that he would have eaten out already and there was no sense waiting any longer. After eating, I cleaned up the kitchen and did the dishes, wondering where he was.

It was now well past ten o'clock and I was looking for something to do. Still pleased with the return of my ability to read and feeling that I had a lot of catching up to do, I got a book and sat down in front of the fire. About an hour later, deep into the book, there was a sudden, sharp, stabbing pain in my abdomen. It was so painful that I threw my head back and gasped for air, closing my eyes and trying to relax the pain away.

The instant my eyes closed, my inner vision opened and a scene spread out before me like film footage from a movie. There was Ben, dressed in slacks and a short-sleeved white shirt or sweater, sitting in a bar somewhere on the East Side, laughing and talking.

Across the table, a slim black woman wearing some kind of yellow or light-colored outfit was smiling back at him with an intimate look. They finished their drinks and decided to leave, heading back to her house, or perhaps her apartment, I couldn't tell which. In horror I watched the usual courting behavior, the playful invitations, the build-up of passion and Ben's indecision, his guilt, his desire to make love to her.

"Please, oh please, don't do this," I cried out to him feeling like an unwilling voyeur in some awful theater seat. "Oh no, please, no…" I begged as he and the woman began to make love.

I tried to blot out the scene but it remained. I told myself it was just my imagination, that I didn't want to see, didn't want to know, that I was making it all up and he would probably drive in the driveway any moment now, wearing his work clothes, having had too much to drink and smelling of smoke. "He's out with his buddies," I told myself over and over.

But the scene would not go away. I got up, paced around the house, looked at the clock and saw it was after midnight. I went back to the sofa and sat down, tried to read, tried to sing a little song, tried to watch the fire, but the progress of events between Ben and the young black woman remained clearly in front of my eyes. Helplessly I cycled between reading his thoughts, then her thoughts, then feeling their feelings, then my own.

"It's not true!" I sobbed in a dry, tearless way when it was over. I jumped up again, cursing my perception and trying to erase the sickening apprehension in my stomach. It was now after 1:00 a.m. and I was still try-ing to tell myself that I was wrong, it was one of those dreams I thought was real and I was going to wake up any minute now and discover that Ben was probably just out celebrating with the boys and would be home after the bars closed.

Unable to clear the scenes from my mind I watched them get up, get dressed, and say goodbye. The clock said almost 1:30 a.m. and I was feeling a sense of shock as I looked at where he was, estimating that he would be home in about half an hour. I watched as he drove home calmly and thoughtfully, parked the car in the drive, and walked through the front door at 2:00 a.m.

Unwilling to believe what I had just seen, unable to erase it, and unprepared for that moment, I sat there on the sofa and stared. He was wearing dark slacks and a short-sleeved white sweater, his hair was neatly combed and he had obviously not been out drinking with his buddies all evening.

He looked surprised to see me but smiled softly as I gazed at him. As if in a trance I got up and walked toward him, able to smell the strange perfume when I was only halfway across the room. He thought I was coming to give him a hug and he reached out to hold me saying gently, "Let's go to bed, it's late." I followed him up the stairs silently, unable to say anything, and was awake for much of the night.

The next morning I felt unnaturally detached, as if my mind had been frozen in space and time. Ben was acting as if nothing unusual had happened. We sat on the bed talking and drinking our morning tea. I asked him where he had been the night before and he said he had gone out with the boys.

The subject changed then and for a while we talked about other things. Then my mouth opened as if someone else were directing it and I heard myself say, "There's something I'd like to share with you. It happened last night, and…I'm just wondering, if I asked you some questions, would you promise to tell me the truth?"

"Sure," he said, grinning at me boyishly.

So I launched into a full description of what happened the night before. I told him how I had been reading on the sofa, of the stabbing pain, the clear vision of him in a bar laughing, talking with a young black woman. I described the yellow and white outfit she was wearing, how thin she was, what her front teeth were like, then the trip to her house and making love, what he was thinking, what he was feeling, what she was thinking, what she was feeling, what time he left and how he had arrived exactly when I had expected him to.

Then I asked, "Where were you last night at 11 o'clock?"

He sat there for a long time staring into his tea and finally he said in a quiet voice, "At the bar."

"Who were you with?" I said.

"A woman," he replied.

"Was she black?" I asked.

"Yes," he replied.

"Did you make love to her?" I pursued, holding my breath in the hope he would say no.

"Yes, I did," he answered.

"What time was it when you did?" I asked him.

About midnight," he said.

We both sat there in silence. The stabbing pain in my abdomen had returned. I got up and headed downstairs.

"So much for the confirmation of my psychic abilities," I thought to myself in a haze of rage and pain. "Never! Never again do I want to see!" I screamed inwardly, cursing my clairvoyance and my inability to control my perception. I was hurt and furious, and there was precious little to be thankful for that Thanksgiving.

∞

In anger, I left my job as a bartender, refusing to make it so easy and convenient for him to be away every night while I was working. Inside, I was immeasurably relieved to be out of the loud, smoky environment, but I never admitted, even to myself, that I hated the whole business that surrounded liquor and alcohol for this would have forced me to ask myself why I was pursuing a bar and restaurant business with Ben.

Time moved me painfully onward until it was the week before Christmas. Ben asked me again and again to forgive him, and when I said I would, he invited me to attend his swearing-in ceremony as a Mason.

On the designated evening I got dressed up and drove to downtown Detroit, meeting him after work, then heading for the Grand Lodge where the ceremony was to be held. The city, the people, the Grand Lodge, other Masons, all of it was wrapped in an air of unreality, but I told myself I was getting used to the distance that seemed to exist between myself and the rest of the world.

The ceremony began on time and I watched Ben move through the impressive ritual as if I were watching from another planet. When it was over, we gathered in the hallway, laughing and talking with a group of older Masons as we all prepared to leave. I suggested that we go out and get something to eat, but Ben said it was late and that he had to get up early the next morning. Since we came in separate cars, Ben hugged me and said he'd be home shortly so I drove off. Once back home I waited endlessly, but he did not show up all night. Later he claimed he had gotten drunk and stayed the night with a friend, but I knew where he had been. I felt shattered, at a breaking point.

A few days later, needing someone to talk to, I drove into the city to visit some old friends. After a long evening of tearfully telling them my troubles and feeling sorry for myself, I climbed in my truck to drive home. I was feeling old, tired and drained, and couldn't get the faltering relationship with Ben off my mind. I wanted him to stay with me, to love only me, and I had no intention of quitting the love I felt.

As I drove toward the expressway I began to cry, then to sob, hardly able to see where I was going. Suddenly my truck began to cough and choke and jerk back and forth. I stopped crying momentarily and looked at the various dials and the gas gauge on the dashboard. There were no warning lights on, the gas tank was full, the emergency brake was off, and everything had started up smoothly five minutes ago, yet now it was acting like there was something seriously wrong. As I turned onto Cadieux Road I nearly stalled, but with a little coaxing the truck finally got going and I drove to the expressway with no further problems.

As I headed down the entrance ramp to the expressway the truck started running smoothly and all worries about its mechanical condition faded. I turned my thoughts to Ben, and again I began to cry. Immediately the truck started to cough and choke and backfire again. In irritation I accelerated fiercely, thinking that the engine wasn't getting enough gas, and glanced at the dials and gages again. Everything was fine except the gas gauge – on which the needle was dropping rapidly.

In a panic, I pulled over to the side of the expressway and sat there staring at the gas gauge. I thought maybe I should get out and see if the gas cap had fallen off, or if there was a leak, but as soon as I pulled over and sat there for a minute, the needle climbed back to the full mark and stayed there just as normally as ever.

After an uncertain moment, I took off toward home again, wondering what was going on and wishing I had started the trip home a little earlier. It was almost eleven o'clock at night and if there was a serious problem it would be a real nuisance to run out of gas, or end up having to call and ask someone to get out of bed and come and get me.

Once back on the expressway I drove with careful attention to the truck's sound, motion and feel, trying to sense what might be wrong. When everything went smoothly for a short distance, I dismissed the truck problems and returned my thoughts to the problems with Ben, his affair, the pain, the anger.

Shortly, my tears began to fall again, and soon I started to sob. As soon as my sobs returned, the truck began to jerk and cough. I glanced at the gas gauge and saw that it was dropping rapidly. It was already past the one-quarter mark and moving toward half-empty. Since the coughing and jerking had started and stopped twice already, I kept driving but kept my eye on the gauge. I was sure I had not paid attention long enough to figure out what was going on, and that everything would right itself in a moment or two.

Instead, the gas gauge kept dropping. I wondered if there really was a hole in my gas tank and panic ran through me at the idea that I might run out of gas on the expressway on a cold winter night. I glanced in the rear view mirror, searching for a telltale trail of wet gasoline on the cold, dry pavement, and then glanced back at the needle. Now there was less than one-fourth of a tank of gas left and the needle was still moving down.

I decided I had to get off the expressway and get to a gas station for help so I got off at the next exit. The needle was now almost to empty and as I watched it still going down, my panic increased to ridiculous levels. I drove to a gas station, stopped the truck and got out, half crawling under it to look for leaks, cursing Ben's infidelity and wondering if I called home for help if he would be there. There were no leaks, the gas cap was securely in place, and when I got back in the truck, the needle on the gauge registered at the full mark. Now I was feeling stupid. What was going on?

As soon as I asked the question I heard Edgar answer in his soft, hillbilly twang, "The truck is feeling like you are. As long as you are going to spend time and energy feeling hopeless and de-energized, that will be the effect you will create on everything around you."

The concept that my emotions could be disrupting the operation of my truck left me dumbfounded. For a few minutes longer I sat there watching the gas gauge and wondering what would happen if I started up and took off. Finally I decided to try it but keep my mind quiet, away from Ben and the shifting sands of our life together. There was no further trouble with the truck that night and I drove home wondering if what Edgar had said was true and just exactly how my mood and feelings could effect the machines and technology around me. I watched the truck for several weeks after that but no further trouble appeared; finally I dismissed the possibility of a mechanical problem and realized I would have to accept Edgar's explanation. ✃

10 &

A Past Life

*"I do not fear death.
I see what has gone before,
through eyes that are not of this body.
When I dream, my visions are of days yet to be."*

Kathy M. Donnelly

OVER CHRISTMAS AND INTO JANUARY, THE PRESSURE IN THE RELATIONship between Ben and I increased dramatically. Our financial situation became entirely depressing, and worse, our fight to get the city of Pontiac to approve our location became a public fight at the city council meetings and in the newspaper.

As if this was not enough to deal with, I began to have a recurring dream that I was a tall, bronze woman with long black hair and a Polynesian or Hawaiian face. When the same woman appeared for the third time in visions in which her feet were rooted in my right hip and her head was sitting on my right shoulder whispering in my ear, I began to take serious notice of her. When I had a dream in which the tall, bronze woman told me that I had been herself in a former life, I began to experience long moments when I felt her presence. It was as if she was inside me, looking out through my eyes at the world I lived in.

Even after I started my classes in psychic development I was very skeptical about the subject of past lives, but when the dreams continued, I began to be very curious about the possibility that I'd had a past life and if the tall, bronze woman had been in it.

One day I had the distinct impression several times that someone was talking to me in my right ear and each time I became aware of it, the image of the Polynesian or Hawaiian woman came to mind. Finally, late in the day, I was alone in the house, so I sat down on the bedroom floor at the foot of my bed and cleared my mind of everything. I gave myself directions to go backward in time and see if I had any hidden memories or experiences of life in Polynesia or Hawaii.

I didn't really expect anything to happen but in my mind's eye I began turning calendar pages backwards and shortly I found that the calendar had disappeared and I was sitting cross-legged on a wide, black sand beach, looking out toward the sea. For a split second I was unnerved, partly because I did not expect such a distinct transition, and I had never seen or heard of black sand. But I steadied myself and continued into the experience.

The sky was gray, the waves were huge, the smells were completely unfamiliar, and the air was surprisingly warm. Unexpectedly, I heard a voice coming to me from inside, yet it seemed like it was coming from far away in space and time. Absolutely motionless, I listened and watched.

"I am in a place where there are islands and I am sitting on the beach of a small cove with my legs folded, looking out to sea. There is a small entryway to this cove and no one can get into the cove without going through a narrow, difficult inlet, which makes this a good place to come and speak to the gods alone.

"I am a woman and have come here to pray and learn. I am sitting on what appears to be a broad, flat rock that forms a low shelf all the way to the water.

"I have been sitting here for several days now, and at the present moment a storm is pounding the sea, the cove, and the beach. The tide is coming in again, and in combination with the storm, causes large waves to wash onto the rocks and over me. This does not bother me as I have been taught how to root myself in the rock and so the water simply washes over me. Because of my great size, strength, and learning, I can form this root to earth and the rock, and this way the water does not harm me or wash me into the sea.

"I have been taught to see the future, and at this particular time I am searching for coming events. This is done by first setting a goal – in this case to learn the future of the next seven years – then going to my place of power and prayer where I pray and fast for the next seven days. This is called inhabiting the time structure. In this case, each of the seven days is equal to one of the seven years and so for seven days I will sit rooted on this beach and listen to the wind and the rain and the waves and the sun and the voices of the gods. They will tell me and show me what the next seven years will bring for my people.

"The present storm is a reflection of the stormy problems coming for me and for our village. I am here to see what I can of our future so I can lead my people right. The problem with which I am concerned in my village is that my father has told me he has seen men of another color coming to our land. Now I am sensing a threat to our way of life and many changes for our people.

"My people are wonderful, but they are so foolish at times. I feel some fear, but it must be used to find direction. The storms that have passed through this cove have told me of much conflict for us, and now in the huge waves I see wave after wave of these strangely colored men and much sadness in the gray color of the water."

There was a brief pause, and then I had the sensation of standing up and stretching.

"It is now the end of this meditation and fast and I am standing up. I am a very tall woman, about six feet by your basis of measurement. In years I am about nineteen if we use your idea of time, although we use a different way to reflect time here. I am the daughter of the man who would be considered the chief in the villages. He is very powerful. He does much healing, and from him and several others whose abilities are kept secret, I have learned many powers. I, too, do much healing of a kind that is not given to all the people of the villages, but I do not do as much as my father.

"At times there is much disagreement between myself and my father. He says we will have much to learn by following the ways of the strangers. In concept he may be right, but I have just seen that there will be many things we will be forbidden to do, in our work, in our ceremonies, in our healing, and in every aspect of our lives. There will be much confusion among the people of our villages.

"Now I am leaving the cove. I have a small boat or canoe which I paddle myself. I am physically powerful because of my size and training."

At this, I had another sense of movement and transition both in location and time. Abruptly I found myself in a village where the first impressions were a shocking mixture of smells. There was warm earth, fire and smoke, food cooking, and an assortment of unknown aromas. The homes had thatched roofs, many had a mostly open framework and I was struck by the thought that they didn't really live in houses, but rather lived in something that looked more like a porch! There were sick people laid out everywhere and some looked already dead, or in the process of dying.

Then the tall woman continued, this time with the sound of anguish in her voice.

"I am now in my village and the strange men have arrived. People are getting sick and some are dying, yet we are being told not to use our medicine. The essences and secrets of our medicine are very valuable, and what is more, the new medicine does not work. I have been forbidden to do the healing I have been trained to do. My father stresses patience. He says we have much to learn from the white man. I feel he is wrong but I cannot go against him.

"As I wander among the sick who are laid out in our public gathering place, the large central fire in the village is burning dimly while my mind is on fire with anger. The sick ones cannot even be counted as they lie there, row after row of them, and I am torn inside because I am not in favor with the light-colored men. I have too much knowledge and many healing powers, for I am Keilani, daughter of the chief, and always being watched. I have made my own decision that I must practice my healing and defy my father.

"To do this healing I must become both male and female, for the union of the self contains the necessary power for healing. To create this union I become a young male, though I am still the tall female as well. I am not sure if you will understand how this is done, but the two are both alive in me even though I have the form of a very tall female. This male who is also part of my body has his own personality, and is at times sulky and defiant, while at other times he is fun-loving and very active. He has a very tall frame, like myself, with a slim, unbearded face, and he is lighter in his color, but he is still part of myself.

"This male who is in me was created in several of the secret rituals practiced by the healers of our people. This young male who is part of me is also involved in some of the rituals in which a child of my blood heritage and power is produced. It is our tradition that I will only conceive and give birth when it is necessary to carry on the blood of my family, as we carry the knowledge of life and death in our family blood. This ceremony can be conducted only at certain times during the year. It is a sexual ceremony between this male who is part of me, and myself, meaning the female part of me."

Again there was a pause and I experienced a sense of relief in the quick transition because I was having difficulty grasping what she was trying to share with me.

"I am now in a later time, some years from the time I was speaking of when we began on the beach in the cove. It is as I saw then, wave after wave of white man has come to our land. I am now an official prisoner although I am allowed to roam the villages and live in my house. Many have died, many are still dying, and I have chosen to perform what healing I can in secret, and to take care of as many as I can for as long as they survive. I have also decided that I will leave this place and time if I begin to suspect that there is any physical danger to me. I will leave even though I have not yet passed on the powers I have, and of which it is my duty to do so. Part of the knowledge that has been handed down to me is the ability to simply transport myself to another place where life is not threatened.

"At this time, however, I am choosing to stay here. I have not been allowed to perform the secret ceremonies for the continuation of our blood-heritage which would produce a child to continue our knowledge of life and death. I live without a partner, but have taken many of the men of the village, and indeed, I have my choice. It is expected for one of my position to do so. But it is not the ritual of the union of the male and female self and thus I may be one of the last of my line."

There was one more transition with a sense of great passage of time and when she continued, it was as if there was a slight haze in my ability to perceive her and her surroundings.

"My body is much older now, and I am much changed in physical appearance. I am somewhat thicker but still statuesque, and have come to value sheer physical size for its impressiveness and its impression of power. Many of the white men who have come in such numbers are much smaller than myself. I decided when I was younger that I would leave my people if my family heritage was threatened, if I was not able to perform the secret rituals of power or carry on my healing activities. But over the years there was always someone new to take care of and I am old and believe perhaps my father was right, there is much to learn here.

"In some of the journeys I have taken into the future, I have found myself in new form in you. Our times are different, but we are similar in sympathies, in vibration, in seeking, and in the many changes within our villages that we must deal with. Perhaps we can continue our journey together, guiding and sharing with one another where we can. I am you. This is my chance to pass on the powers that I have been given as a result of my blood heritage, thus I will be able to fulfill the requirements of this great knowledge. I am Keilani. You may call me by that sound.

"I will be available to you in this vibration for what would be approximately ten more years of your time and then I will have changed my vibration, but my energy form can still be reached by the sound 'Keilani.' Because we are one, this communication is always going on between us and always changing as we change. You may consider it as a bank or source of continuous energy and expanded knowledge from which we may each draw when needed. This is the legacy of us.

"I will be silent for a while, and when you have an experience for which you need assistance, I would be pleased if you would call on me, perhaps we can help one another fulfill our destinies."

Suddenly she was gone. I sat, still and motionless, except for a few shivers. This was not what I expected when I sat down to see if I'd had any past lives. Looking around the twilight-filled room, I realized I had just been somewhere full of sunshine, water, mountains, broad beaches, huts and open fire pits. People with bronze-colored skin and black hair had been everywhere and the young woman, Keilani, had been as real as the body that now sat stiffly on the bedroom floor of the house on Jefferson Avenue.

After a few minutes I got up and went downstairs to begin preparing dinner. I had no idea what to think of the experience, so after dinner I wrote down as much as I could remember and put it away. I intended to explore the possibility of other past lives, but first I had to come to grips with this one. ✂

11 ⍟
Solving A Piece Of The Mystery

"Men stumble over the truth from time to time,
but most pick themselves up
and hurry off
as if nothing happened."

Sir Winston Churchill

IN THE LAST HALF OF JANUARY, THE LITTLE MEN IN BROWN ROBES returned and this was the start of what was to become a long and intense series of visits over the rest of the year. Each time they appeared, they brought 'pictures' of events and circumstances to come in the future. I never mentioned their visits to anyone, not even Ben, for fear someone might bundle me into a small white jacket and tell me I needed a rest, but I began to develop a sense that doomsday was approaching. At times, I could think or talk of little else.

Occasionally I retrieved various pieces of the information they had shown me, turning the events over and over in my mind.

"How could the Berlin Wall possibly come down...or the nations somehow not be there?" I asked myself. "Who was in charge of making such decisions? Was anybody?"

In the pictures they showed me, it looked like ordinary people chipping away at the Wall, but I was sure the Russian or the East German soldiers who patrolled the border would never allow it. Who would want to risk getting shot? No one in their right mind, I was sure. Then I would feel overwhelmed, dropping any attempt to come to grips with the information. I needed to deal with my own life and I was barely coping.

Whatever energy I had available after worrying and weeping over the relationship with Ben, was going into phone calls and letters, meetings with accountants and lawyers, and completion of paperwork for Pontiac regarding our bar and restaurant or for our small corporation.

The city of Pontiac had been seriously stalling and I couldn't understand why. They kept asking for more details, more plans, more promises, more paperwork. What started as a confrontation at the city council meetings was turning into a lengthy fight and this added to the drain on my energy. In February, the situation reached fever pitch. Not only were Ben and I fighting between ourselves, the city of Pontiac once again voted to deny the location of the bar and restaurant.

At the height of this frustration it occurred to me for the first time that I might try to use meditation and the psychic abilities that seemed to be built-in to my mind to look for answers to the many problems I was experiencing. I did not have much success in this inquiry into the issues around Ben, or the question of why Pontiac kept turning us down. I could see everything else, why couldn't I get help with these two areas?

Frustrated, the problems remained without answers just like the mystery of what had happened to me to produce such a profusion of anomalies in my perception, consciousness and awareness. The biggest difference between the two areas was that I could discuss Ben and our relationship with my friends, and I could talk over the bar and restaurant problems with Ben himself. But as far as the strange physical experiences were concerned, there was really no one to talk to. Although my fear of psychic experiences had diminished somewhat, my fears regarding the physical difficulties of heat, pressure, and sensuousness had not.

I brought the subject up at different times to different people thinking they might help me understand what was happening. Once or twice I tried to find an acceptable way to tell someone I occasionally had a spontaneous orgasm in my head without benefit of foreplay or sexual activity. The few people that I told either thought I was joking or dismissed my statements as unreal. At other times, trying to talk about the intense heat that felt like liquid fire moving through me, the pounding heart, the sound of wind and thunder, or the explosion of lights almost always brought a question like, "Well, what brought this on? How did it start?"

I didn't know how it started. If I knew how it started I might have been able to figure out how to turn it off. So when I said, "I'm really not sure how it started…" the usual answer was a shrug and a comment like, "Sounds crazy to me," which only reinforced my fears. If I brought up the connections to sexuality, or the exquisite pleasure, the conversation came to an even quicker end. Eventually I realized that people were frightened at a deep, intuitive level. They went blank, turned silent, and even changed the subject as if we had been talking about something else altogether; but I could not change the subject; it was happening in me!

I was plagued with questions and I could make no sense of the things that came to me as answers. I suspected that the sexual experiences had something to do with the perceptual changes I was still experiencing, as well as the psychic abilities that had mushroomed.

Over and over I asked myself, "What happened during those first monumental sexual experiences when I had been carried into a world of silent, empty awareness with its sense of eternal fulfillment? Had I found myself *in* a world of brilliant stars and pulsing waves – or had I *become* those lights and waves. What caused the roaring sound and the powerful sensation that something was plowing its way up the center of me? What caused the shaking and the explosion of light? Why the orgasm in my head instead of its usual location? What happened to physical reality, and where did it disappear to? How could I describe the apparent paradox of a sudden expansion of my perception when there had been no physical reality to perceive or describe? Why did consciousness seem to have *opened* only to find there was nothing there? And what on earth was causing the recurrence of it all, again and again?"

I was still taking classes in psychic development, and one night a tall, gray-haired man joined us as a guest speaker for the evening. Before arriving at class, I had decided that when the evening was over I was going to talk at least briefly to my teacher about the unusual physical experiences since my terror during them had not eased. The gray-haired guest was standing next to her, listening, as I tried to explain my dilemma without sounding ridiculous. I was so nervous about the whole subject that my explanation was neither smooth nor very coherent, but immediately my teacher and the gray-haired man looked at each other in a meaningful way and one of them said, "Sounds like kundalini, doesn't it?"

I had come across the word *kundalini* about two years earlier in one of the books by Castaneda, who referred to it very briefly as some kind of female sexuality. At the time, I tried to look it up in the dictionary, but no such word was listed, so I forgot about it until I heard the word that night in class, after which my mind fixed on it. Now, instinctively, I knew it had something important to offer by way of explanation.

When I questioned my teacher, asking for more information about the subject, she mentioned a book by Gopi Krishna and suggested I read it. She had it in her personal library and let me borrow it. I took it home

and began to read that very night. When I came to his description of the
kundalini experience, gooseflesh rolled over me in wave after wave.

> "...Suddenly, with a roar like that of a waterfall, I felt
> a stream of liquid light entering my brain through the spinal
> cord... The illumination grew brighter and brighter, the
> roaring louder, I experienced a rocking sensation and then
> felt myself slipping out of my body, entirely enveloped in
> a halo of light. It is impossible to describe the experience
> accurately. I felt the point of consciousness that was myself
> growing wider, surrounded by waves of light. It grew wider
> and wider, spreading outward while the body, normally the
> immediate object of its perception, appeared to have receded
> into the distance until I became entirely unconscious of it. I
> was now all consciousness...a sea of light simultaneously
> conscious and aware of every point, spread out, as it were, in
> all directions without any barrier or material obstruction." [2]

I was stunned, caught between tears and an inexpressible gratitude.
I could have written his description of the experience and he could have
written mine! The only difference was that instead of using the metaphor
of a roaring waterfall of liquid light, I had described it as an roaring freight
train that moved up the center of my body and exploded in my brain.

I read through the night without stopping, relief and fear alternately
pulling at me, and put the book down only when I finished it in the wee
hours of the morning. I sat there for a long time, and then got a piece of
paper and scribbled a letter to Gopi Krishna, hoping to get in touch with
him. More than anything in the world I wanted to talk to someone who
would understand, perhaps give me some guidance on what to do.

After the letter was written, I re-read it, only to feel embarrassed.
The letter sounded desperate and half-crazy.

"Why would he even respond to this?" I thought, and ended up
putting it in my drawer with a feeling of loneliness and depression. Still,
it was comforting to think there was at least one other person in the world
who might understand what I was going through.

Since it was often possible for me to get information and experience
in my dreams, I tried several times to give myself instructions to 'learn
about kundalini.' Nothing happened other than a series of incredibly erotic

2   Gopi Krishna, *Kundalini, The Evolutionary Energy In Man* (Berkeley, CA.;
Shambhala Press, 1971) pg.12.

dreams. I already knew sex had something to do with it, but I wanted clear and specific, virtually scientific information.

One morning after Ben left for work, I went back to sleep, telling myself to return to the dream I had just left. Instead I found myself in a very dark room or cramped space. Then, right in front of me, a small door or slot opened and an exceedingly bright white light hit my eyes. Startled, I backed away from the small two- or three-inch opening, thinking someone had lit a fire in the furnace and I didn't want to get burned. When I backed away, the miniature door closed.

Immediately after backing away, I had a flash of recognition flow through me and I thought, "Hey! There's a fire in there. I've been trying to find the fire…maybe that's it!"

The small door or slot opened again and once more I was surprised at how incredibly bright the light was. It was like a tall column of fire, white in the center and sort of gold and reddish along the edges of the column. It got brighter and bigger and seemed to come toward me. It reminded me of a long shaft of light, similar in shape to a feather in the way that the light seemed to be coming out of some central column. The light continued to come toward me until I was floating upward on a column of fire that didn't burn but was extremely bright. Then I couldn't remember any more.

This experience raised more questions than it answered and I made up my mind to find out as much as I could about kundalini. Unfortunately, there was pitifully little information available. The one book I did find was filled with a lot of esoteric terminology I didn't understand, and it was written as if the author was hiding something between the lines. I was frustrated because I wanted a nice, neat, complete description, and all I could find was a lot of condescending spiritual posturing.

What was worse was that the book contained all kinds of warnings about kundalini that got out of control and people that went insane or burst into flame and self-incinerated because of it! In the end I became even more frightened. What if this mysterious heat and fire decided to incinerate me? What if it really could drive me insane? That was just what I had sensed and been afraid of all along!

Feeling a need for a veil of protective self-defense against the possibility of harm, I began to question the validity of my own experiences and perceptions. Maybe I had just imagined it all. If I was experiencing kundalini, why had I never heard of it before? Why were there no books or pictures on the subject? Why didn't the doctors or the priests or the professors know anything about the condition? And why was the little bit of material I had found so vague, so threatening?

After considering the many issues, I calmed myself a bit and decided that, whatever it was called, I had definitely experienced something that altered my life and my consciousness almost overnight, and in a way that had not reversed itself yet. If it was a sickness, I was still sick. If it was an evolutionary energy, as Gopi Krishna had called it, I hadn't the slightest idea what I was evolving into.

In spite of the renewal of worries about what kundalini could do to me, reading the two books I managed to find did help because they provided me with the comfort of knowing that I was not alone in experiencing the phenomenon. They also raised the possibility that the experiences had a purposeful outcome, or that they could be approached and managed sensibly. After incessant pondering, I began to wonder if there was so little writing on the subject because of the explicitly sexual nature of the experience.

The more I thought about this, the more convinced I became that the sexual angle was a stumbling block. Even plain old sex was tangled up in literally dozens of sticky, peripheral issues – and what I was experiencing was definitely not plain old sex. Thus, beyond the conviction that I had experienced kundalini, that kundalini and sex were somehow linked, and that no one would talk about it because no one was comfortable talking about sex, I remained frustrated as far as further explanations were concerned.

My search for an answer took on an air of hysteria when a man in Port Huron, Michigan, burst into flames while sitting on a bar stool in a local bar one day. Port Huron was only a half-hour drive up the expressway. Reports of eyewitnesses offered little insight or information about the incident; everyone agreed he was just sitting there minding his own business when he burst into flames and went up in smoke!

Here and there, I found other obscure reports of individuals who had self-incinerated, all of which confirmed my deepest fears, but none of which offered any kind of explanation or advice for protection. I continued to search and stew. ⚬

12 ❦
An Ending

"The end of a melody is not its goal:
but nonetheless, had the melody
not reached its end
it would not have reached its goal either."

Friedrich Nietzsche

MEANWHILE, EDGAR BEGAN INCREASING THE URGENCY OF HIS MESSAGE to "Buy a year's worth of food and a wood-burning stove." He was now telling me that I should do this by July, and that I had very little time left to accomplish it, thus it was important to begin. I had developed quite a measure of trust in such things by this time, but I balked at the idea and the expense, and struggled with justification for taking such a dramatic step. No amount of logic seemed to make sense of his directions. I didn't have a lot of kitchen storage space, and yet as the time left to accomplish the task became shorter, I found myself more and more inclined to take action.

Finally I sat down and made out a comprehensive grocery list. When I thought it was complete, I put it away for a few days and started a second list of things that were not really groceries, but were items I might buy at the grocery store over the course of a year. The second list included things like light bulbs, a spare pair of mittens, a box of matches and the like. Then I got out the first list and compiled the two, revising and editing as I went along. I put the compiled list away for another day or so, and then got them both out for finalizing.

When it was close to what I thought I would actually buy over one year, I divided the list into three sections. The next evening I piled myself and my two girls into the car and drove to the grocery store where we spent the next half hour simply filling in prices next to the items on our lists. When that step was completed, we went back home and I figured out what the total cost of such a shopping trip would be. When I had that final amount, I divided it by four and decided to make four smaller trips rather than one large one.

The next week I completed the first one-fourth of the grocery shopping for the year's worth of food. Once home I marked everything with the date of purchase so I could rotate my stock appropriately. With that accomplished I set up a plan to do one of the remaining shopping trips every two months. The next one would be in early May, the third one was scheduled for the first part of July, and even though I would be past the deadline Edgar had given me, I set the final one for September.

Somehow calmer after having begun the purchase of the year's worth of food, I turned my thoughts to the idea of a wood-burning stove. We already had a beautiful freestanding fireplace in the living room. I loved it and the fact that it helped heat the house a bit; thus I stood in front of it again and again, wondering why I should be told to buy a wood-burning stove when I already had one. Finally I made the decision to consider the existing fireplace as my wood-burning stove. I didn't have the money to buy a wood-burner that would do any serious heating, I had no place to set up a unit like that, and I couldn't justify the purchase of a second stove to myself, let alone Ben. A friend across the street cut down a tree and offered me the wood so I took that and figured I was ready for whatever was coming.

03

By now it was 1981 and spring was approaching. Two years had gone by since the initial opening of my mind had occurred. The struggle that followed had taken on a life or death quality quite often. However, little by little, except for the physical experiences of great heat, pressure and light, I felt I had gained enough experience and understanding of the mind and intuition to begin working with others.

My own teacher of psychic development was moving to California and I did not want to be without a group of people with whom I could share, discuss and practice using my psychic abilities. So I decided to try teaching a class of my own, thinking it would force me to get myself and the extraordinary perceptions organized. Such a broad and fascinating range of skills seemed built-in to the mind that it was a shame not to both receive support for my own abilities, as well as teach others how to develop them and put them into practical use.

In addition, I was anxious to see if other people could be taught to recognize and use their own psychic abilities without the intervention of kundalini. I was sure that almost anyone could do so, and ready to test my theory, I began putting together a series of classes and lesson plans.

The class began in February and I was pleased to have seven people sign up. Weeks later when it was over, I was gratified to discover that, in fact, people *could* be taught to develop and use intuition. Even more surprising, I discovered I was an excellent teacher.

Then, unexpectedly, all of my pleasure fell to the background in late March when our dream of a bar and restaurant collapsed. After the last refusal of the Pontiac city council to approve our location, we discovered that one of the city council members had an uncle who owned a bar on the same street we had chosen for our location. The uncle didn't want our bar and restaurant competing with his, and the city council members, in allegiance to one of their members, had been deliberately and quite successfully blocking us all this time by telling us they needed more paperwork, more planning, this survey, or that referendum vote.

Giving up on our original location, we took on a silent partner and were tentatively looking at other locations in Orchard Lake or Birmingham. Weeks later, with Ben still insisting that he really wanted the original location in Pontiac, the silent partner withdrew. When Ben heard the news he fell into a strange sickness. He vomited, then went to bed where he tossed and turned feverishly, sweating and moaning in a series of private nightmares that haunted him through the night. The next morning as I looked at his tired face, I knew in that moment that some spark of life in him had been extinguished.

My outward reaction to the collapse of our dream was one of disappointment and sympathy with Ben. But my private, inner reaction was one of explosive relief and a sense of boundless freedom. I knew in my gut that the bar and restaurant was dead. Ashamed of this reaction, I tried to hide it by encouraging Ben, telling him what *I* really wanted him to tell me – that we were now free to pursue something else, something that wouldn't take years to get up and running.

Ben was silent and inconsolable. As he slowly recovered from the shock of his lost dream, he withdrew even further from me. Gradually, my burst of freedom was followed by a terrible, ruthless clarity that filled me with panic as I saw that while the bar and restaurant may have been the source of many of our problems, it was also the force that held us together.

CB

In early May I purchased the second one-fourth of the groceries Edgar had urged me to buy. I also applied to teach a class titled *Psychic Development* in our local community education program. Even though it was just an attempt to do something that would make a few dollars, I was pleased to be accepted and scheduled for the coming autumn. So I busied myself putting my lesson plans together, using what I had learned in that first shy class back in late February-March.

I also decided to take lessons in professional massage therapy. My goal was to work with the entire body/mind system, experimenting with the bright lights and hazy clouds of color around the people I knew. Finally, although the going was slow and the growing was fitful, I had the feeling I was moving ahead in my ability to manage my mind. I was putting my life together again, even though it was completely different from what I had envisioned only a couple years ago when moving up the Chrysler ladder had been my determined decision.

Summer came and it was time to go back to classes at the university. The bachelor's degree that I intended to hurry and get at the time of my divorce was now six years in the making. I had a bad case of 'senioritis' but there was only one more semester to go and I would have that blessed piece of paper.

Ben and I were carrying on, but the relationship was a shadow of its former self. He was again working afternoons and every time he walked out the door I found myself perched precariously on the cliffs of hope and despair. Was he really going to work? Had he given up the other woman? Why did he seem to look right through me these days? Often I mused about the days when we had first met and fell in love. Back then I had thought I was on top of the world. Now it felt as though the world was on top of me.

In mid-July, I took my girls and Ben's two children and went to the Blue Water Festival in Port Huron one night. It was well after midnight when we finally arrived home and I was disappointed to find that Ben was not home yet. I was still plagued by the constant sexual desire that nothing seemed to quench and I had looked forward to the possibility of making love.

The kids were tired and got themselves off to bed, and when it was quiet, I put on the teakettle to make myself a cup of tea. When my tea had finished steeping, I took the cup, went upstairs, and sat down on the edge of the bed to relax a bit before tucking myself in. The window was open and peaceful night sounds filled the room. I became caught up in the faint lapping of the water at the edge of the docks and the sighing of the wind through the trees just outside the window. Closing my eyes, I drifted with the sounds, daydreaming about Ben. The sighing became louder, and louder, then distinctly rhythmic. There was the sound of heavy breathing, of low moans and then a voice cried out in sensuous release. I snapped out of what I thought was a daydream and in a moment of paralyzing shock, I heard Ben's voice and that of a woman. They were talking to one another, murmuring like lovers, saturated with the tenderness of lovemaking. It was the same woman he had been with the previous Thanksgiving.

It was my turn to cry out and a long, despair-filled "No-o-o-o…" rolled out of me like some alien sound. I tried to cover my ears, to turn off the hearing, to stop the knowing, but like a radio stuck on a single incoming channel, I continued to hear what was going on with Ben in some distant bedroom across the city for more than an hour.

Just like the clairvoyant experience of the previous November, I was now caught in a clairaudient experience that wouldn't quit. Since the clairvoyant episode, I had fearfully done everything I knew to block my own clairvoyance, telling myself that I didn't want to see anything that would bring pain. And I had been fairly successful. It had never occurred to me that some hidden and banished part of me *wanted* to know the truth and, honoring my wish not to see anything painful, would seek to present that truth to me via hearing.

By the time Ben finally arrived home exactly when I predicted at 6:00 a.m., I had realized two very important things, one of which was that *you can't NOT know what is yours to know.* The other was that the relationship was over. ◌

13 ♋

Face-to-Face With My Self and My Life

*"You have to leave the city of your comfort
and go into the wilderness of your intuition.
What you'll discover is
yourself."*

Alan Alda

AFTER THE CLAIRAUDIENT DISCOVERY OF BEN'S CONTINUING AFFAIR,
I again confronted him angrily. The following morning he announced he
was leaving, and each of us began to dissolve into private, lonely tailspins.
He insisted we sell the house, and for the rest of that hot, lonely afternoon
I sat contemplating the fact that the worst had finally happened. I was now
facing the loss of Ben, our small family, a place to live, and the entire
financial investment I had made in the house. Sick at heart, I realized I
might have to send my daughters back to live with their father because
there was no money, no job, my once excellent credit was in a shambles,
and I had no financial resources to fall back on. Not only was I deeply in
debt, I found new lows in the pit of heartache as I realized that I still loved
Ben and could not pretend otherwise. To do so would have been a lie to
myself and about myself.

The cauldron of my life now began boiling over. Edgar kept telling
me not to give up the house, and my daughters were extremely upset at
the prospect of having to return to their father. After weeks of indecision
I decided I was going to keep the girls with me if they were willing to
go through some uncertain times. I was going to call the man who held
our land contract and see if I could get a six-month extension before the
balloon note on the house came due. I thought this would give the girls and
I time to settle down and figure out where to go from there.

Before I could tell them of my decision, however, they got into an angry fight with Ben while I wasn't home. They called their father to come and get them, their clothes, and their few possessions immediately, and when I got home, they were gone. I was crushed. It seemed like everyone was leaving me.

Getting myself together as well as I could, and picking among the remains of what had once been an expensive wardrobe, I went out to get a job and took the first offer that came to me. The man who interviewed me wanted me to accept so badly, he offered me the use of a company car when he found out my truck was in the repair shop for some bodywork after a minor collision two weeks earlier.

Once hired, no one bothered to train me, or even explain the whole picture of what the company was about, and the schedule seemed to require a continuous, unnatural race against the clock. Briefly, I was relieved to have an income, but the work I had to do to make that money was totally without meaning, and all the things I really thought were important, or needed to be done at home, or for my personal self didn't get done.

The whole business seemed disorganized, the priorities shifted in confusing ways, and I didn't understand their goals or deadlines at all. Complicating this was the fact that since the appearance of my psychic abilities and my tendency to wander in and out of past, present and future, I paid even less attention to clocks and deadlines. Over the last months I had counted myself as fortunate to be able to stay in one place and time at a time! Worse, I felt shockingly dishonest working there, as if I was part of a gigantic scam designed to channel money toward the few people at the top.

"Where did I get such awful attitudes…? What happened to my competitive spirit?" I berated myself. "Why can't I make myself care? I need this money badly!"

Instead I sat at my desk every day wondering why we were all playing such a senseless game. Even though I was finally bringing in some cash for myself, the paycheck had lost its power over me.

Exhausted one morning after a night of tears over Ben, I just didn't go in. At the very moment that I should have been walking in the office door, I called and told them I was quitting without notice and would turn the car in the following weekend which was the earliest I could deliver it and get the necessary ride back home. The woman who shared the office with me seemed relieved that I wasn't coming back and I hung up convinced I was a complete failure at everything. Ben was disgusted with me, almost as much as I was with myself, but I felt that I needed to do something that was real, that would lead to security and the ability to survive, something that meant something to me, even though I didn't know what that was. Everything I thought I *might* do didn't make enough money, or make it fast enough to get me out of the serious crunch I was in. Yet anything that would have put me back on my original career track seemed unattractive and left me cold.

The days dragged by, the house seemed stuffy and every sound echoed without the presence of my daughters. I felt paralyzed, and although Edgar kept telling me not to give up the house, I was slowly losing any incentive to hang on to house, truck, furniture, appliances, a job, or even the little things I once worked so hard to get. I did not know what would happen to me or how I would survive and wandered from room to room, wondering what to do, unable to focus.

For a while I asked myself repeatedly, "Why is this happening to me?" But every time I asked myself this question, the group of little men in brown robes would reappear, offering to show me some information they said was sure to help. Instead of giving me ideas, suggesting better decisions, or telling me the actions that I should take…instead of helping me to analyze what had gone wrong in my life so I might understand how to fix it and know what to do next, they always had immense visions. These pictures of the future were like movies, with fully telepathic surround-sound, that showed where the world was going, not where *I* was going. They had tons of information about global changes that were coming, why these changes were going to happen, what sorts of choices we would have to make, and where the danger points were for all of us. [3]

In their first few visits long ago, I tried to make them go away or ignore them altogether. In later visits I acknowledged them and watched the things they wanted to show me with a combined sense of resignation and curiosity. Now, sitting on the picnic table in late September, crying about the disintegration of my life and wondering why it was happening this way, they appeared again and as usual, offered to show me some information that might help.

Having no other resources at the moment, feeling terribly lost and alone, they struck me as old friends, and I welcomed their presence. Closing my eyes so I could see better, I watched quietly and intently as the pictures and sounds rolled by. Halfway through, I still found it necessary to ask them why everything had fallen apart.

---

3   For further information about these global changes see *Robes: A Book of Coming Changes* by Penny Kelly, published by Lily Hill Publishing.

"Because the life you keep trying to set up has nothing to do with what you came here to do," they answered.

"But what did I come here to do?" I asked for the first time.

"You came here to be part of the group that will work to keep the world from destroying itself during the coming changes and to help pull the world together in a new way," they said. "Would you like to see how?"

What they tried to show me wasn't what I expected to see, nor was I comfortable with it. At first I revolted, but when they returned and asked again if I wanted to see where I was going, I nodded mutely, closed my eyes, and watched.

After they left, I cried solitary tears for the mess I had made of my life. The information I had seen was nothing at all like I had thought my life would be. The course of events they showed me did not seem to have any connection with the past thirty-three years so I assumed that these occurrences had to be in the distant future, since it was obvious that they were not going to happen tomorrow. Worse, most of what I had seen verged on the impossible and when they left, I went in the house, threw myself across the bed and cried myself to sleep. Some of the tears were for the lost relationship with Ben, some for the loss of my own dream of rebuilding my home and family with a new love, and some at the sheer improbability of the visions presented by the little men in brown robes.

∞

We had to be out of the house by December, or pay off the balloon on the land contract. Ben would not sign for any kind of mortgage with me, the bank would not lend the money to me on my own, and finally the Realtor who had listed it offered to buy it for exactly what we had paid for it. The $10,000 cash that I myself had put into remodeling it went down the drain, not counting whatever cash Ben had put into it on his part, or our labor.

When Ben moved to Arizona over Thanksgiving, the last shreds of hope that we would be able to reconcile disappeared. Feeling sorry for me, an older woman friend living in Royal Oak, a suburb just north of Detroit, offered to let me stay in her basement for a few dollars a month. By moving, I left behind the small client base I had established for my budding massage therapy practice and soon had no money left. Collection agencies began calling; a few even came to the door, and in the depths of despair I made several firm decisions. The first was to finish my last semester of school at Wayne State University. The second was to continue my new career of teaching people how to develop and use their intuition. The third was to continue doing massage therapy. And the last was to pay back every cent I owed even if it took me the rest of my life.

I set up my massage table in the middle of the basement room I lived in, and even though this seemed extremely humble and unprofessional, I was determined to start again. The basement was so cold my toes were often numb, and it was during this period that I realized the value of Edgar's urgent messages to buy a year's worth of food and a wood-burning stove. I had made only two of the four grocery purchases planned, but I had originally been planning for four people. Now there was only me, and by stretching and conserving, I lived on those groceries and made them last until well into the next summer.

The wood-burning stove would have made life so much more comfortable, but I ended up borrowing a kerosene heater and putting up gratefully with its smelly operation and constant refilling over the winter in return for the bit of warmth it provided.

During this time I ached for Ben to return. To pass the days I alternated between crying, a detailed study of the notes I had made over the past two years, and keeping track of what was currently happening in my dreams and in my mind.

Toward the end of winter I met several other professional women who were also in crisis for one reason or another and we tried to be supportive to one another. With the unflagging encouragement of one of them, I rented a small office, put my massage table in it, and practiced my massage therapy more professionally. A couple of months later she joined me in the office and we shared it for a while. When we began to disagree on things after three or four months, I left, giving her the entire office, and went back to working in the tiny basement room I lived in.

C８

It was now the summer of 1982. I came face to face with myself and my life only to discover that there was nothing left. The woman I had once been was gone, the life I planned and pursued so aggressively had disintegrated piece by piece. One husband, four children, a college degree, a great career, a new love, my dream home on the water, my furniture, my appliances, my expectations and plans for the future, even the way I had once seen and experienced the everyday world – all were gone.

I existed moment to moment, caught in the clutches of a mind that still seemed to be awake virtually all of the time, and struggling with perceptual abilities that seemed to know no bounds. Unable to explain the peculiar sexual experiences, I was suddenly taxed to my physical limits in an attempt to keep a roof over my head, food on the table, and a sense of connection to the reality I found myself in. I was convinced that no matter what I touched would crumble into failure and disappear as if it had never existed in the first place.

One day a woman who had taken one of my classes in *Developing and Using Intuition* called and asked if I had ever considered making an audio tape of the things I was teaching, or perhaps writing them down. She was going to move to Hawaii and wanted something that would help her continue her efforts at self-development. I told her I would try to put something together and after hanging up the phone, decided to begin writing and compiling not only what I was teaching but my notes and observations about what was happening to my own mind and body. I was sure there was a better explanation than just the word 'kundalini,' but I had no idea what it was, nor did I know where it was taking me.

Little by little, the few students I'd had before my move, got back in touch with me, asking me to continue teaching. They also began to tell others of my psychic abilities and people began calling to ask for help with all sorts of things. When a nearby suburb advertised their coming 3-day summer fair and said they were looking for unusual vendors and concession stands, I took a friend up on a dare and applied to play a gypsy fortune teller just for fun.

On the first night I dressed up in what I hoped was something gypsyish, dragged a card table and a borrowed crystal ball to the fair, and set up a sign that said "See your future, $3 for 5 minutes." By the end of the night there was a line that stretched two hundred feet from my table and around the gym. By the second night it stretched out the door and down the sidewalk all the way to the parking lot. By the third night people were lined up before I even got there and by the end of the evening several policemen were still trying to disperse the line of people long after the fair had ended. Finally I gave out my phone number and what I had thought was just going to be a few days of fun, turned out to be a steady flow of appointments and a serious change in my image of myself as well as my direction in life. ✑

14 ∞
Questions and Explorations

*"There are no facts,
only interpretations."*

Friedrich Nietzsche

SUDDENLY AWARE THAT MY ABILITIES COULD BE QUITE HELPFUL TO others, especially if they were polished and clarified a little, I began to put things together in ways that I hoped would make sense, based on what I had observed and experienced. It all had to be going somewhere, I told myself as my experimentation became extremely complex and carefully deliberate. I didn't know what more I would learn or conclude, but I realized I'd already learned a lot and it was time to organize it in some way. There had to be a reason for it all.

Soon I began going through my Dream Records, taking them apart one at a time, frame by frame, until I had a deep understanding of the kinds of consciousness that occurred in dreams and the many significances of this special form of reality. I studied them until I could interpret any dream for anyone, no matter how garbled, inane, or confusing. I came to see that many of the dreams I'd had were not really dreams in the usual sense. I'd just called them 'dreams' because they took place at night. In reality, many were visions, and some were experiences in other dimensions and realms that had given me considerable expertise in understanding a wide variety of realities.

I realized that the people, the objects, the scenes and the events that appeared in ordinary dreams or visions all had important reasons for appearing and carried many levels of insight and kinds of messages. None were accidental or unrelated to waking consciousness or our everyday experience. We were creating realities at night in the same ways we were creating our reality during the day.

I began to try different things with dream consciousness and within a short time I was able to decide what I would dream and what I would learn from it. I found I could easily program myself to have three, four, or even five dreams with diverse or specific contents. Once I gave myself the necessary directions, I went to sleep and had the first dream. As soon as it was over, I would wake myself and write it down. I would immediately go back to sleep, have the second dream and then wake to write it, too. Often I would go on to a third and a fourth dream in the same way.

Soon I taught myself to have a dream, and when it was time to wake and write it down, I would simply become lucid instead of waking up. Once I entered the lucid state I would memorize the entire dream while still asleep. When I had memorized it, I would return to ordinary sleep and have the second dream I had programmed. Later, when this second dream was over I would again become lucid. After memorizing the second dream, I would review the first dream, and then return to sleep to have the third, fourth and fifth, handling them in the same way. In the morning, I would make a cup of tea and spend the first hour or two of the day recording all my dreams and studying them for help and insight.

Eventually I learned to program a dream, have the entire dream while in a lucid state, and then analyze the dream right there on the spot. After extracting the desired information or experience, I would decide, while still asleep but lucid, what kind of dream experience I needed to program for the next dream of the night. Then I would go on to have that dream, to analyze it while in the lucid state, and go on to the next one. I got to the point that if I programmed four dreams, and one of the dreams had information or experience that affected the directions for the remaining dreams, I could reprogram the rest of the dreams while I was still asleep.

I even played around with what I called multiple levels of dreaming. I found I could go to sleep and have a dream in which I went to sleep and had a dream, and in that 2nd level dream I would go to sleep and have a dream (level 3) in which I would go to sleep and have a dream (level 4). In the 4th level dream I would actually have the experiences I had programmed, then bring the information back out through each level of dream experience and waking.

℘

Another thing I experimented with was time. "Exactly what is time?" I asked myself. Like most people I grew up believing that time was something measured by the clock. Now, having completely discarded the importance of clock-time, I thought of time as some mysterious element that couldn't be seen, heard, or touched. Yet it continuously moved us and our lives into the future while constantly creating an impression of something called the past. This understanding was not enough though; I wanted to understand the structure and workings of time, as well as its hidden effects in the world around me.

As I studied my dreams, I was astounded at how often they displayed information from the future. My experiments with past lives and the many experiences of seeing things before they happened had taught me that time did not work the way we thought it did.

Even more than this, my experiences of being in two places at once, sometimes the present and past, other times the present and future, created many questions about the true nature of space and time. It also greatly increased my curiosity about the nature of reality and whether there were any limitations on how to move about in it.

My experiences, and the possible concepts that arose from them, did not fit the conventional picture of reality I once held, and yet I could find little or nothing written about the subject of time itself. It seemed to be something that was just there, too obvious to notice. Going back to my books on physical science, chemistry and physics was not much help either.

One day, however, I gained what I felt was a critical insight. For weeks I had been conducting a series of experiments with perception. I would set up a timer or small alarm clock and practice moving to various levels of consciousness known as alpha, beta, theta, and even delta. These were the names given to specific ranges of brain wave frequency.

In the first series of tests, I timed how long it took me to get to each level of consciousness, say alpha, for instance. Once there, I kept track of how long I would naturally stay at that level. Then I would try theta, then delta, or perhaps high beta.

In a second series of experiments, I would go to each level of consciousness and see how long I could force myself to stay at that level. In the next series, I would go to a chosen frequency level and attempt to perform various physical or mental tasks, noting the differences in physical movement, attitude, and perception.

In a fourth series of explorations, I would go to each level of consciousness and make careful notes on the kinds of thoughts, feelings and perceptions that occurred there. And in yet another group of experiments, I entered two different realities and compared the kinds of perceptions there, then tried to achieve beta in one and perhaps alpha or theta in the other.

Over the time that I was conducting these explorations, I continued my search for an explanation of time, what it was, and how it worked to create the past, present and future.

One day, in the course of one of my experiments involving being in two places at once, I was calmly moving back and forth between them. Each location had different activities going on in it, and the objects or events in each seemed totally unrelated to the other.

I was caught up in the act of viewing not just the two places I was focusing on, but a myriad of sub-choices within each place that I could choose to pay attention to. Unexpectedly, without any sense of transition, I became involved in a third location with all its own unique events and details...and in quick succession, a fourth, and then a fifth. Suddenly everything in all of the locations, plus dozens of others, coalesced into one big picture that included the long, undulating waves of color that I had first seen in the initial kundalini experiences.

These waves were crisscrossing one another in many places, creating pockets, holes, and all sort of spaces resembling a honeycomb. Nestled within each pocket of the honeycomb were the various locations, objects, and events I had just been switching my attention back and forth among! Each event was going on in its own little pocket of space and time. Each pocket was not only a different location, but each location was distinguished by what appeared to be a characteristic set of wave frequencies. In fact, the location was defined and maintained by those wave frequencies.

Because of the way this honeycomb of frequencies was constructed, everything was connected to everything else. It was all responding to everything that was going on in every other pocket and pigeonhole of space. The long, undulating bands of wave frequencies separated things, yet these separations were transparent from the point of view of the many events going on within the various pockets. The things going on in one pocket seemed to occur without conscious reference to what was going on in other pockets, even though I could see the changes and shifts in all of them as actions and reactions took place, all held in place by the long waves that resembled the threads in a giant weaving loom. Each thread carried information while also holding everything in its relative place.

It looked something like a huge, living, vibrating, pulsing honeycomb of spaces, with each little pocket of space having a unique set of fields and wave frequencies in it, and each set of fields and frequencies determining the forms and activity in that space.

In the odd way that something suddenly takes on profound meaning to someone, I understood many things in a single flash of insight. These wave frequencies were not only the basis of individual perception – they were also the basis of the illusion of time.

This huge network of waves forming intervals and spaces, each location with its own unique set of frequencies, forms, and activities, made it possible for us to have linear perception. Since there was too much to focus on at once, we were forced to focus on one location or pocket at a time, stringing the perceived objects and events together, one after another, in a very personal way.

Linear perception was simply the act of focusing attention on a sequence of things found in the various locations. Awareness of the change that occurred as we moved attention from person to person or activity to activity in the pocket in which we lived gave us a sense of passing time.

Time as we know it is also related to the fact that the frequencies that make up our world are moving at approximately 186,000 miles per second. The kind of light produced by frequencies moving at 186,000 mph is the kind of light that makes up our space-time dimension of reality. Other worlds are made of light frequencies moving at a different base rate. In other words, everything that can be perceived in our reality is made of energy that is moving at roughly 186,000 miles per second. This includes physical humans.

We are most likely to perceive things formed from frequencies that are associated with the spectrum of light moving at 186,000 miles per second, and our sense of time is related to the average speed required to perceive the form, action, or intent of things going on in a location. Because other realities are based on different speeds of light, time there is correspondingly different.

In addition to the sequential patterns of perception and the speed of light factor, time is also derived partly from the length of time our attention stays focused on any one thing. Additionally, although this is less of a factor, time is affected by the relationships that exist between the various dimensions. When we daydream, time is altered because time is different in other dimensions and because we are moving between dimensions.

Everything is really happening at once and time is merely a concept that allows us to apprehend space in the way that is characteristic of our particular reality. If we did not move our perception from object to object or event to event and experience the change of perception, feeling, and action that results from our response to each one, there would be no variety in our experiences and no sense of passing time.

As I gazed at the gigantic honeycomb, it dawned on me that in an effort to communicate and share parts of our reality with one another, we had given names to everything! A tiny sampling of familiar names for these varying frequency sets was "One, two three, four… Father, mother, sister, brother… A, B, C, D… Red, blue, green, yellow… Minute, hour, day, month… Car, truck, bike, plane… Loving, fighting, eating, singing…" and so on into infinity. In fact, the word *infinity* implies endless intervals and is a verbal attempt to express the concept of eternity.

I also understood that for all of us, only the barest framework of reality is universally agreed on. Beyond this, each of us embellishes that basic reality by responding to it with personalized words, thoughts, attitudes, habits and reactions.

For me, time had always been something precisely calculated by science, something measured in terms of seconds or years. Now I could see that our sense of time was based heavily on the processes of perception and the frequency fields of wave energy that created the illusion of intervals in space. Within these freestanding fields were all sorts of activities and forms that we could pay attention to or ignore.

ᘓ

With these new perceptions in hand, I formulated some rules about time. The first was that since our sense of time was based on the movement of perception among frequencies, time must have movement, direction, speed, frequency, depth, amplitude, and duration and was, therefore, a form of energy. Changing any of these factors would also change our experience of time and what was possible within it!

Since time was based partly on wave frequency patterns, it could certainly speed up, slow down or disappear altogether, depending on the range of frequencies we perceived or existed within!

Another obvious rule was that our physical reality was based on the wave frequencies that were associated with visible light moving at approximately 186,000 mph.

The next was that all activity based on the particular kind of time that is happening within our space-time continuum is occurring continuously and without stopping. It is only our perception that changes. The characteristic of continuously ongoing frequency patterns is what makes memory possible, for if the energy did not exist in this way, we would not be able to tune and re-tune our brain cells to a given set of frequencies and experience the phenomena we call 'remembering.'

And finally, since all time is happening in the same place, at the same time, and continuously, we can string linear perceptions together in a myriad of ways – forward, backward, sideways, in repeatable, alternate, duplicate, triplicate, or other ways. By stringing together moments of perception within space-time, each of us is able to create a personal working reality that gives the impression of being sequential, and thus presents us with the illusion of a past, a present, and a future, all of which is creatively individual.

Once I reached this understanding of time, I became more comfortable with the fact of my psychic abilities. My travels out of the body had taught me that other dimensions and realities existed and were based on other frequencies that may or may not be visible to us unless we learn to shift our own brainwave frequencies enough to tune into and perceive them. I understood how it had been possible for me to see things before they happened, or to look back and see the past experiences of myself and others. I knew, finally, how it was possible for me to experience the private feelings, thoughts and perceptions of others and to often see where they were going with their lives. It was simply because I had become adept at tuning my own brain wave frequencies to almost any set of space-time intervals and observing what was happening there.

Not long after this I began to see whole patterns of sequencing associated with a particular time, place, or nation of people. For the first time I began to see the deep relationship between the way people chose to use their perception and the reality that became possible within the framework of thought, desire and action they were using. Like a light bulb going off, I suddenly grasped the old concept of karma.

Karma is an ancient way of expressing what we in the modern world call cause and effect – except it might be better expressed as choice and results. People were stringing together sets of perceptions and experiences chosen from pockets in the space-time continuum whose patterns had difficult, painful, or unhappy results. This became habitual, and they ended up choosing the same kinds of perceptions and experience over and over. They were caught in karma – meaning they were caught in the same old choices, the same old strings of perception. Not only did they fail to see any other pockets of possibility, they didn't realize that they were doing it to themselves by the choices they insisted on.

Sometimes, as they moved from life-time to life-time, they alternated the roles in their chosen drama but they were still selecting from the same old boxed set of experiences, those that produced sorrow, frustration, unhappiness, and guilt.

Without warning I was bowled over by an understanding of the experience of being raped, suffocated, and murdered on the morning of February 6, 1980. This was an effort of my own consciousness to present me with a dramatic preview of the coming results of the choices I was consistently making regarding Ben and the bar and restaurant business! It was also why I hadn't been able to successfully use my own psychic abilities to find out why I was running into so many difficulties. I was determined to have my way and didn't want to hear or see anything else!

It was also quite possible that I wandered into another dimension of existence that congruently displayed an example of the kinds of creating I was doing. Chasing after the bar and restaurant suffocated my own natural development and purpose, choosing Ben over and over was about to leave me feeling raped and tossed aside. And the follow up vision in which I had seen a young woman dangling from the ceiling of her room contained a clear message for me, "She did it to herself." In other words, these were reflections of *my* decisions, *my* choices.

Not only did I make quite a leap forward in understanding time and what it was, I came to have a better understanding of my abilities to see forward and backward in time. I also had a growing appreciation of the way the mind and consciousness worked. It was clear that when we made a major error in our choices, the mind, which could pick up information anywhere in time, would try to present us with information that would show us the outcome of that choice so that we could change it for a better outcome.

The goal was to keep us balanced and bring us quickly back to joy, peace, and confidence while moving us along our own personal path toward development of our highest human potential. With this new under-standing, almost overnight my mind began to be more of an intimate, trusted, friend and counselor in almost the same way that, overnight, it had become a shifting, untrustworthy enemy three years earlier. ∞

15 ∽
"Turn on your heart light..."

"Turn on your heart light,
let it shine wherever you go,
let it make a happy glow
for all the world to see."

Neil Diamond

DURING MY TIME IN THE CRAMPED BASEMENT ROOM, I FINISHED my course work at Wayne State University. The next requirement for my degree was a research paper of at least fifty pages. Considering my experiences over the previous three years, I was intent on writing about the possibilities of revamping our failing educational system to be more in line with the capabilities of the mind that I was learning about.

It seemed to me that my unusual homework techniques, the ability to take tests without reading or grueling study, and the synthesis of understanding that created such a wonderful change in the quality of my learning would be a welcome change for those in school. I thought that if the learning and teaching of facts and concepts were made much easier, teachers would have time to address the wider development of the whole person and our educational system could produce truly intelligent, wise, and capable people who were infinitely adaptable.

I outlined the paper over and over but I could not find a way to express what I knew was possible with the mind in a way that would not be dismissed as so much occult hogwash. I kept telling my advisors that I wanted to revamp the whole system, and they kept telling me this was too broad an issue, certainly one that couldn't be covered in fifty pages. Finally I decided to begin a deeper study of the existing literature on the brain, along with writings on perception, mind, cognition, and related areas. Once I had some idea of what was already written I could decide what I wanted to write.

I ended up focusing deeply on brain structure and function. Yet even as my picture of the mind/brain, consciousness, and intelligence became more sophisticated, I realized I was really looking for answers to the questions surrounding the strange sexual experiences, the stabbing pains and the heat. Although they had gradually become less frequent and much less threatening in their intensity, as my skills in managing the mind increased so did my need to understand how I had gotten from 'there to here.'

I grouped all of these experiences under the term *kundalini* because I was inwardly certain that, so far, it was the best label I had for what had happened to me. Certainly, whatever kundalini was, it had a profound effect on the brain, mind, consciousness, perception, and intelligence. That was obvious.

Yet, in spite of the fact that I was now teaching people how to develop their own intuitive abilities, there were still many gaps in my own understanding. What was intuition based on? Why did it appear so inconsistently? Why were there so many differing manifestations of it? How could I reconcile what I knew was possible within space-time with what was taught in our sciences? More than anything I wanted to be able to explain the sporadic presence of intuition in relatively large numbers of people, and the fact that these psychic abilities might be the result of an event called *the awakening of kundalini.*

There had to be others who experienced this phenomenon, and with them, I wanted to compare notes and explore the fact that this event just happened to generate anomalous sexual experiences. For a time I relied on the traditional 'occult' framework of answers. These included explanations like, "Intuition is just something that you're born with," or, "It's a gift from God." But these answers were no longer enough. I had not been born with any abilities that were even remotely psychic, and my early experiences of this 'gift' had been a continuous nightmare that didn't resemble anything taught by the God or the church I had gone to for the first thirty-one years of my life. Thus, even the most basic questions, like "What causes psychic abilities... or psychic phenomena?" went without the neat, satisfactory answers I wanted.

Now, ostensibly trying to write a thesis paper – but really engaged in research that would answer some highly personal and very driving questions, I spent hours thinking back over the events, reading and re-reading my notes. I had one clue, but I didn't know what to do with it.

It had come to me just before my life with Ben came to an end. I had been tormented by the sexual experiences and obsessed with trying to figure out their cause, their explanation, and their control.

One day I had driven home after a class session in which I emphasized the importance of 'the question' to my students. Forming the right question was half of the success in using one's psychic abilities. Recognition of the answer or answers was the other half.

In mulling over this advice to my students, I realized I ought to try deliberately applying it in this situation. So, testing the hypothesis I had formulated earlier, I posed a very careful and deliberate question, then put it out there into the universe for the mind to solve.

First I cleared my mind, then asked my simple question with intense concentration. "What *is* kundalini?"

I waited to see what the mind would come up with for an answer, but nothing recognizable came to me. Since I was now used to almost immediate answers and ideas, the lack of response was more than frustrating. I continued to stew and chew on the question.

The next day I walked down to the edge of the bay and stared out at the water. The waves on the surface seemed to move effortlessly, endlessly. I sat there for an hour, wondering why there were waves, until I felt chilled and had to return home.

As I walked home the wind began to blow harder and harder until it was nearly screaming and I found it necessary to push my way through it. Trees were bending and waving wildly and I wondered how something as invisible as wind could make such a roar and create such commotion.

Several days later I went to the park where my attention was caught and held by children swinging on swings. Up and down, back and forth they went, just for the experience of the rocking motion.

The next day, while driving my car on the expressway, I was nearly hypnotized by the motion of cars whizzing by me. Later the same day, while sitting on the picnic table in my back yard, I was entranced by the slow effortless drift of a swan on the canal and its slow lift into the air, powered by its own wings.

On Sunday afternoon of that same week there was a small, brief earthquake, a shocking kind of movement I had never felt before. It was centered in Kentucky and rocked areas that did not usually experience such things.

That evening I was relaxing with a cup of tea and felt it had been an intense week but couldn't put my finger on why. Musing again about the question of kundalini, I thought of the fellow who had discovered the benzene 'O' ring from a clue that appeared while he was dozing.

Wondering if I could just get a clue by copying him, I gave my mind directions to produce some information that would just get me on the right track. Then I sat back and relaxed, closing my eyes, intending to doze in order to let the familiar vagaries of consciousness present an answer, or at least some new information.

To my amazement, it reproduced, in one flashing scene after the next, all the scenes involving endless, intense, or exaggerated movement that I had experienced over the previous week!

To my surprise I had an answer – *motion*. To my dismay it meant nothing, and I found myself up against the second shortcoming I had frequently told my students about, "You are as limited as your ability to recognize and apply the answer." I resolved to discover the hidden meanings, the connections, and the knowledge offered in the clue, but over and over I ran into dead ends.

Finally, I left the question and its clue standing there like the monolithic stones on Easter Island, huge, real, and a mystery, until the research for my senior thesis brought the mystery back to center stage where it again became an obsession. Once more I searched for answers to the question, "What is kundalini?" And once again there was no satisfaction and no further insight beyond the original clue of 'motion.'

ల

As the autumn of 1982 approached, I was still researching and writing, and had resigned myself to living in the basement room forever. Then my dreams began to indicate that someone new would be entering my life unexpectedly and changing it rather quickly. In the dream I was told that he would be a 'city farmer,' that I would recognize him because he would sing music to me about his farming, and that he would be more than a husband, he would be a life partner.

For months I had hoped that Ben and I would get back together, but by now I knew it was not going to happen and that I was going to have to do something more active to rebuild my life. I was in the basement literally and figuratively.

Gradually a newfound sense of practicality took root, and for no particular reason, one day the external world was as new and exciting as if I had been away on another planet for several years. Although my perception was still unstable from time to time, the strange sexual experiences had calmed into gentle rivers of luminescent sensuousness that occurred mostly when I was relaxed. They were not really a problem in themselves any more, rather it was my desire for an explanation that plagued me now.

Since answers were not forthcoming and work on my senior thesis was stalled, I pushed both the search and the writing to the background and looked about for some way to get my life on track again. After exploring several paths I might take, I decided to investigate the world of computers. In September I enrolled in a class and began to learn word processing, which I turned out to be very good at. Meanwhile, I continued to see people who wanted personal consultations because of my psychic abilities.

On a Sunday evening in early October a telephone call came in from a man I had been introduced to back in May at a meditation gathering of people who met regularly. I only attended the meditation once and yet I remembered him. I even recalled thinking when I met him that he seemed like a 'stuffed shirt,' out of place in such a group.

His name was Jim, and he was requesting an appointment and some guidance for a lawsuit he was involved in. The following Friday we met at the end of the day, and when the appointment – which went on for nearly two hours – was finished, he asked if I would like to go get some-thing to eat. Breaking a rule of my own which forbade any socializing with clients, I accepted and we walked a couple of blocks to a Mexican restaurant.

Over dinner we talked about our personal dreams, and to my surprise he told me he had wanted to meet me for some time. He said he owned a large building with six stores, and six apartments above the stores. He also knew I had a small business in massage therapy and personal counseling, and he asked if I would be interested in moving my massage business into one of his empty storefronts.

He was, he explained, already running a sound and recording business, and he was selling restaurant shelving, but he owned a couple of computers and wanted to start not only a service that would offer to type and print professional word processing documents, but a mailbox service. He offered to give me one of the apartments rent free if I would consider running his two current businesses and starting up the two new ones while I ran my own, since he already worked a full-time job.

When I told him I would consider it, we walked back to his office where he handed me a notebook full of business plans and operation manuals.

"Look this over and let's get back together Sunday evening," he suggested. "Maybe we can put together a plan."

"Okay," I said, then took the notebook and drove home.

Two nights later on Sunday evening, I drove over to the building he owned and told him I was interested. We talked for a couple of hours about this or that aspect of what he was trying to accomplish, and finally came to a financial agreement.

As we picked up the notes and papers and I prepared to go, he told me that he had once been a farmer and that farming was where his heart was but it was impossible to make any money at it. He had already mentioned that he was born and raised in Harper Woods, a Detroit suburb, and I wondered what on earth had attracted him to farming. I didn't tell him that my whole family had come from the farm and I couldn't imagine why anyone would want to be a farmer.

Then he went over to a tape player saying, "...so even though I can't see going into farming again, I think of my businesses like this..." and he started up the music.

It was John Denver singing, "Inch by inch, row by row, gonna make this garden grow, all I need is a rake and a hoe and a patch of fertile ground. Inch by inch, row by row, someone blessed these seeds I sow..."

I thought it was a neat little song and listened with enjoyment as I prepared to leave.

Just then Jim said, "You know, I've been looking for a business partner for a while, and I've been looking for a wife, too. But I've really always wanted my wife to be my business partner... and uh...you wouldn't be available would you?"

I turned around and stared at him, goosebumps running over me. The music of *The Garden Song* was still playing, and standing in front of me was this strange man who was born and raised in the city but wanted to be a farmer, and who was casually asking if I would be interested in being a business partner and a wife.

Shock rolled through me as I remembered the dreams I'd had, while my mouth opened and I heard myself say, "Yes... I would."

"When could you move in?" he asked.

"How about Tuesday?" I replied, my mouth opening and closing without conscious volition on my part.

"Good!" he said, "I have a trailer; if you can be all packed up, I'll be over to pick up your things about 3:30 in the afternoon. Does that sound like it'll work?"

"Sure," I said, still in shock.

He walked over, gave me a hug and said, "I'm a little nervous about dating or living with a psychic, but I suppose I'll get used to it."

I left, moving as if in a trance, and went to get in my truck. A few blocks from Jim's building I sort of 'came to' and began to argue with everything that I had just agreed to do involving the move, the business, the relationship.

"Good grief! What am I going to do?" I said aloud as I reached out and turned on the radio.

"Turn on your heart-light...!" came the answer, blasting back at me as Neil Diamond sang the theme song from *E.T.*

Startled at what seemed like such a direct answer to my question, I turned the radio off immediately and decided to begin planning.

I spent Monday packing, Tuesday moving, and literally overnight, everything about my life changed. Jim turned out to be wonderful and a year later, Thanksgiving of 1983, he and I were married.

My life filled up with issues surrounding computer technology and I got interested in everything from how the hardware was built to the software that ran it. I sold computers and their related peripherals, taught people to use the software, and continued my massage and counseling practice on the side. The two careers seemed incongruent, but at the time it seemed the thing to do.

All the while, in the back of my mind, I wrestled with the question, "What is kundalini?" One by one I tried to line up factors such as heredity, environment, education, spirituality, biology, sociology, diet, exercise, health, emotions, IQ, and every other thing I could think of but none of them seemed to fit or offer an explanation that satisfied me.

One day while riding in the car with Jim, I turned the tormenting question and my single clue of 'motion' around and around in my head. The window was open and I stared out at the passing cars and scenery, irritated at my inability to figure out my only clue. Finally I dropped the idea and started a conversation about a technical course we were putting together for a client. I had great difficulty paying attention to his end of the conversation because 'the question' and 'the clue' were still rumbling around in the back of my mind as we talked about just how basic the technical course should be.

"Well, how much do you think they know about the electrical system? Should we include a section on basic electricity? Or maybe, do you think we could cover the subject of electricity in ten words or less? In fact, how could we do that? Could you define electricity in ten words or less?" I said to him.

"Well," he said, "basically, electricity is motion..." and the rest of his statement was drowned out by a passing truck.

I froze. The conversation about the technical course was over. Somehow I knew I had another piece of the answer I was searching for. ଔ

16 ∾
Eureka!

"Some mathematician has said
pleasure lies not in discovering truth,
but in seeking it."

Tolstoy

TAKING OFF WITH THE NEW CLUE, I WENT DIGGING THROUGH PHYSICAL science books, chemistry, and anything else I could find that had something to say about electricity. I had studied the basics of electricity in my early college days but with the typical handicap, "I'll memorize enough to pass the test." Now the motivation was entirely different, and what had seemed so impossibly boring was fascinating reading now.

I read a considerable amount of material about basic electricity and its uses before I realized I was getting nowhere. None of the books or articles were dealing with the subject in terms of the body. They were talking about how to wire houses, build machinery, or conduct scientific experiments.

Weeks later, I was discouraged. Again, over a cup of tea, I asked for more help or another clue. To my surprise I heard a small voice answer almost immediately, "Kundalini is perfect relativity of all motion within a defined frequency range."

This clue was as difficult as the first one had been. What in the world was 'perfect relativity' or a 'defined frequency range?' I picked at the various words, tackling the idea of *relativity* first by reading Albert Einstein's Special Theory of Relativity, and then his General Theory.

Nothing clicked, so I spent some time wondering exactly what was meant by the term 'defined frequency range.' When this led to no insights,

I went back to the idea of electricity and went searching for materials that dealt strictly with electricity within the body.

This proved to be more rewarding, at least in terms of how interesting the information was. I learned that within the body itself, the nervous system ran on electricity. In the brain, electrical impulses triggered the release of neurotransmitters. These were chemicals that made us feel hungry or full, tired or wide-awake, sexually active or uninterested! Too little or too much of a particular neurotransmitter could cause either serious forgetfulness or hyper-memory; it could make us feel irritable or joyful, depressed or ambitious, attentive or daydreamy.

"Good grief!" I thought with an edge of disbelief, "our emotions are the result of our electro-chemical activities!"

I discovered that electrical stimulation of specific areas in the motor cortex of the brain would cause a hand or a leg to move without the individual consciously deciding to move; and electrical stimulation of dead muscles would sometimes bring them back to life again. Even more amazing, electrical stimulation of the hypothalamus in the mid-brain area would cause the elimination of short-term memory traces.

I was momentarily ecstatic when I came across Wilder Penfield's work. He had discovered that electrical stimulation of areas in the temporal cortex could produce the sensation of being in two places at once. [4]

From the work of Roger Sperry and Michael Gazzaniga, I learned that too much electricity resulted in uncontrolled 'electrical storms' in the brain, and these were the cause of epilepsy. In addition, I learned of the left hemisphere's preference for linear processing, and the right hemisphere's knack for pattern recognition and intuitive processing. [5]

I discovered that the entire electrical circuitry of the body had been mapped out hundreds, maybe thousands of years ago, by the Chinese in their practice of acupuncture. I watched films of surgery, birth, and other supposedly painful events take place painlessly just by controlling, re-routing, or interrupting this flow of electrical energy. These were all interesting ideas, but none even came close to explaining what I was looking for.

Meanwhile, two and a half years went by as I continued to search and to study. It was now spring of 1986. Jim and I had just moved across

4 Wilder Penfield, *The Mystery Of The Mind* (Princeton, NJ; Princeton University Press, 1978) pg. 22.
5 Michael Gazziniga, "The Split Brain in Man" from *Language*, ed. Virginia P. Clark, Paul A. Eschholz and Alfred F. Rosa (New York, NY; St Martin's Press, 1977).

the state, and I decided I was going to write the story of what happened to me in the kundalini experiences, and then submit the manuscript to a publisher somewhere. This decision brought me face to face with the fact that I still didn't know and couldn't really explain exactly what kundalini *was*. Thus the search became an obsession; while, without an answer to the mystery, little writing got done.

One day I sat, discouraged and forlorn, at my desk. I had spent hours going through books on electrical applications in medical research without being able to put anything together. Nothing seemed to fit and I wondered if I had gotten off track. Maybe there was something more basic that I just didn't understand.

I got up and wandered into the kitchen for a snack and a cup of tea, absentmindedly taking one of my basic Physical Science books with me. I made the tea, got some crackers and peanutbutter, and sat down to nibble. Without thinking about anything in particular, I turned the pages of the science book, browsing through chapters on the atom and light.

Suddenly a sentence jumped out at me, "…light itself is a form of electromagnetic wave motion." Instantly I recalled the explosion of light that occurred in the kundalini experience. Snapping into place alongside this were the clues of 'motion' and 'electricity.' Deep inside I knew I had hit something important. Kundalini had something to do with light, electromagnetic wave fields, and electricity.

For the rest of that day and into the night, I read and re-read, studied, thought, wrote and re-wrote, working to put the pieces together. Finally, almost in shock, I reached the point when I knew I had a major piece of the puzzle I had been trying to put together. Some of it was rough, all of my questions were not quite answered, and the implications seemed staggering, yet I was sure I knew what kundalini was.

I considered the facts. I had always known that electric wires could get hot; and it was general knowledge that electricity was used to create light, as in the light bulb. I also knew that wherever there was an electrical current flowing, an electromagnetic wave field was created at right angles to the direction of current flow, and that the frequencies found in any wave field would determine the colors that appeared in that field. For instance, red light has a wave frequency of about 261 cycles per second (cps), blue light has a frequency of about 392 cps, while purple is around 493 cps, and so on.

Earlier, as I had struggled with my clues of motion and electricity, it had not occurred to me to put these into the actual context of what I had experienced. Thus I had not given any thought to possible connections between the *heat* I experienced during the kundalini episodes, the explosion of *light*, and the beautiful *waves* of color in that eternal expanse of complete and fulfilling nothingness.

Now it was clear. *Kundalini was a spectacular electromagnetic event caused by a dramatic acceleration of electric current within the body!*

As electricity accelerated through the nervous system during a kundalini experience, it created heat in exactly the same way an increasing electrical current in a wire would cause the wire to get hot. A relatively low increase in the flow of the electrical current created that occasional tingling, itchy feeling that something was crawling or creeping around my head, up my side, or down my leg. When the rate of flow was increased, great internal heat would be produced. And when there was a sudden, massive acceleration of electrical flow, a flash or explosion of light would be produced.

Heat and light were both forms of electromagnetic wave action. In fact, an electromagnetic field could produce an electrical current. The reverse was also true; an electrical current would produce an electromagnetic field. Where you had one, you would find the other.

The thing that I had completely missed was the fact that the human body/mind system was – just like every single other location or object in space – a matrix of wave frequencies in the space-time continuum. We were running on electrical power just like the machines at the Chrysler plant. The nervous system was our electrical wiring, and the colors and lights I saw around people were part of the electromagnetic wave field in which they existed!

I recalled the little bits of information I had been able to find and read about kundalini, information that always described it as a spiritual energy that moved up the spine. Since my experiences generally created the sensation of something moving up the front, or occasionally, the center of me, I had frequently questioned myself as to whether my experience could be a real kundalini experience since it didn't seem to be moving up my spine.

However, when it became apparent that what was moving was electricity, this question was resolved. Anyone who has touched a live wire and become a convenient conductor for the current will experience anything from a tickle to a serious jolt, depending on the amount of current moving through the wire. As the massive currents of the energy of kundalini moved up my spine, they had jolted one nerve plexus after another. Since each nerve plexus had its responding, sensory ends in the organs and tissues that lay stacked up in front of the spine, the actual *feeling* was that something was running up the center front of me.

Although the first few times I had described it as a 'freight train that hit my brain and kept on going into outer space,' it had eventually quieted down to become a river of heat and pressure. And as my system gradually became accustomed to it, it had turned into a gently flowing stream of light, always accompanied by sensations of shimmering pleasure.

Defining kundalini as an acceleration of the electrical current moving through the body helped shed a much clearer light on what had happened to the man in Port Huron who had burst into flame. He had experienced a spontaneous awakening of kundalini with its massive acceleration in the frequency of electric current. Unfortunately, it proved to be too much for his physical system. Something had shorted out, an electrical fire had started, and he had self-incinerated.

Finally satisfied, I put my papers and books aside and headed off to bed in a euphoric state of mind. In the magical space of only a day, nearly seven years' worth of tormenting questions were answered. And to say that I was grateful to have survived my own experience of kundalini would have been a monumental understatement!

೦೩

Getting this far gave me a certain amount of satisfaction and for a couple of days I thought about how simple it all seemed. As always there were major gaps in my understanding, and remarkably soon I was wrestling with a whole new set of impossible questions. Where had physical reality disappeared to during the experience? How was it that I remained conscious if my bodily self and my everyday reality faded away? And why had I experienced such fulfillment in such an empty space?

These questions and others were running through my mind as I sat watching the twilight deepen over the lake one evening. Still basking in the satisfaction of my newly pieced-together theory about kundalini, I didn't really expect any answers. To my surprise I found myself listening to a small lecture going on inside my head that concluded with "…and read Walter Russell's *Polarization and Unified Field Theory*!"

I had been given a copy of this theory some years earlier by a man who knew Russell's widow and who encouraged me to read it. I tried, but after the first few pages I'd given up. It was extremely complex and full of equations that went far beyond my ability to comprehend. Now I dutifully got it out again and started reading, certain I was wasting my time. It took me hours just to get through the first couple of pages as I read and re-read, took copious notes, stopped to look up unfamiliar or forgotten terms, and tried to create a picture in my mind of what he was saying.

I was thoroughly discouraged when I finally decided to put down pencil and paper and just plow through the words, reading them aloud to myself and hoping my brain/mind would somehow make sense of it. After all, I didn't usually get information or direct instructions to do something this specific unless I was actually ready to start working with it. Thus, I trusted that it was time, and sure enough, little by little I began to understand what happened to physical reality during the kundalini experiences.

Walter Russell, a former contemporary of Einstein, was explaining theoretically and describing mathematically just what I experienced in the kundalini experiences.

He started with the notion of a general class of particles, such as electrons. Then he established the fact that particles have two kinds of motion. One, they spin, which gives them a wavelength (and which he called Angular Motion). And two, they move in a variety of directions with changing speeds, which gives them physical characteristics (and which he called Kinetic-Energy Motion).

According to Russell, these two motions, spinning and directional movement, work in completely balanced equilibrium when in a vacuum.

He then proceeded to work his way through a series of complex mathematical equations and postulates, which demonstrated that no matter how these particles broke up or came together, the total mass of energy and the balanced equilibrium were always maintained. These statements in themselves were not that surprising, they were part of the same theory I had learned in chemistry in college.

But! He went on to say that as the particles collided and broke up, they reached the point of having no mass, and when a particle reached the point of no mass, two things happened. One was that without mass, there could be no inertia, or friction, and thus motion would continue endlessly and infinitely. The other was that without mass there could be no particle to maintain an angular spin. The result would be motion without any mass, and *without any mass it was impossible to have physical matter*. This, he concluded was Absolute Space or Infinity!

In his words:

"It becomes evident that infinity or absolute space is a limitless frame of infinite motion having no mass (no physical particles) and no angular activity (no spin). Since this limitless frame is infinite in all directions, all infinite motions are infinite in all directions. Since all no-mass motions are moving as infinite motions in all directions, any motion, being perpetual and infinite, may be visualized as being in the same point at the same instant, and at each and every instant.

"Therefore, infinity is at one and the same time, and at all times, an absolute *stillness* with respect to matter. It follows that all mass-energy frames (physical objects) are absolutely transparent to the no-mass infinite motion." [6] *(Italics and parentheses mine)*

This rather complex yet carefully worded statement of Russell's became the key to understanding more than I had bargained for, and another piece of the puzzle came together. Kundalini was such a powerful current of energy within the body/mind system that it accelerated both the spin (Angular Motion) and directionality (Kinetic-Energy Motion) of our own particles and molecules to the point of dissolving the attraction and connections between them. As these connections dissolved, so did the constructions and forms of physical matter, the very forms that gave us our sense of being a physical individual. Thus one experienced a growing loss of boundaries, an increasing sense of fluidity, a rapidly expanding sense that one was flowing outward, and finally the experience that one had dissolved into complete transparency in a place of utter stillness. All that was left was a state of total awareness without physical matter.

Kundalini had allowed me to briefly enter the state of no-mass wave motion. In this state, the 'body' side of the body/mind equation, along with physical matter and the familiar world of reality had disappeared. The world of matter became transparent once I entered the condition of no mass, also known as the Void.

In the Void, bathed in a pool of unending stillness and peace, I experienced unlimited awareness – the eternal Source of all things. It was a knowing that could only be described as *I Am*. In this knowing was a sense of completeness and love that was more blissful than words could

6   Walter Russell, *Polarization and Unified Field Theory* (Universal Science Foundation, VA; 1963) p.87.

ever describe. It was now clear that the core of each one of human, plant, animal, or form of any kind was bliss, joy, and a sense of satisfaction that could not be adequately described with words. To really understand, it had to be experienced. ✧

17 ❧
Altered Senses

"...the true miracle is the natural state."

Satprem

FOR WEEKS AFTERWARD I LUXURIATED IN THE TRIUMPH OF MY UNDER-standing. Finally, I knew what kundalini was. It was a serious, even dramatic change in the range of frequencies that formed the basis of the electromagnetic, and therefore the electro-chemical operation in the body/mind system. I knew the signs, I had experienced the symptoms, and I had lived with the effects. It seemed truly a miracle not only that such a thing was possible, but that it happened to me – and I survived!

As I reflected on the whole series of events, I felt as if I had come through some difficult birth. Like an infant born with a whole new mind, a tabula rasa, I had suffered my way through various stages of development and now basked in the profound pleasure of being able to manage my mind, my perception and my consciousness.

I thought about the changes that occurred and the difficulties of trying to navigate what suddenly became a whole new world with an entirely foreign set of rules. As one experience of kundalini followed another, I became more and more sensitive to the world around me. A good analogy of the change in my ability to sense and perceive everyone and everything around me could be found in the difference between trying to see your reflection in a mud puddle on a breezy day, and then trying to see your reflection in a pair of perfectly silvered mirrors placed facing each other, with full-spectrum lighting all around them, and you in the middle between them. You could get an occasional basic idea of shapes and relationships in the mud puddle reflection; while in the paired mirrors you could see forward, sideways, or backwards, with tons of detail and a cascade of reflections that seemed to go on into infinity.

My eyes could now see light of a far finer, fainter nature than ever before. I could even see the magnetic field around electric wires. In addition to the display of flashing lights and clouds of color found in the electromagnetic field around people and objects, I could also see the bright, continuous flashing of tiny sources of light everywhere in the air. Now and then curving, swirling vortices of plain, old 'empty' space appeared here and there.

My ears were another source of amazement. Before the kundalini experiences I never realized how much noise and static went on in my head. Now, inexplicably, I could hear a wonderful silence. I could also hear far better in everyday situations, and at far greater distances than I ever had before. I felt as if I had developed a new ear in the center of my belly and when I consciously used this third ear in combination with my ordinary ears, I could hear anyone almost anywhere in time and space!

My senses of smell, taste and touch became acute to the point of embarrassment, even painful at times. I could smell people in ways that went beyond noticing their perfume or their body odor. I could smell traces of them just before they arrived, and long after they were gone. Sometimes, when I thought I was alone in a particular aisle or department of a store, I would smell someone who had moved quietly into the next aisle or another corner of the department. I also began to smell things I'd never noticed before – things like water, or heat, the earth, or a tree, even fabrics and silverware.

My senses of touch and taste changed in unusual ways as well. Whenever I physically touched someone or they touched me, I was aware of a tremendous current of energy, perhaps electrical energy that passed between us. I could feel people, animals and objects touch me when they passed by yet were six, eight or ten feet away. And words were no longer just words, they were powerful sounds having a certain kind of electrical energy. Words became a physical experience, and sometimes I experienced the sound of words as a physical impact on my body, sometimes so powerful they caused me to jump, to recoil, to rock or to sway in pleasure as they touched me.

Putting something in my mouth was a cross between pleasure of the most intimate sort and an invasion of the deepest parts of me. When this sensitivity began to cross modalities, I discovered I could taste a sunrise, see a song, hear a tree, smell the touch of a stone, and be transported by a peach or a plum to the location of its birth in the sun.

As I listened to news on the radio, odd bits of information triggered my ability to see a whole series of events that were connected, like beads on a string, through time and space. Just hearing the name of a convicted killer or thief would create enough curiosity for me to see the history of the relationship between him and his victim for many lifetimes. Often they were caught in a vicious circle of anger and revenge. Sometimes they didn't know each other very much at all, they just agreed to play off one another in order to grow at the soul level. The 'victim' ended up teaching family and friends important lessons around loss, or caring and unexpected departures, while the 'felon' attempted to gain a sense of appreciation for life, the ability to balance temperament, belief in the self, or the limits of freedom and self-expression. Some criminal-victim relationships had no history and no growth at all. They were simply caught in the mistakes of the time and place, victims of the shortcomings of our culture.

I thought back on the confusion and disorientation I became mired in as my undisciplined mind, running willy nilly, ever-curious and mostly nosey, began to access all of space and time, presenting a continuous stream of information that at first seemed random, unrelated, and uncontrolled. I marveled at the revelation that this stream of information consisted of answers to questions I unconsciously wondered about. And I chuckled as I realized that, just like an infant, I spent two years learning to deal with all the new perceptions and abilities until I finally arrived at the toddler stage where I could say 'no' and turn the mysterious perceptions on or off.

Once I could do this, I was free to pay attention to the present reality, the one that everyone else was paying attention to. In retrospect it was easy to see that kundalini opened my mind, erasing former boundaries and expanding awareness until it unfolded all of my existence, revealing the central Source of my life, of all life, the eternal *I Am*.

I entered into the experience of something the ancients referred to as The Void, I knew exactly what was meant by the phrase 'we are all one,' and I understood firsthand the truth in the old saying that the world is an illusion. But even as the wondrous nature of all this filled me, other questions began to surface.

Was I correctly interpreting what I was seeing and experiencing in my expanded world of awareness? Without anyone to guide me I was left to map the territory on my own. Now that I'd finally pieced together a whole new reality, with all new rules for perceiving in time and space, I was still somewhat uncertain, not only of the labels I had given to events, but of how to fully interpret those events and processes.

Based on what I observed, individual consciousness was a singular but powerful magnetic pattern that formed within the eternal, infinite ocean of electromagnetic waves – and possibly other kinds of waves that I didn't even know of. If this was so, then did the individual magnetic pattern of consciousness help to create the form we called the human body?

I once thought of the body as the source of consciousness and behavior. Now I felt the reverse was true, the body and its behaviors were the result of the magnetic patterns of consciousness. If this was so, why did consciousness need a body to experience individual existence? After all, I had been out of the body enough times to know that I didn't need the body to be aware of myself as an active, living being. So what was I doing here in this time and place, living in a physical body on planet Earth, where so many people and things around me no longer made sense?

In the seven years since the awakening of kundalini, the entire map of this physical reality that I had been building since birth was redrawn and reorganized. I no longer managed my life in the ways I once thought so normal. Whenever I tried to get back into the 'planning and appointment game,' I felt cornered and unhappy. I ended up canceling, which drove people around me to distraction. Their dismay caused me to be upset with myself and wonder what was wrong with me.

At times, I could see and know so much that I was overwhelmed. I wondered frequently exactly what I should be paying attention to. However, what I saw, heard, and decided was guided by some inner knowing, so again and again, I simply observed until something inside of me prompted me to act.

This way of managing my life was in sharp contrast to the way others managed theirs. For them, every hour was planned out for weeks in advance. It was a long time before I realized that the reason I canceled so many things was because I kept agreeing to do things that were pointless to me and, when the time came to do them, I had no heart for them. Once I realized this, I took a long hard look at what the rest of the world was really doing. I was upset at the amount of meaningless activity that was going on. Had I really changed that much? Where was I going? Where were they going? Why did it look like everyone was investing in a house of cards? How had my paths diverged so dramatically from theirs?

In the meantime, I worried about other things as well. If kundalini was an acceleration of electrical current up through the body and the brain, had it done anything permanent to my brain? To my nervous system? To my body as a system of organs and glands? Since it had so completely changed the functioning of my consciousness, my entire view of the world, the way I related to people and events, and the ways I thought the world could be sensibly organized for much greater levels of satisfaction and quality of experience, then surely it must have done something permanent to my physical body and brain!

For the fourth time in my life I decided to carefully interact with and watch people around me to see if I could discern any differences between their physical functioning and mine. I hoped that watching bodies as an expression of consciousness might turn up subtle differences in some-thing like breathing or heart rate or some other factor that showed an alteration of physical function.

For months I watched people all around me. Instead of finding any differences in physical function, what I observed again and again was an endless and ongoing struggle of men and women, both high and low, young and old, to force themselves into molds that didn't fit, to pretend they were happy. They reminded me of myself five years earlier when I was trying desperately to hang onto the relationship with Ben; to open a bar and restaurant business when I disliked bars in the first place, and to spend tons of energy trying to be what I was not.

Why were so many people suffering in the name of love? Was that what love was really about? Why were they pursuing work they had no passion for, or actively disliked? Were they completely unaware of the calling of the heart to the work that fulfilled one for a lifetime? Why were they working so hard to present an image that had nothing to do with who they really felt they were? Was everyone hollow on the inside? These observations caused me some personal discomfort and I wondered if the real problem was myself. Was I was becoming too lazy, or cynical about getting ahead in life? Why wasn't I out there struggling to get ahead, to create an image, to be loved, with the rest of them? The only answer I consistently came up with was a question, "Why couldn't people see they were only fooling themselves, grasping for an illusion?"

Nevertheless, I continued to observe, still hoping for clues that might signal permanent but hidden changes in my body/brain function as compared to others.

As I observed, my mind still presented tons of information to me and sometimes I offered the information to people, thinking I might help. A few were thankful, most were doubtful, some got upset. Even when I cautiously and indirectly brought up the subject of their problem, intending to help, their response was an indignant or embarrassed, "Who told you that?!" But the most frustrating were those people who said, "Why didn't you tell me…?" when weeks or months earlier I had told them what I saw coming.

It was during this period that I discovered people's love of noisy, romantic, and dramatic attention. They didn't want a 'hint' of truth, or even a small piece of quiet, unobtrusive information. They wanted brass bands and trumpets of god to announce their future and the bit of insight they needed. If it didn't come in that form, they missed it entirely. Later, remembering the noise and static that had constantly run through my head before I had discovered the magic of silence, I realized perhaps they still had a lot of noise and static going on in their minds. And perhaps the brass bands and trumpets were really needed just to get their attention in the first place.

During this long period of intense observation I ended up feeling terribly responsible for people and the world and what I knew. If I had all of this knowledge and insight, shouldn't I do something with it? Shouldn't I save the world? Finally I realized that this was grandiose. The world did not act like it wanted to be saved at all, and in the end, I realized it didn't need to be saved. People were not ready to hear useful information until they themselves needed or asked for it. Thus, at the conclusion of my fourth period of intense observation of people and events around me I made two decisions.

One was that the world had been pretty much the same for at least ten thousand years and probably did not need to be saved from anything, thus I was not going to offer anyone any sort of information unless I was directly asked.

The other was that if there were any specific differences between the way my body and brain physically operated and the way other people's bodies and brains operated, I could not tell just by external observation. With this conclusion I completely overlooked the most obvious difference, one which I had been struggling with ever since the first kundalini episodes – the fact that other people did not ever complain about periods of suffering that involved shocking visions, unusual sensory experiences, intense heat, internal pressure, a pounding heart, or backwards breathing. ∞

18 ∽
Saints, Poets, and Presidents

*"Intelligence highly awakened is intuition
which is the only true guide in life."*

Krishnamurti

MORE THAN SEVEN YEARS HAD NOW GONE BY SINCE THE KUNDALINI experiences first began. After years of constant, driving search to figure out what had happened to me, then reaching my goal, I was now at loose ends, dangling and without a clear direction.

It was obvious that I was never going to return to engineering; and as my knowledge and expertise increased in the areas of brain structure and function, consciousness, intelligence and cognition, I became more and more involved in educational consulting as a specialist in brain-compatible and accelerated learning. Still, I had long wanted to write.

Having solved what I thought was an important mystery of consciousness for myself, I wondered if this phenomena might have happened to others, and since there was so very little written about it, perhaps I could help others by writing about the whole experience.

I needed to make a living and doubted that I would ever be able to find time to write. Nevertheless, the desire to write grew until it became a constant thorn in my side. I would start, then stop, then start again, then get distracted by all the other things that needed to be done every day. Somehow I could not let myself write.

One day a friend came over and was obviously blue. He'd had a fight with his wife the night before and they still weren't talking. He had come home from work the previous evening with a number of things to do. His wife, who worked different hours, left a note asking him to clean up the house and please vacuum. He was tired and wanted to take a nap but had to get supper on the table, and in the back of his mind he wanted to avoid what he felt was a growing confrontation with his sulky fifteen-year-old.

Other things on his to-do list for the evening included a little bit of time to put the final touches on a gift that he'd put together for his youngest daughter's birthday the next day, as well as the paperwork he brought home because he was behind at the office. He hoped he would be able to spend some time with his wife when she arrived home at 11:30 p.m., and in the middle of trying to decide what to do, a neighbor called with a reminder. He had committed himself to attending a meeting more than a month ago, and the meeting was that very night.

These were all worthwhile goals, but each one pulled him in a different direction leaving him scattered and overwhelmed. Taking a nap was in conflict with getting supper on the table, which was in conflict with cleaning up and vacuuming. Getting supper on the table and vacuuming were two things the sulky fifteen-year-old could have helped with, but this would have meant doing battle with his combative son. Doing the paperwork was in conflict with finishing the birthday gift, both of these conflicted with the scheduled meeting, and the meeting conflicted with the energy he needed if he was going to spend time with his wife when she finally returned home from work in the middle of the night.

Even if he had managed his time well and worked his way through every task, he would have been exhausted, with or without the nap, because of the stress of being constantly drawn in conflicting directions. Needless to say, he hadn't managed anything well. He ended up in a fight with his wife and felt resentful.

I offered him a soda and tried to cheer him up, although I really wasn't sure what to say to him. My own life was going in twenty directions and I was looking for the same kinds of solutions, especially something that would simplify my life and allow me to write. We started to chat and somewhere in the conversation, almost as if someone else was doing the talking, I heard myself say to him:

"Do what you *want* to do. Follow your heart, and do what you most want to do at any given moment. This isn't being selfish because *you never want what you're not supposed to have.* You must do whatever is in your heart because heart-based experiences generate the lessons you personally need in order to grow. It is your own natural intelligence, based on your original life plan that draws you to want these experiences. Through them you learn to balance your life and find joy. People who shy away from something they really want or feel they need, are not doing themselves, or anyone else, a favor. In fact, they usually remain immature, undeveloped, and afraid. What kind of favor is this to anyone!"

After my friend had gone, I thought about what I had heard myself say to him and wondered where such counsel had come from. The words "You never want what you're not supposed to have," kept running through my mind. Was this the truth? At this point in my life I wanted to write more than anything else; but once, long ago, I had wanted Ben more than anything in the world. And where was he now? Gone! Perhaps I hadn't really wanted him... maybe I had only wanted what I thought he offered. What had he offered? I thought it was love, but in the end he had walked away. So what was it I had really wanted from him? Suddenly a clear voice inside me rang out, "You wanted the expansion of consciousness!" Unexpectedly a large chunk of understanding about the relationship with Ben became clear.

I had been making love to Ben when the first signs of kundalini began to appear. Not knowing anything about what was happening, I simply assumed that *he* was responsible for the incredible sexual experiences we had. I wanted to hang onto Ben because I was confusing the effects of kundalini with what I felt for him. I thought he was turning me on, when it had really been the kundalini that left me so passionately sensuous, aware, and in a state of love. I thought things were the way they were between us because we were very much in love. As it turned out, I was the only one in love. Kundalini unleashes our inherent capacity for intense, unconditional love, and so I let myself love – without judging, without holding back, without reservation, criteria, or hesitation. Suddenly I could see that love and caring were the basis of all intuitive consciousness and psychic awareness, and that Ben had only distracted me from the truth and understanding of what was happening to me.

After he was gone and the mysterious sexual experiences went on, I moped about, hoping he would return, still unaware that the sensuousness I felt was the result of the increased electrical current moving through my nervous system.

Now I realized that I originally wanted him because some deeply anchored part of my whole being really wanted the vaulting lessons of consciousness that were the result of the kundalini experience. Perhaps, in my life plan, Ben had simply agreed to be the trigger that helped make the whole metamorphosis possible, and after it began, I lavished my newly prodigious capacity to love on him.

This realization brought a new avalanche of questions. What was it in me, what part of me had so intently wanted the leap in consciousness that kundalini brought? Had I really planned my life and its lessons before I actually got here? And was the whole experience of kundalini a latent human potential that was built-in to each of us, waiting to be triggered at the right time and place? If kundalini could happen to me, wouldn't it seem natural to think that it could happen to everyone? So why didn't it? What conditions had to exist for the event to occur? Was the missing connection a sexual one? If kundalini and sexual experience were related, and if kundalini resulted in an expansion of consciousness, then somehow sexual experience was tied to the expansion of consciousness and the development of psychic abilities.

Now doubt overtook me. There couldn't possibly be a serious connection between sexual experience, consciousness, and higher intelligence... or could there? I was off to research and explore again, curious about the connections between sexuality and consciousness, and this time the path took a few surprising turns.

Ever since the winter I had spent in the basement, I had been slowly working my way through my Dream Records. Whenever I had a block of time I went back to them, reading and analyzing, carefully noting how my mind had put the dream experiences together and how, afterward, I had perceived and described the dream in my written record. Now, looking for connections between sexuality and the mind, I came across an old dream I had written down years earlier and ignored. When I came to it this time, I skipped over it as irrelevant, but it kept coming back; I couldn't get it out of my mind.

It had been a very intense dream about either working with or following someone called Theresa of Avila. After wondering who she was for several days, and being unable to forget the name, I got out the dictionary thinking that maybe she would be listed as a famous person or something. To my surprise she was listed as a saint and described as a Spanish Carmelite nun, mystic, and author. I had gone to a Catholic school for most of my school years and vaguely remembered a saint named Little Theresa who had something to do with roses, but I couldn't recall ever reading or being told if she was from Avila.

In spite of the fact that I always believed saints and sex were at opposite ends of the spectrum, the dream about Theresa of Avila sparked something in me and a new dawning began. Had any of the saints experienced signs or symptoms of kundalini?

I began to search through stories of the saints and other prominent historical figures, looking for clues, or for anything that might suggest they had suffered through strange sexual experiences, displayed unusual psychic abilities, had visions that presented powerful messages or lessons, or entered into that silent, blissful place I called the *I Am* state of awareness. As I searched, I also began to look for anything that would support my growing suspicion that sexual experience was a major key to the evolution of consciousness and the mind.

To my surprise and gratification, there were a number of famous historical figures that could easily be classified as having psychic and intuitive abilities. People like Walt Whitman and Edgar Allen Poe were well-known for their intuitive natures and the mystic flavor of their writing.

Famous writers I had been required to read in high school, writers like Thoreau and Emerson, were members of a large group who believed in higher states of being and called themselves Transcendentalists, a term that was now more than just a label to be memorized.

George Washington, our national father, left many writings that contained detailed descriptions of his visionary experiences, including one in which he described being in his tent during the Revolution and very discouraged about his ability to win the battle against the English army. He reported being at a low point when two angels entered his tent and talked to him, encouraging him to go on, and showing him visions of what the United States was meant to become, including the role it was meant to play in the world of the future. This gave Washington just a little more determination, he pressed on, and everyone knows the rest of the story.

Among the saints, there were a number of figures with psychic as well as paranormal healing abilities. In fact, continuous demonstration of psychic abilities, paranormal healing skills, and a wide variety of unexplained phenomena were the most powerful arguments for achieving sainthood! Some of their writings held surprising statements of their experiences with phenomena that sounded exactly like the signs and symptoms of kundalini.

The writings of St. Theresa, as well as the beloved apostle John, mentioned that their mystical experiences were accompanied by hearing a buzzing noise, like the buzzing of bees, or thousands of birds and crickets chirping at once. It sounded similar to the buzzing noise that accompanied all of my own experiences with kundalini!

St. Hildegard's visions were always accompanied by a flash of light, and St. Paul's description of being 'struck by lightning' sounded remarkably like my own 'explosion of light.' The fact that Paul's 'lightning' was accompanied by a voice asking him why he was persecuting Christians did not sound much like an actual strike by real lightning caused by bad weather. Indeed, it sounded exactly like some of my own kundalini experiences that proved to be powerful moments of direct learning.

St. Theresa, along with St. John Of The Cross, a priest and contemporary of Theresa, wrote powerful poetry and meditations that spoke of having been virgins, then going to 'meet the bridegroom' (in Theresa's case) or to 'meet the bride' (in St. John's case) and of the bliss in these encounters, surprisingly sexual metaphors for a nun and a priest!

Now other symbolism from my earlier, church-going years came back to me and I couldn't shake the memory of all those stained-glass windows with a halo around Jesus, Mary, and Joseph; or the apostles after Pentecost with the tongues of fire depicted above them. Even in their church window settings there was an amazing resemblance to all the people I was observing with swirling, glowing lights around them.

It startled me when I recognized that the Bible actually contained a book of predictions about the future in the apostle John's *Apocalypse*. For some reason, I always thought Christianity frowned on predictions, lumping them in with occult matters, which were also frowned on.

However, the sudden realization one day that Jesus himself was probably the most famous psychic, paranormal healer, and metaphysical teacher of all time was truly unsettling. How had the church managed to gloss over this particular fact? Why had I never noticed this side of religion before? Was heaven, with its promise of joy and bliss, just another term for The Void, or what I called the *I Am* experience? Had the idea of prayer once been rooted in the idea that anyone could see, hear, and know most anything in space and time and all you had to do was clear your mind, form the right question, ask, and the answer would come to you?

Abruptly, many religions and their rigid teachings began to look like gaunt skeletons without any meat on their bones. For centuries they had been teaching a bunch of do's and don'ts based on a meager framework of rules, rituals, and statements of belief. Yet they were almost uniformly unable to offer any substantive experience of which they preached, and they were unwilling to allow any questioning of their dogma. Had they just wanted control?

Because of my experience with kundalini, I could see that real religion was aiming for transcendent experience and the enlightenment that came with it. It saddened me to see how far off the mark most churches were.

As I prowled the library and bookstores in my continuing search for more clues among religious writings, I was delighted to come across a few more non-religious books whose subject was specifically kundalini. I read these at the same time I was going through works that discussed not only St. Theresa and John of the Cross, but Mechthild von Magdeburg, the teachings of Meister Eckhart, and other western mystics.

In all, there were many references among these modern western writers, as well as ancient Christian writers, to the lights, the buzzing sounds, the visions, the conditions and the experiences common to kundalini and its resulting paranormal abilities. But the word that was always used when referring to these phenomena was the word *grace*. Gradually, the more I read, the more convinced I became that the concept called grace was just a Western name for the Eastern event that was called kundalini.

The similarity in the two concepts took me back to the library one Sunday afternoon to take another look at the writings of St. Theresa and John of the Cross. By seven o'clock that evening I was still at the library and was certain that they had both experienced kundalini with its sexual ecstasy, the explosion of lights, the disappearance of physical reality, the sense of eternity and the overwhelming bliss. And I was convinced that since each of them was heavily culturalized within the institution of Roman Catholicism, each tended to write flowery descriptions of their experiences as 'manifestations of grace.'

Staring out the window of the library, I realized that kundalini and grace were simply two different words for the same event, an event that expanded consciousness, created the intense physical energy that we described as orgasm, and triggered further evolution of the individual body/mind.

Finally, tired and hungry, I packed up my papers, books and purse, put on my coat and began walking through the west wing toward the stairs. I was half way there when, for no reason, I veered suddenly and sharply to the right, as if pulled by a string, and headed down between two rows of books. I came to a stop as if on automatic pilot, and my hand reached out for a book on a shelf. I looked curiously at the book I had selected to see what it was about and discovered it was called *Christianity and Evolution.* It was written by a man named Pierre Teilhard de Chardin.

As smoothly as if I had planned the detour to this particular book, I turned to the back and looked up the word *grace* in the index. There were a number of pages listed that referred to the concept of grace so I chose one and opened to it. It read as follows:

"There can be no hiding the fact: In the present teaching of theology... the most prominent tendency is to give the word 'mystical' a minimum of organic or physical meaning... Whatever the reason, the official Church normally shrinks from emphasizing the concrete, realistic character of the terms in which the Scripture defines the state of unification attained by the consummated universe."

And further on, in a section with the heading *The organic nature of grace,* he stated,

"Under the unifying influence of divine love, the spiritual elements of the world – souls – are raised up to a higher state of life. They are super-humanized. The state of union with God is, accordingly, much more than a mere juridical justification (a statement giving oneself legal authority) associated with an extrinsic increase of divine benevolence (an outer show of goodness). From the Christian, Catholic, and realist point of view, grace represents a physical super-creation. It raises us a further rung on the ladder of cosmic evolution. In other words, the stuff of which grace is made is strictly biological." (Parentheses mine.)

Nodding in agreement, I added half aloud, "And the stuff of biology includes human sexuality." Then thanking whomever or whatever had led me to Chardin's book, I put it back on the shelf and walked out of the library. I went home knowing unmistakably that grace and kundalini were the same thing, that somehow they transformed consciousness and the physical body, and that heightened sexual experience was clearly a part of the process. ♋

19 ❧
East vs. West

"We face neither east nor west;
we face forward."

Kwame Nkrumah

ONCE HOME I WAS TIRED BUT FEELING GOOD. IT WAS LATE BUT I WANTED to re-copy a few notes on the research of the day so I sat down at my computer. Instead of re-copying notes, something else poured out.

"Step back for a moment as if the planet Earth were your hometown and you were trying to understand some of the stories and legends that have been passed down through time, stories that the old-timers talk about when they watch the youngsters and shake their heads patiently.

"At one end of town you have the eastern hemisphere, and at the other end you have the western hemisphere. According to old town records, the houses on the East Side of town have been around since at least 27,000 BC. The West End, whose homes and historical records were destroyed through too many wars, is relatively new. It has been almost completely rebuilt since the start of the Industrial Revolution and it continues its suburban sprawl today. Between these two hemispheres is the New Center Area, the Middle East, a maelstrom area between East and West, which has been continuously torn down and rebuilt physically, mentally, emotionally and spiritually.

"If we were to examine the habits, ideas and beliefs of the old-timers on the East Side, we would find that they believed in a power greater than themselves – a Creator who looked after them and to whom they could pray and offer sacrifice to. We might also be surprised to find that this God to whom they prayed and dedicated their lives was personified as a woman, strong, benevolent and caring, who would lead them to the bliss of nirvana if they lived according to her laws of goodness.

"Times do change, however, and so do belief systems. As old structures began to break down, people started fighting among themselves. Blight and discontent moved across the East Side of town, neighborhood gangs roamed around, and there were a number of serious wars as people looked for someone and something to believe in. After a few centuries of hassling, the town settled down and began to grow and expand again.

"Many of the old-timers on the East Side kept their ways, their habits, and pieces of the old belief systems. You can now visit this end of town and see examples of their ways of life, their rituals and mystics. If you do, you will immediately notice how the Orient, as this section of town is sometimes called, has a prevailing sense of femaleness, and how the women of this area seem so potently feminine and mysterious. This is because of the many years this section spent being culturalized with the idea of the supreme deity as Woman.

"You will also hear talk of a mysterious feminine energy force called kundalini. People in possession of this power have reportedly been able to heal the sick, touch electrical wires carrying thousands of volts of electricity, walk through fire, make it rain or survive attacks and assaults on their physical bodies that would quickly kill the ordinary person.

"Meanwhile, over in the New Center Area of town, a baby named *Jesus* had been born. His neighborhood had been rough and extremely unsettled so his parents sent him to school back East, hoping he would get a good education, and this gave him some firsthand experience with the ideas, rituals and powers of the old feminine ways. Upon returning to his hometown, which was still in upheaval, he became a well-known teacher. Being strong and practical as well as a good teacher, he started pointing out what wasn't working and began translating some of the ancient ideas that had worked for the old-timers back East into practical thinking that fit the new times and helped shape some new ways in the West.

"As Jesus tried to restore and reinterpret the basic order of caring that had once prevailed long ago, he naturally did so from his own perspective, and thus he talked about it from a man's point of view. He talked about a power greater than himself and personified this power as God the Father, the exact opposite of the former personification of an Earth Mother. God was seen, again, as The Creator, benevolent and caring, someone who loved us just as we were and would guide us to the bliss of heaven if we lived according to his laws of goodness.

"Jesus talked a lot about grace and will power while he was around and did some spectacular things such as healing the sick, raising the dead, walking on water, feeding thousands with just a couple of loaves of bread. He also was able to control the weather, and appeared around town after having been publicly executed, all of which convinced quite a few people that there was some validity to the ideas and the grace he had talked about.

"Some people began to apply the new ideas he talked about and a few even learned to do some of the things Jesus did. Gradually his ideas and ways of teaching spread all across the West End of town and became the standard for new religious practices. These have been in effect for about two thousand years now, and if you visit the New Center Area or the West End of town, you will notice a prevailing sense of masculinity because of the many years spent culturalized with the idea of the supreme deity as Man.

"If you compare the search for power that went on in the East, with the search for power that went on in the West, you will see that while on the East Side there was always talk about somehow becoming possessor of the mysterious kundalini power, at the West End there was frequent mention of being blessed with the power of grace.

"On the East Side, mystics and yogis long advocated total cleansing of body and mind, high levels of discipline and self development, and absolute control over bodily processes normally considered to be autonomous. Along with special diets and exercises, an extreme ability to concentrate was cultivated; and there was a willingness to risk pain and mental derangement in order to waken the kundalini power in the individual. Whatever the risks, the benefits of becoming a recipient were the great psychic gifts, the healing abilities, the powerful love that kundalini bestows, and an invitation to enter the experience of Oneness and live forever after in the *I Am* awareness.

"At the West End, priests and monks strove to attain a state of grace through intense study of spiritual teachings, prolonged fasting and limited diets, the renunciation of worldly goods, and a willingness to sacrifice the self. A high degree of physical discipline over pain was cultivated, regular prayer and chanting was practiced, and long periods of celibacy were prescribed in the hopes that when enough sexual energy had built up it would release naturally, awakening their consciousness and carrying them into the state of grace. Entry into the *I Am* state of awareness, and an experience of their own Oneness with all that exists would make them the beneficiary of the many visionary and healing gifts that the blessing of grace provided. Basically there were – and are – very few differences between the two belief systems.

"Today, much of this has been forgotten. Only a few are blessed with the reward of having awakened the power of kundalini or entered into the blissful state of grace; and modern religions teach the rest that they must be content with believing they will find nirvana or heaven in the afterlife."

∞

When my writing finally came to a halt, I was amazed at what I had written. For me it was a synthesis of a lot of loose ends and the solidifying of a lot of senseless teachings that I had observed and struggled with over the course of my life. It was also the beginning of my understanding that for many years, whether in the East or the West, people had been searching for something they could not even articulate. Everyone wanted the same thing, but because of their frustrated inability to describe what they were after, they foolishly took out their frustrations by attacking the methods, beliefs, and dogma that others were using in efforts to reach the same mysterious and undefined end.

I looked back at my childhood years in the Catholic school and felt sad. If I had understood with even the faintest glimmer what religion was talking about when referring to 'grace,' if I had thought it was anything other than being gentle, kind and thoughtful, I might not have been so devastated when this spontaneous change in consciousness occurred. To me, grace had always been something that Jesus and the apostles had. It was something the saints either caught or developed.

I was never taught and, until it happened to me, nothing I ever read even hinted at the fact that grace was a powerful, physical, life-changing experience that could reduce the physical body to ashes, or open the mind so wide that you could see, hear, feel, and know what was going on anywhere in space and time. As for the nuns, they would probably have fainted away if they suspected that reaching a state of grace included the sexual experience!

Through all my years of going to church, 'grace' was just a word that was heard somewhere in the background, behind the clamor for more financial support and the demands for compliance with the church rules and rituals. 'Grace' was an obscure concept, something that happened to saints back in the Middle Ages, and it had no connection to physical reality or life in the 20th century.

As for the eastern religions and the concept of kundalini, back then they had not existed for me either. Not only did I know nothing about the East or its belief systems, I had swallowed the Catholic rule that other religions would take you straight to hell and were to be avoided at all costs.

Even after the first kundalini experience or two, if someone had told me that I had experienced something called *grace*, or even *kundalini*, that it was a form of electromagnetic energy based on a set of high-powered frequencies that moved through the body, generating a sexual experience as it traveled, and opening the mind to whole new realms of consciousness, I not only would *not* have understood, I would have thought they were nuts.

Back then, the idea that sex was an electromagnetic event in the body that united you with Source, realigned the polar orientation of all your molecules, and restored the body to health and peak operation would have ruined my entire sense of romance. Before my experiences with kundalini, I believed that sexual experience was tinged with some kind of shame, and orgasm was brought on solely by making love, not by some journey into the Godhead. In fact, no two subjects had been farther apart in my mind than God and sex.

Suddenly the meaning of the Trinity was clear. The concept of God as Father was simply a human personification of the Source or Ground of all Being. God as Son was the individual man, woman, plant, or animal who emerged from that Ground of all Being to live a life. And the Holy Spirit was the breath of life that kept us in relationship with that Source as well as all other beings. It was the spirit of oneness, of wholeness that flooded the individual when there had been an awakening to the Source via kundalini or grace. The symbol of this awakening was, appropriately, a small tongue of fire, symbol of heat, light, and transformation of matter. Thus it was said of the individual, that he or she was 'filled with the Holy Spirit,' or, as I had come to think of it lately, had been introduced into the spirit of wholeness and had become 'wholly' spirit.

Now I moved into a new phase of my learning. I began studying religions old and new around the world. In the process I learned a little bit about a whole lot of belief systems. To my amazement, all of the major religions had a creation story like the one in Genesis, and some version of Noah's Ark and The Flood.

They almost all had a virgin-birth story, they all had some kind of messiah-teacher, and they all had some kind of heaven-like place for people to live in or for the dead to retire to. There were an amazing number of characters I always thought were exclusive to the Catholic religion, but the most surprising fact of all was that they *all* preached the same thing – the evolution of the human being toward a state of existence that returned him to his original condition of joy and love, peace, and the power to know and to heal.

Nearly every major religion celebrated the life and teachings of some evolved human, someone with uncanny powers of mind and body. And all held up their example of this evolved human to the world, trying to convince the masses that they could achieve the same level of development, but of course, only if you followed their rules and contributed money to their organization.

I thought about the sexual nature of the kundalini experience and how incongruent this was with current religious attitudes. Sex was strictly forbidden unless you were married; and for some, even that was not enough – sex was only permissible if you were trying to have children. Nothing I could think of, except perhaps money, had created as much general woe for mankind as the senseless taboos around sex. How had we come to put so many shackles on something that was obviously a powerful spiritual energy and apparently such an important key to human evolution?

Was it possible that the early priests understood the power hidden in the sexual experience and decided to put some limits on sexual activity? Since priests and popes had great power at that time, maybe they wanted to curtail the possibility that the masses would ever evolve and become powerful enough to run their own lives! Perhaps it was just the opposite and the early churches didn't want people to squander their sexual energy. Perhaps they thought it better to limit sexual energy, letting it build up to a high degree, increasing the possibility of activating the kundalini mechanism.

Whatever their intent, as time passed, the original reason for banning sex had certainly become cloudy and misunderstood among the priests themselves. Especially since the real thing, a kundalini experience, never happened for them. It was easy to imagine a group of priests, raised under a host of sexual restrictions, trying to decide later on what was sinful and what would get you into heaven! Sex wouldn't have been understood at all. Obviously, sex had become more and more synonymous with sin. As the church fought to maintain power in the face of growing nationalism and the spread of economic power, evidently more and more things had been declared sinful in an effort to control the common man – including sex.

Whatever the reason, sex had definitely gotten a bad reputation. As the dark ages progressed, it was likely that fewer and fewer men and women, whether clergy or common, understood what kundalini or grace really was, or how to spontaneously trigger this tremendous form of energy. And without the actual experience and its aftereffects of enlightenment, it would be easy to proclaim that sex was sinful, then place all kinds of restrictions on sexual activity.

The truth that got lost in the process was that sexual energy was the energy behind the evolution of the Self, and through its door one could enter the *I Am* state to experience the Source from which we were all created.

The great tragedy of all this was not the misunderstanding of the electromagnetic nature and healing potential of sex, nor the fact that we had ignorantly linked it to immorality and guilt. It was not the fact that we had misguidedly declared that the true purpose of sex was for making babies, and not the fact that we had lost most of our rituals for integrating and celebrating true sexual purpose. It was that the sexual experience was a doorway to the *I Am* awareness, and the legacy of barred entry to this awareness was the flourishing of anger, competition, fear, and guilt. The tragedy was the loss of love, joy, peace, wisdom, insight, and compassion for both the Self and others.

With a new clarity I saw that no matter how you looked at it, sex was a major key to human evolution. We could use sex to create a whole planet full of people, and thus have an ongoing selection of bodies to come back into here on Earth. This would allow us to slowly and painfully evolve through a series of physical lives.

Or we could take a much more powerful and direct route to human evolution via the awakening of kundalini, or the manifestation of grace, which generated enlightenment along with its own sexual experience. Either way, sexual experience was the key to the continuing evolution of consciousness. ❧

20 ෪
Mind, Space, and Thought

"Isn't it amazing that we can think,
not knowing what it means to think?"

Marvin Minsky

EACH TIME I REACHED THE END OF AN INTENSE PERIOD OF OBSERVA-
tion or research and study around some aspect of kundalini, and each
time I came to conclusions that seemed important to my understanding
of the deeper issues related to kundalini, I entered a brief period of quiet
relaxation.

At the end of my quest for information surrounding kundalini,
sexuality, saints, and religion I entered into just such a period of quiet
peace. As usual, I believed I had figured out everything I would ever need
to know. As always, I was relieved by the cessation of questions. But this
period of respite was, like the others before it, only temporary.

As I began to grasp the implications of what all religions were
really about, I began to wonder if the religions of long ago once held
any simple keys to unlocking kundalini and triggering the transcendent
experiences that brought further evolution of body and mind.

I reasoned that religions could not have been designed for one or
two special individuals. It was implicit in the practices and rituals of all
religions that anyone and everyone could trigger kundalini or reach the
state of grace, and thus the mechanism for experiencing kundalini, for
activating grace, had to be built-in to every human being.

I was certain that kundalini could be triggered in several ways. One was a spontaneous triggering, a sort of top-down approach in which the experience just exploded into your life, which was the way that I had experienced it. The other was through a deliberate and disciplined bottom-up approach, using the prayer practices and meditation techniques found in many religions. The spontaneous awakening I had undergone, with its link to sexual experience, suggested that the mechanism for triggering the awakening was in the body, perhaps in the sexual experience. In contrast to this, the disciplines and rituals practiced by many religions suggested that the mechanism was in the mind. But what, exactly, triggered it? What did the mind have to be doing or not doing? And just what was the mind anyway?

Reviewing the whole sequence of events and acknowledging my conclusions about kundalini, I asked myself frequently, "How and why would an acceleration of electromagnetic frequencies in the body have the impact of creating peace, joy and overflowing love in the mind? What did electromagnetic wave frequencies have to do with mind, with consciousness, or perception?' The more I turned this around in my head reaching for an answer, the more I decided I could not locate the mechanism for triggering kundalini in either body or mind until I understood what the mind was.

Facing the fact that I really had no clear or satisfying idea of what the mind was, my brief period of quiet relaxation ended. I began to search for answers again. Over and over I thought about the kundalini experience, the exquisite bliss, the sense of perfect fulfillment, the absence of physical reality and its accompanying wants and worries. The impact of the *I Am* experience was so extraordinarily powerful that I felt as if I was now living with one foot constantly in that world of bliss. I could not forget it. I did not want to, either. But what I had always thought of as 'my mind' now seemed to contrast sharply with the minds of other people.

Among other things, there were serious differences in perception, in perspective, and attitude. One very noticeable difference was around the subject of anger. Other people seemed to me to be experiencing an inordinate amount of anger. They seemed caught in bitterness, filled with resentment, carried away by petty rages. Fears, angers, and aggressions pervaded their thought, their words, their actions and expectations.

For me, anger was just an occasional tool, something to be used when appropriate. Even when someone directed his or her anger at me, I often failed to respond properly. I did not feel attacked, I did not feel defensive, and I seldom got angry in return unless I felt it was a useful move. Most often I was curious. When someone became suddenly angry, I became watchful, listening carefully, for I had discovered that 99% of people's anger was really an unconscious frustration with *their* lives, *their* inadequacies, and *their* rigid set of basic assumptions about how life should be. The small remaining percentage had what I considered to be justifiable anger, and these I tried to honor and learn from.

There were other differences between the emotions and thinking of other people and my emotions and thinking. I watched how hard people worked to get through everyday activities, how they struggled to maintain a sense of control, a feeling of usefulness and productivity. They were always hurrying, worrying, dealing with some problem as if their whole life depended on it. They were so thoroughly caught up in the world that they were like actors who had been hired to stage a play and forgot it was just a play.

Not only were their own wants and needs upsetting to them, the wants and needs of others were even more upsetting, often interfering with their already poorly maintained self-esteem. I, too, worked hard, and I hurried, sometimes worried, or had to deal with difficult people. Yet, always, in a corner of my mind, I had one foot in that eternal pool of quiet peace I had experienced in the *I Am* state, while other people did not seem to have access to the pool of peace at all.

Occasionally, still trying to formulate a satisfying definition of mind, I would ask students, friends, or acquaintances what they thought the mind was and I got all the same answers I had come up with myself.

"Something in the brain...my invisible side...the part that knows stuff...the part of me that gets upset...what I think with." People everywhere, no matter what their cultural, educational or financial background, had some opinion of what the mind was, and believed that they had a mind!

After getting nowhere for some time, I decided to go about my search in a more scientific manner. I would try to fully reactivate the kundalini as it had occurred in my earliest experiences with it, my intention being to remain aware and observe what was happening as it unfolded. I felt that there must be an orderly but hidden sequence of changes that triggered the mechanism of kundalini in the body/mind and carried me into that eternity of peaceful bliss and light. I thought that if I could maintain a careful awareness of the exact sequence of body/mind events, I might not only discover the mechanism, I would better understand just what the mind was and why kundalini affected it so deeply.

I never asked myself why I needed a more scientific explanation of all the things I had experienced, but I did. From the very beginning, my search for an understanding of kundalini and what was happening to me was not satisfied until I understood what was happening, why it happened, and how. Although all of my searches surrounding the experience had strongly reinforced the fact that reality was far different from what I once thought it to be, the empirical methods of science had proven to be very useful in exploring spiritual reality. Thus, I felt it was ignorant to think that science and spirituality contradicted one another.

I also had high disdain for spiritual mumbo-jumbo and lopsided explanations. In the same way that I eventually come to an explanation of kundalini that offered more than "It's the awakening of the serpent power at the base of the spine," or "It's a spiritual experience that changes your life," I assumed that somewhere there was a more complete or coherent explanation of what the mind was, something more than either I or the dictionary could come up with.

My mediocre background in science, along with my deep curiosity about how and why things worked, anchored me through those long first months of the changes in my mind. It was my scientific side that had first given me the idea of empirically observing all the strange phenomena going on in my life, looking for a common thread. This approach had resulted in many of the discoveries I had made so far, including the important premise that my mind would produce tons of information for me whenever I was curious or needed to know about something.

Now, off on a new quest, I didn't know what the outcome would be when I reactivated kundalini, but once again I was about to learn that my mind would produce some deep teachings tailored especially for me.

To reawaken the kundalini I set up a fast that was to last forty days, asked my husband if he could live without sex during that time, and embarked on a comprehensive meditation and exercise program.

My goal was to see what I could do with forty days worth of preparation and to extend the time if I needed to. But I was only six days into my fast, meditation, and exercise program when the first reawakening of kundalini occurred.

In spite of this, I continued for another 32 days and then stopped because I was losing too much weight. I had reactivated the buzzing sounds and the rocking sensations, and I was very afraid of reactivating the experiences of great heat. I was also becoming less and less interested in maintaining a presence in physical reality.

The experiment was both a success and a failure. I succeeded in reactivating kundalini in the ways that it had first occurred, but I found the experience far too powerful to maintain any sort of double consciousness that allowed me to track the specific sequence of events in either mind or body. After several attempts, I realized that kundalini was an experience of oneness, and trying to maintain a dual awareness to observe what was happening while it occurred would be a contradiction in terms. So I left off my attempts to combine kundalini with dual awareness.

Still unsatisfied as to what mind actually was, I began sorting through the few pieces of information I had about the mind, attempting to arrange them into a coherent framework of explanations. For weeks I turned the pieces every which way I could think of, but nothing that I could come up with made any real sense, nor did it satisfy the intuitive knowing I had come to recognize with an 'Aha!' each time I hit upon the truth.

One night, at a complete standstill in my efforts to come up with a definition of mind, I sat down at my computer to edit some old poetry. To my surprise, my hands began to move, typing out the following:

"Although you usually think of the mind as something that is in you or goes along with your body, for a few moments set all of that aside. Realize that your brain is not your mind. If you die you no longer have a working brain, but you still have your mind with all its knowledge, awareness, and personality. In fact, you don't have a mind, you are mind.

"In its broadest definition, *mind is the awareness property of space whose natural condition is that of absolute peace and stillness.* Mind and space cannot be separated, they are like two sides of one coin, different, but one. You could also say that space is mind whose natural condition is absolute peace and rest. When someone returns to the original condition of mind, they experience something that ancient literature refers to as The Void, which simply means that they experience absolute, unlimited space in its natural state.

"When space begins to move, the motion is referred to as energy. When energy is compressed, basic particles of matter are created. And when these basic particles are gathered together into one place at one time, a complex pattern is created, from which duplicate – but individualized – forms can emerge. Now let's take a little journey that might give you a better sense of how this all happens.

"To begin, close your eyes and imagine you are floating in open space...space that is absolutely empty. There are no boundaries, no edges, no horizons. It is absolutely quiet and still. Silent. Empty.

"Now, like water flowing out of a glass that has been turned on its side, feel your entire body flowing out in every direction and become space itself. You are not just floating in space, you are space.

"You have no body, there are no other people, no planets, no wind, not even a speck of dust. Your attention cannot wander about... yesterday and tomorrow do not exist... nor do concerns like health or life, ethics or morality. There is no curiosity, there are no questions, no sense of waiting, no worry, no boredom. There is no awareness of the weather, the dog, your job, money, the neighbors or objects of any kind. There is nothing but pure awareness. It is just the very simple, very basic awareness that you exist. And this awareness is the single attribute of your entire existence.

"You are absolute space... you are mind, that is silent, peaceful and at rest. You have nothing but a sense of being aware, and no awareness other than *I Am*. Because there is nothing to see and thus nothing to want, no one to complain to and nothing to wait for, this condition of basic awareness is a state of complete and total fulfillment. It *is* ecstasy. To say that all needs are filled would be to miss the point entirely, for there is no such thing as need. There is only *I Am*, and that is all, nothing more and nothing less. Mind is the awareness property of space, and you are space... whose only attribute is awareness.

"Suddenly a force comes rolling through you, pushing and pulling, moving and lifting you, creating waves, whirls and eddies in what was formerly absolute stillness. The power of this force transforms you into vibrant, shimmering motion.

"Now you are different. Your existence is no longer characterized by absolute stillness and peaceful awareness. You have been transformed by the singular attribute called motion, and you are no longer known as space; instead you go by the name energy.

"In your conversion from space into energy, your awareness is also converted. You leave the basic *I Am* awareness and enter the condition called consciousness. You have moved from the quiet awareness of pure existence to the experience of Self-and-Something-Happening-To-Self. What is happening is the new experience called motion, and thus you are aware of both Self and movement of Self.

"You have taken the first step away from the quiet bliss of Oneness and into the state of mind that is characterized by duality. And in this first splitting of the awareness of oneness, you now experience the reflective property of space known as consciousness.

"As energy, you are a sea of motion and will wend your way as a wave, caught up in the flow of movement. Your movement is fluid, swift, and you vibrate, undulate and tumble at different speeds... on and on... endlessly. Gradually, forces and pressures caused by your very own movement begin to seriously squeeze and wrinkle, or pinch and fiercely stretch you.

As the intensity of your motion mounts, the power of your own seething increases until, in some areas you becomes densely compressed and, getting in your own way, you find yourself running into yourself...slowing down...moving slower feeling more compacted...pressed upon...until you feel heavy, momentarily solid.

Suddenly you are no longer just energy, moving crisply about. You discover you have transformed again, this time into a particle. You are slow-moving, weighty and massive, and you float along, born on the waves of energy that weave endlessly through space. You are a tiny speck of matter with dimensions, with weight and characteristic movement, and thus you begin to experience the substantive property of space known as matter.

In your new state as a particle you discover that this most recent transformation has changed the character of your mind as well. Instead of the simple consciousness of motion, of Self-and-Something-Happening-To-Self, you now have intelligence, which brings you a basic knowledge of yourself as form, how to maintain your form, and your own cycles of activity. You are an intelligent being.

"And so you drift and float and spin, riding waves of energy that carry you along, that sweep you back and forth, this way... and that way... until, without warning, you discover there are others! Your path and those of neighboring particles cross in a head-on way. Collisions abound, and you are bombarded from every side.

"Some just hit and bounce away. Others hover nearby, and still others seem to cling to you, changing your speed, your weight, your direction, even your very sense of form. With a rush you find yourself swept into fields of tangled, densely compacted wave frequencies, accompanied by an assortment of other particles.

"You huddle about, along with all the others in the group, swarming in close congregation, as if unable to swim back through the fine, frothy net of wave frequencies to where the rolling waves of energy swell and dip gently. And as you make the effort to adjust to this new, crowded environment you realize you have changed again. You are no longer a single particle riding the ocean of energy, you are one of many particles working together as one. Together you form a unique pattern of energy fields, wave frequencies and other particles. And you discover that this exquisitely balanced arrangement of waves and particles is capable of creating a physical entity with a very particular shape and characteristic activities.

"With this latest transformation, you find your mind has also transformed once more. You no longer have the singular intelligence of a simple particle, you are now part of a powerful and highly interactive condition called thought, which is the creative property of space.

"Millions of particles gathered into one composite pattern gives the whole group of you access to an immense amount of intelligence which can be used to work together, to reproduce yourself as a physical entity, and then help maintain the form of the Entity.

"And so for a while you will exist in this way, identifying with the composite pattern you have become part of. During this time you will learn to think according to the thought patterns common to its form, whether your basic pattern is that of a tree, a human, a mosquito, a catfish, or something else altogether.

"If you could look back and recall all that you have been, you would see that you began as *space* with only the simple awareness of your existence. You then began to move as a wave of *energy* and to enter the motion of consciousness. Next you suffered the pressures of transformation to form and became a *particle*, with intelligence and knowledge of self as an individual creation. And finally, you metamorphosed into an exquisitely complex form, a *pattern* capable of thought and the ability to create.

"The experience of kundalini is simply the movement of the individual Self back through all the stages of existence until you arrive at the source of yourself which is absolute space, eternal mind. Once the individual form has been reacquainted with this Source, it is once again in possession of the peace that characterizes absolute space, the energy of love that characterizes consciousness, the recognition of all other forms of intelligence, and the power to create inherent in all thought patterns. Thus oneness with all that exists is expressed in and through that Self."

∛

When the writing was finished I felt as if I were returning from a long journey. Looking back at what had emerged from my fingertips, the statement, "Mind is the awareness property of space," touched something deep inside of me. I had experienced the pure awareness of mind and this statement expressed the nature of that experience perfectly. I had been searching for an answer to the question "What is mind?" and there it was. This was an answer that satisfied all sides of me: the side of me that needed sensible, practical answers and the scientific side of me that wanted to know what was happening, and how, and why. It also quenched the hunger of a more recent aspect of myself; that intuitive, unnamed Self in me that experienced the very uncommon event called kundalini and was suddenly unable to accept pat, meaningless answers and descriptions.

I recalled the silent, empty stillness of the kundalini experience at its most profound. In the first experiences I had described it as being catapulted into outer (or perhaps inner) space, but it would have been just as accurate to say that I had momentarily *become* space, which had seemed silent, motionless and empty. Nothing existed in that space except pure awareness and thus, early on, I had been forced to sum up the entire experience in only two words, *I Am*.

Not 'I am female' or 'I am five feet tall' or 'I am going shopping later' or 'I am in love.' Just two simple words – *I Am* – and the exquisite ecstasy and completeness that *was* this basic state of existence.

To enter this state was to transcend the illusions of reality, and upon re-entry into everyday life, to find your mind and your consciousness wholly transformed. An explanation that consisted of, "I Am... I am everything...and there is nothing outside me," could easily seem to be the height of narcissism and self-centeredness. But the truth was that once you accelerated through the door of kundalini, there was no 'other.' There was only a singular, unified awareness of your existence and an unbounded sense of love and peace.

Momentarily, I imagined myself as pure space with some kind of force moving through me, creating waves of motion and transforming me from space into energy and from energy into a particle. I pictured the leap that would carry me from the quiet *I Am* awareness into the motion of consciousness, the first step in the long journey toward recognition of the self as a physical entity, a singular individual. It felt like a natural evolution of steps and stages.

Even though our existence as a physical entity allowed us to think of ourselves as separate beings, we all arose from the same ocean of absolute space. We were all formed from that same oneness. Each of us only appeared to be different, because once here in this reality, we prided ourselves on building an individual existence full of personal characteristics and unique attributes. It was much the same as the way people prided themselves on driving unique cars, defining oneself with fancy fashions, or creating a newly decorated family room with its unique colors, fabrics, furniture and collectibles.

"Mind is the awareness property of space," I said to myself again and again. We were all made of mind and space. We then evolved unique expressions of creative thought, floating in a sea of intelligence, powered by the energy of consciousness.

03

My thinking about *thought* went on for days. Thought was considered to be an exclusively human activity, but it wasn't! Every kind of form had its own characteristic thought patterns whether it was human thought, plant thought, animal thought, insect thought, soil thought, water thought, or even cellular thought. Thought was the activity of mind that was inherent in the basic pattern of the form.

Humans used thought for all sorts of things: when talking to others, deciding what to eat, who to love, what to wear, how to solve a problem, how to create a career, or even 'the meaning of it all.' But these were only surface uses. It was clear to me that the primary activity of thought, was really meant to maintain the individual mind. This individual then expressed in a personal way a few of the characteristics and potentials that were inherent in the basic pattern from which he or she had emerged. Thought, in its essence, was supposed to stimulate one's creative individuality and respond to the individuality of others.

Because of the unique patterns of thought that were characteristic of every form, any form immediately recognized what was part of its individual self, what was not part of individual self, and what was similar to the self. This deep recognition of the self as a unique, self-maintaining form was the (thought) barrier that prevented the cross-breeding of a dog and a cat, or a spider and a blue jay. It was 'thought' that caused the initial rejection of a kidney or a heart that had been transplanted from one physical being to another.

Thought made all interaction possible and it was the basis of all relationships, whether people-to-people, animal-to-animal, plant-to-plant, insect-to-insect, cell-to-cell, or any combination of these. It was also a very powerful tool for limiting oneself and one's experience, for once you became part of a physical entity, you were bound by the customary patterns of thought that were integral to that form.

Thought allowed us to grant one another the illusion of privacy. It also allowed us to overlook the fact that we were all made of mind and could, theoretically, know or experience anything and everything.

Awareness, consciousness, intelligence, and thinking were all variations on the theme called 'mind.' They were all related processes in the oneness of mind, and because of this essential oneness, any activity going on anywhere within it would be communicated everywhere at once.

This was what caused a mother in Denver to experience the birth pains of her grown daughter, now married, living in New York, and about to deliver her first child. It was the factor that caused a father in Georgia to be painfully aware that something was wrong with his son in the Army. This was what prompted a woman living in England to suddenly call her sister in France to inquire into her health, only to find out that her sister had fallen and broken her leg that very day. And this was how it was possible for a man to know that his father had been hurt in an auto accident half way around the world. Mother and daughter, father and son, sisters – all were made of mind.

I had never granted the capability of thought to anything other than people until my conversations with the tree in the park, and my experience with the little spider on the dock. Not too long after these unusual conversations, I had seen a film called *The Secret Life Of Plants*.

In some well done research, trees and plants in a public conservatory were wired with sensors that would detect any frequencies of sound that the trees and plants gave off. These sounds were then amplified and fed back, via computer, to the visitors passing through the gardens of the conservatory.

Not only was the frequency range of sounds they produced amazing, but the plants seemed to react to people with a whole range of sounds that, when heard over the speaker system, seemed to express everything from chatter, curiosity and enthusiasm, to nervousness and fear.

When hooked up to a sprinkler system whose on-off switch had been wired to respond to a few key frequencies, these plants quickly learned to turn on the sprinklers when they wanted a drink of water.

In another bit of interesting research, two large plants were placed in a sunny room where they were well cared for. Then, according to plan, a set of sensors was hooked up to one of the plants and these sensors were then wired back to a computer and some gages. The plants were monitored for a while, to see what was the natural range of operation for their sensors.

Then one day, one of the researchers, dressed in a white technician's coat, rushed into the room and grabbed one of the plants, viciously ripping it from its pot, smashing it, breaking the stem, tearing the leaves off, and finally leaving the destroyed mess on the floor. During this whole episode the sensors on the neighboring plant began to relay an extreme reaction with the needles on the gages rocking back and forth violently.

Later that week a succession of people walked nonchalantly, one at a time, through the room while the surviving plant's reaction was carefully monitored. Several of the men who strolled through were dressed in a white technician's coat but there was little or no response from the surviving plant to anyone in particular – until the man who had actually 'committed the murder' of the plant's companion walked in. Instantly the plant who had witnessed the destruction of his neighboring plant reacted. The sensors and gages shot all the way over into the distress zone indicating fear, recognition of the 'murderer,' severe stress, and shock on the part of the plant![7]

When I thought about it, I realized I had seen animals, too, ex-pressing both emotion and thought. The cat who jumped quickly off the

---

7   There is an excellent book by Peter Tompkins and Christopher Bird titled *The Secret Life Of Plants*, published in 1973 by Avon Books.

cupboard at the approach of his owner then went slinking away in a most guilty fashion not only knew he was not supposed to be on the cupboard, he knew that if caught, things could get uncomfortable, even painful.

I had seen dogs try to comfort their owners when they cried, and I knew of several birds that would only sing for certain people. I had listened to mother cows bawling for days when separated from their calves. And I had watched as an old cow, chosen to be slaughtered from a herd of about twenty others, was urged on by the frantic calling of her companions – who knew exactly what was going to happen – until she managed to get over a high gate. Once over it, she was quickly and protectively surrounded by them and the whole herd raced away until they were at the other end of the farm and as far away from the barn and the shotgun as possible.

The more I thought about *thought* and the whole process we called thinking, the more I felt that human beings misunderstood the whole basis of thinking and were misusing the creative power of this important process of mind.

Thinking, as practiced by many, was not really thinking at all. It was shallow, habitual jumping from one subject to another. It was allowing oneself to be bombarded by a continual stream of input from radios, televisions, office gossip, news, advertising, trivia, fads, neighborhood squabbles, national causes, troubled relationships and family demands, and then worrying and obsessing about what they'd heard. What most people termed 'thinking' about all of this was really just knee-jerk reacting. And the purpose of thought, which was to create and maintain individuality, ended up being used to maintain the Self in the most clumsy and ineffective of ways. The true creative power of thought was seldom used, or used well.

Instead, we set up little, selfish, personal realities like little castles and kingdoms. Then we expected others to agree that this was what and how a reality should be. Like tyrant kings we sat in our solitary realities and passed judgment on everyone and everything that crossed our attention lines. How ruthless we were with those who saw things differently or thought otherwise! Most of our time was spent trying to control and manipulate one another. When that failed, we condemned each other, or sometimes declared war, but always we suffered the stress of constantly judging and attacking other realities, or needing to defend our own reality. Millions of people spent whole lifetimes of energy struggling in this way, never realizing that they had often accepted someone else's version of reality in the first place (our parents, the Jones's, Uncle Sam's) and never discovering the wonder and magic of a personally-designed-and-built-reality of their own.

It seemed to me that in too many cases, the more energy people put in to extending their personal realities and then getting others to recognize and validate them, the more lonely and isolated they became. Somewhere along the way too many people lost their sense of inner authority and now their private reality was not legitimate or allowed unless someone else said it was okay. They were no longer able to create, maintain and enjoy a personal, private reality of their own design and making.

Attempts to communicate information about personal realities often degenerated into competitive arguments over whose rules of communication would be followed, or over whose reality was more important. It was clear that the need to communicate was very important to all of us, but given the results, I couldn't help wondering why we bothered.

Why didn't we just slow down, back off, and let ourselves become aware of others and their realities? And then it came to me. Through communication we were all trying to re-establish, or at least simulate, the natural condition of oneness with its characteristics of natural joy, deep caring, and love. We had gotten off track and started arguing about who was right when we started believing that a single version of reality was a reasonable replacement for oneness. ◌

21 ☙
Symptoms of an Awakening Consciousness

"Serious spiritual practice is more than serene walks
in the woods, lit candles, and incense. You have to be committed.
You have to be willing to enter into your own
darkness and transcend it."

Maria Erving

TEN YEARS HAD PASSED SINCE THE FIRST AWAKENING OF KUNDALINI or the first manifestation of grace, as I occasionally thought of it. In the beginning, I thought surely I must be the only one in the whole world ever to endure such experiences. However, by teaching intuition and intuitive management, I found others who had similar experiences. Most occurrences were not nearly as dramatic or disturbing as mine, but even if there was just a single experience of kundalini, it always had a life-changing impact.

Without exception, those awakened by kundalini became extremely sensitive, intuitive, and psychic. Many reported that their life and habits became chaotic for a while. For some, the onset of disturbing perceptions was not as disorienting as for others, and there was seldom an immediate conversion to an entirely different lifestyle or belief system, but the event always proved to be a turning point.

I discovered an interesting parallel in people who had been struck by lightning and survived this powerful electromagnetic jolt. They tended to experience the same aftereffects as kundalini. Survivors developed exquisite sensitivity to others' presence, thoughts, and intentions. Powerful psychic abilities often surfaced during recovery from the lightning strike and this shed a consistent light on my theory that kundalini was an electromagnetic event in the body/mind system.

For years, I lived, ate, worked, and slept immersed in the subject of brain structure and function. Nothing was as interesting to me as the brain/mind processes of perception, intelligence, consciousness, and cognition. I was certain that exposure to specific electrical currents and E-M fields would induce changes in consciousness, and I was convinced that with the right amount of current or the correct frequency, we could trigger the changes that were supposed to happen in all of us.

I thought often about Eastern stories telling of the power that came with awakened kundalini. There was no doubt in my mind that the power referred to was the power of consciousness and intelligence. This was not the ordinary consciousness or cultural intelligence measured by I.Q. tests and other educational measuring sticks. These were natural forms of so-far-undeveloped human power that we knew nothing about. I was convinced that true intelligence was an inborn gravitation of the body and mind toward perfect balance in health, a deep peace, and love that flowed from you like a fountain. I was also convinced that in the West, this power was known as grace.

Whether you called it kundalini, awakened consciousness, or grace, it bestowed great power and creativity, and demanded that you live true to the purpose of your life. Developing a more natural intelligence resulted in a steady awareness of the Source of life and an unlimited communication with everything existed. It also brought a growing awareness of your power to create or adapt to the surrounding reality while remaining in a state of peace and joy.

Anyone undergoing the phenomena of kundalini would experience specific changes in perceptual ability along with wide-ranging changes in physical, mental, emotional, and spiritual life.

Physically, there would be periods of heat or icy cold, internal pressure, especially at the base of the spine or in the skull. There could be odd stabbing pains here and there, especially in the feet, toes, and legs. Currents of electricity and light might run up and down the body, and there could be a greatly quickened heartbeat. Sometimes great sensuousness or feelings of orgasmic pleasure moved swiftly up through the body and exploded in the brain, bringing the loss of physical boundaries, fading away of the physical world, and the entry into something that could easily be described as complete emptiness, a total void, except for the bliss and the twinkling intelligent lights there.

Perceptually, there would be an exponential increase in sensory experience along with the development of senses you may never have noticed before. Although there might be a period of time in which it was difficult to focus, this would be followed by a deepening of the ability to concentrate, and a rich increase in awareness of the smallest details of everything whether color, sound, shape, texture, movement, smell, or interaction with the surrounding world.

At times, there could be the experience of being in two or more *places* at one time, of being in two or more *times* while in one place, or of having the ability to see and hear forward or backward in time in a very clairvoyant and clairaudient way.

There might be sporadic occurrences of transmodal perception such as tasting with the eyes or hearing with the skin. Sometimes there was an inability to perceive where your own skin ended and an object began. You could easily find yourself out of the body, or hearing clear messages from family or friends who had died and were living on 'the other side.' There might even be times when you would hear messages from distinct voices you had never heard before.

Mentally, you could discover an ability to know things without being told. You would often understand sophisticated material processes and scientific concepts without being taught. Initially, because of the many changes in perception, you might experience great personal confusion and a total inability to handle ordinary personal chores and routines. There might be a complete change in thinking, and things that once held meaning for you become meaningless. You could be suddenly unable or unwilling to keep a job or deal with family and other matters.

As life rearranges itself into an entirely new constellation of habits, people, career, and goals, there is usually a broadening of one's perspective into something that can only be described as a global view, or even a universal mindset, with a falling away of much useless trivia or righteous judgment of others.

Emotionally, there is the development of compassion for all living things and a deep desire to contribute to the general good in the world. During the period of havoc in your heart, you might be driven to take up causes or pursue paths that you never paid attention to before, or even actively disliked. This is fueled by the opening of your heart and an ever-expanding sense of love for everyone and everything, as well as an interest in honesty and justice.

Sometimes, instead of experiencing chaos, your feelings become clear, focused, and powerful, and you might simply step into a whole new set of ethics, values, and morals – completely befuddling those who have known you all your life, leading them to say they no longer know who you are.

There could be the ability to feel what others are feeling and to help them redirect their thoughts and feelings to something more useful or meaningful. And the overall range and power of your emotions could easily be experienced as limitless, whereas before, you may have allowed yourself to feel very little.

Spiritually, your whole life comes under review. Spiritual development has little to do with religion, memorizing the Bible, or allegiance to a church. True spiritual development has to do with discovering the *meaning and purpose of your existence.* You discover the spirit of yourself. As spiritual development occurs, you end up asking yourself, "What is my reason for being? What is my life about? If you have been following others because you didn't have a direction of your own, you may shock family and friends to no end as you take charge of your life. If you have been mean-spirited and self-centered, you may surprise yourself as you change over to love, generosity, and joy.

Entry into kundalini not only re-introduces you to the world you have always lived in, it introduces you to a world that can't be seen with physical eyes or touched with your hands. This is the world of spirit, the world of feeling. The spirit of your life is a feeling and passion that fills you and this is embedded in everything you do. It includes your intent, the way you appraise and respond to others, and the meaning you give to your own life and actions. You begin to ask, "Who am I... and why did I come here? What did I hope to accomplish, or learn?" Sometimes, everything that you did prior to your awakening becomes meaningless.

Spiritual development brings gifts – compassion, love, patience, peace, wisdom, a sense of humor, insight, gentleness, vision, healing for your soul, and wholeness are only some of those gifts.

The love that wells up from within is a deeply-felt caring for all others and not a romantic version of love based in immaturity and drama.

You find you have true patience, are seldom irritated, and exchange manipulation for directness. You reach a place of peace, and forevermore recognize the difference between 'peace' and a mere 'absence of conflict.' True compassion fills you, and you no longer get caught in feeling sorry for others or hooked into taking responsibility for them.

The benefits of wisdom surround you as you see how many people are trying to fool themselves into feeling successful with smart, contemporary choices. A true sense of humor allows you to drop sarcasm and cynicism, see the excitement of life, and laugh at yourself.

When the gift of vision arrives, there is no longer any need to be canny or sly, because insight and understanding begin to replace self-centered dreams and goals. You are now fueled by a commitment to life. You discover that there is no temporary salve or anesthesia that will pass for true healing. No set of habits geared to smother the unsettled heart will make you feel whole. Only truth will satisfy and make you whole, and yet you will be gentle with yourself and others.

The gifts brought by spiritual development create deep, joyous shifts in the way you experience the world and everything in it. If there has been no previous awareness of having a purpose in life, if the day-to-day routine is just an empty, automatic habit, spiritual development highlights these glaring gaps in your existence and you end up turning over your own apple cart to find and establish real meaning for your Self.

ℭ

I had been through all of these changes and much more, and although I felt I knew what kundalini was, again and again I asked myself *Why?* The changes brought about by kundalini were all good, but did it follow that these changes were the reasons that kundalini existed?

If yes, what were these changes leading to? There had to be a biological preparedness or critical trigger point built-in to the body/mind system, but what triggered it? What lever, when pulled, resulted in the experience of kundalini and its evolution of consciousness?

I had done nothing that I knew of to precipitate the awakening of kundalini. At first, I had been so terrified that I did everything I could think of to circumvent the experiences or turn them off. However, once begun, they recurred as if driven by some scheduled unfolding of their own.

This led me to assume that a biological preparedness did exist, that I somehow reached the appropriate stage, and that I happened to pull the needed trigger. Therefore, the awakening of kundalini had taken place, along with its deep changes in consciousness and perception, all of which transformed my entire life and the world I thought I lived in.

Every time I started thinking along these lines, I found thoughts about Jean Piaget hanging around in the corners of my mind. I had read very little of his work, but in a college psychology class I learned of his theory that we all went through four developmental stages on our way to maturity. The four stages were known as *sensorimotor, mental operations, concrete operations*, and *formal operations*. These stages closely matched what I observed while raising my own four children.

For quite some time I ignored the hint my own consciousness kept giving me in the form of Piaget. I pushed him and his work to the background with the attitude that his work might be good, but there was nothing more to say. He was dealing with the development of children, whereas I was dealing with kundalini.

Still, he continued to pop into mind whenever I wrestled with questions surrounding the purpose of kundalini and how the results of this experience fit into life in this reality.

Finally, I wrote down his four stages and a brief definition of each one as I understood it. I turned them over in my mind, reviewing what I knew, but the words only sat there on the paper.

When nothing noteworthy came to me after a week, I drove to the bookstore and bought a book on his work. Perhaps there was something in it that would point me in the right direction and satisfy whatever kept bringing him to mind.

I brought the book home but never opened it. Perhaps I 'read' it in the same way that I'd 'read' my college assignments – by putting the book beside my bed. Regardless, it simply occurred to me a few days later that Piaget's four stages of development were not the end of the story. The stages we pass through in constructing a reality do not stop at the age of fourteen with the achievement of *formal operations*, sometimes known as 'abstract reasoning.' It was suddenly clear to me that there were additional stages of development that led to becoming a wise, powerful, mature human being.

The problem with most people was that development *did* stop in the teen years, sometimes even earlier, and this left most people with an adult body and an undeveloped mind. Thus, the reality we construct has many of the flaws of a half-grown adult with immature, unrealistic thinking.

As if the issue were suddenly painted across the sky in big, bold letters, I realized that we humans were suffering from arrested development!

Very few of us enjoyed the benefits that the later stages of development offered – the transcendent love, the expanded perceptual skills, the sense of meaning and purpose, the inner authority, the experience of continuous joy, and the ability to construct a life based on a more natural intelligence, deep common sense, and creativity.

In a flash, I saw that giving birth and raising a child was really an exercise in teaching a new human how to perceive and operate in the reality of space-time. Yet, in doing so, we pass on all of our limitations. We teach children what to notice, how to respond, who to interact with, and how to think and feel about people, objects, and events in the world. This is how cultural biases, habits, shortcomings, gifts, lifestyles, beliefs, and attitudes toward others, the world, and God are perpetuated. When the parents live an unexamined life, the children go on to do the same, never questioning how they came to perceive, think, feel, or act the way they do and often unable to see the value in the ways that other cultures think, feel, or act.

Lots of parents think they can create a good human by giving lip service to our reality. So, for the first few years, perhaps the first decade, we are constantly telling, directing, urging the new human to pay attention to particular things, especially rules, behaviors, and roles.

Of course, this approach completely ignores the fact that the young human brain, like the root system of a plant, is absorbing everything in the field in which it is planted. In addition to of all the things we *want* them to absorb, children intuitively take in all the subtle, unspoken, meaningless, angry, and unrewarding patterns of thought, feeling, and action going on around them. These patterns become their basic definition of reality and form the hidden boundaries of what the individual will consider to be 'normal' experience.

Sometimes, what is most obvious is least acknowledged, never evaluated, and thus most powerful – the proverbial elephant in the living room. Parents who stay in an unhappy, miserable relationship for the sake of the children are teaching their children how to stay in an unhappy, miserable marriage. Parents who pretend they are happy are teaching their children how to pretend to be happy when they grow up – the perfect recipe for depression. Parents who don't believe in and pursue their own dreams teach their children to abandon their own dreams and not believe in themselves. Parents who settle for inequality or injustice yet whine or complain about it are teaching their children to whine and complain without taking any action.

Suddenly I was seeing babies, children, teens, adults, and the construction of reality – personal, social, and cultural – in a whole new way. I always heard that children were 'the hope of the world,' now I realized that children were just copies of their parents and because of this, real change was minimal, inefficient, and painfully slow.

The entire stream of human life on earth looked like an amazing carnival ride through a continuously changing fun-house (or house of horrors) that began with birth and continued until death because no one realized what was really happening or how reality was created.

I began to feel that adults were the hope of the world. If they could reach the later stages of development, there might be a chance for many more of us to share health, peace, love, and the joy of finding our own purpose for being here. We could become much more creative and free in living our lives.

Finally, my thoughts and understanding of how we built and perpetuated our reality began to reorganize, integrating the new perspectives with the stages of development. ❀

22 ↶
Early Stages of Development

"To believe in your own thought,
to believe that what is true for you
in your private heart
is true for all men - that is genius."

Ralph Waldo Emerson

AS YOU ENTER THIS REALITY AT BIRTH, YOU IMMEDIATELY ENTER THE
first stage of development – the *sensorimotor* stage. During this stage,
you (and everyone else, including animals, for reality takes the same path
for all mammals) are introduced to sights, sounds, feelings, tastes, touch,
smell, light and other sensory input coming in through the physical body.
Sensory information that stimulates perception comes in from everywhere! Your attention is captured by any little touch, sound, or movement.
Nothing is familiar at this point, and thus nothing is more important than
anything else.

Reality is not just experienced through the medium of your body
– reality *is* your body, and you quickly report your pleasure or displeasure
with that reality regardless of time, place, or social approval.

Little by little, you begin to discover yourself. Those hands waving around in front of your face are yours and you can control them. You
begin to move around, always attracted to whatever it seems will provide
pleasure, for the basic orientation of all living things is toward pleasure
and away from pain.

As your mobility increases, you go about exploring as many
shapes, textures, colors, sizes, sounds, tastes, and objects as you can find.
As you explore, you become accustomed to voices, to being touched and
handled, to a variety of smells and textures along with a general sense of

safety and security, or whatever life offers, including fear and apprehension.

Together, these experiences form your first impressions of our space-time reality. In these earliest months and years, reality is pouring the foundation for its rules. Forever afterwards reality will be a *space* full of people and objects to explore, and a sense of *time* will come from the changes in perception that occur as you move about and see sequences of action. Many of your very first linear sequences will immediately be incorporated into the structure of a cause-and-effect reality, and you will be on your way to mastery of that reality.

If things progress reasonably well, you will be allowed to explore freely and to experience a wide variety of objects, sounds, smells, tastes and situation. During this stage, your brain cells will be stimulated to encode data rapidly and well, creating millions of neuronal connections. If your day-to-day life is fairly safe and secure, your central nervous system will produce the neurotransmitters, chemicals, and hormones that nurture a calm yet curious and observant learner who experiences life as a pleasure, all of which contributes to ongoing maturation of both body and mind in a healthy manner. With love and support from parents, a good foundation is laid for grasping a deeper, more complex version of reality later on.

Lasting until about age two, the *sensorimotor* stage culminates in a concrete, practical, hands-on, but quite limited knowledge of the world of objects and actions.

ᱬ

You then enter the second stage of development, *mental operations*. In this stage of your development, you will take all the objects, images, smells, sounds, and behaviors that you discovered in the previous stage and practice recreating them in your mind. Thus, you move from needing the actual physical object in order to perceive or think about it, to being able to conjure it up in your own mind...a very important skill necessary for a stable reality system!

During *mental operations* you expand your awareness of what you've observed and experienced during the first two years and add complexity, subtle nuances, and new meanings to everything. The size, shape, color, and texture of objects, the arrangement of those objects, plus all sorts of new ones, the tone and loudness of certain words and sounds as well as when to use them, the words and attitudes with which certain body motions are carried out – all take on finer, more distinct shades of meaning as you refine and network the data you have accumulated so far.

Mental operations is that joyous, creative, almost hilarious stage of play that is so entertaining to observe! All of the input that has gone into your mind is retrieved and creatively rearranged using *mental operations*, which deepens the development of your individual reality and begins to express your personality. You will copy all of the behaviors, daily rituals, and activities that you see going on around you while adding a few of your own ideas and spice!

If you are not allowed to play with certain objects, you will make suitable substitutions wherever necessary in the scenario you are creating. A Lincoln log becomes an airplane, an old purse becomes a lunch box, and a crayon becomes a hypodermic needle to give shots to the family dog.

This is the time when mothers and fathers begin to see themselves reflected in the words, actions, and attitudes of their three- or four-year-old. Sadly, very few parents realize that they are using their own flawed version of reality to program a brand new human...which is why this way of evolving a reality is extremely slow. It allows few changes or improvements from the parents' original version and perpetuates many mistakes for many years, even centuries.

As you play with the reality around you, your brain produces specific chemicals and hormones that will forever accompany the objects, words, and events that you are exposed to. Thus, for the rest of your life, the ability to conjure up and stabilize reality will also conjure the chemicals and hormones that produce familiar feelings – even when the feelings are not good – which is why some people are never able to climb out of misery. It is not whether the feelings are good or bad that is important, it is whether or not they are *familiar*...because anything not familiar means you do not know the world you live in, and this is a very upsetting thing for most people.

The bottom line is that in this stage you are literally creating a storage bank of perceptual symbols – images, sounds, movements, and feelings – that you will work with for the rest of your life. The more symbols you are able to perceive and play with as a child, the more mental energy you will have as an adult simply because it takes a great deal of energy to add to your storage bank once you are fully grown. You will be less prone to depression because the more symbols available to you, the more likely it will be that you will be in the habit of working with this rich data. Thus, the more options you will have.

The ability to recognize and reproduce mental images is a form of spatial intelligence and is recognized by cognitive scientists. This skill will help you to pick up visual cues and be sensitive to the moods of the people around you because you can recognize the difference between a smile and a frown, or a look of fright versus a look of curiosity, both of which involve slight differences in spatial arrangements of the eyes and mouth.

The ability to notice subtle differences in sound, pitch, loudness, rhythm, and the feeling embedded in all of this is a form of musical intelligence, and again, this is a recognized form of intelligence. In this stage, all children love to sing, dance, and clap their hands, and if you are encouraged to join in such activities, you will soon begin to repeat a great deal of what you hear. You will learn to make many sounds, to speak with feeling, to sing, shout, and even berate the dog or the cat with the appropriate words and tones of disapproval. All the time this is going on, you will be assessing the effects of what you do and say, matching your results with various feeling states in order to find out what works best for you in your attempts to come to grips with the world.

The appreciation of these subtleties adds immensely to the richness of your imagination (pictures in the mind's eye), tones (sounds in the mind's ear), and sensations (feeling states) available to you.

The stage of *mental operations* reaches full development around the age of six or seven, although continued encoding of your brain cells, as well as increasingly complex networking, will go on for the rest of your life. When it is complete, you have the ability to stabilize this reality system in your mind.

෴

Assuming that development has gone well so far, somewhere between the ages of six and eight you will enter the third stage of development, that of *concrete operations*.

Having already gained a good basic acquaintance with the world of objects and sounds, having learned to make those objects permanent by re-creating them in your mind, and then practiced all sorts of imaginary scenarios, you begin a further exploration of what can be accomplished with those objects and how they interact within concrete physical reality. To successfully navigate this stage of development requires a great deal of hands-on making, creating, breaking, repairing, dancing, drawing, building, cooking, painting, growing, preserving, exploring, arranging, and re-arranging of the material items that make up our world.

During this stage the quest becomes the development of abilities that will lead to mastery of the physical world and the ability to survive on your own. This stage offers an important opportunity for you to stretch your original perceptions, and to test these perceptions in the expanded reality of the seven-to-fourteen-year old child.

Until now, you have known that hot is hot…but just how hot does the stove have to get before the water will boil or the fudge will burn? Ice is solid water, but how thick does the ice have to be to skate on? A dress is made from fabric, but what shapes must come together to get it to look and feel right? Seeds will sprout into vegetables and fruit, but how much can you ignore or interfere with the process and still end up with something to eat? A tree house is just a few pieces of wood and some nails, but what do you nail to what? And what is the pressure tolerance of a thumb when smacked by a hammer?

The period of *concrete operations* is the time for you to personally experience what works and doesn't work. It is a time in which imagined possibilities must be explored to find out how much work it takes to make something real, which images don't transfer to reality, which don't, and why. *Concrete operations* allow you to practice manipulating the real objects and processes that will eventually support your life and your ability to make your own living in the world.

Frequently your favorite objects and processes will become part of your career. During *concrete operations*, it is essential that you practice using the objects of reality for some time before you are allowed to strike out on your own.

During the time of *concrete operations*, you play and experiment with many kinds of objects, as well as a variety of sequences and processes, exploring – then comparing the real results with those you originally dreamed up in your mind. What you learn will teach you to be practical and will nurture creativity while allowing further development of your image, sound, and feeling banks. It will also anchor you securely within the reality as you learn the basics of survival. It coaxes your own ideas, interests, and capacities into the foreground so that you will feel comfortable offering these to the world when you are older. It encourages you to explore and to find out for yourself what is true. And it enhances critical thinking and your ability to depend on your personal experience for a clear map of what is true. This then leads to the blossoming of personal authority within you.

As you learn to trust yourself and your ability to navigate a continuously expanding reality, your confidence expands, which supports a flexible approach to learning and life. Besides teaching you to trust in yourself, *concrete operations* teach you to observe and respond to the fine differences necessary for successful navigation of the many unique situations you will encounter as you mature. For you, reality will be organized in a common-sense fashion, and you will be alert for new ideas and solutions to emerge.

In this stage, useful creativity and purpose-oriented activity help to define and enrich your quality of life. Along with learning how to survive in the world, you learn self-esteem because you participate and contribute. You learn the value of useful play, also known as *work,* and you begin looking forward to the time in your life when you can step into the adult world and be responsible for your own life.

When *concrete operations* have been successful, you will have a detailed and highly personalized map of reality based on your individual experience.

ɕ

With this map, a good supply of self-esteem, trust in your ability to survive in the world, and some individual creativity, you enter the fourth stage of development, that of *formal operations.*

During *formal operations,* which begin between the ages of twelve and fourteen, you will cycle around to a renewed emphasis on development of abstract capacities, as opposed to working concretely.

You move from handling, making, and exploring concrete items and processes to once again manipulating reality using the abstract abilities of your mind. Your goal will be to carry out ever more complex sequences of operation on entire groups of people, objects, numbers, or processes and assess the probable results *before* spending the time, energy, or money to carry them out in reality. As in *mental operations,* this stage refines your ability to predict realistic outcomes.

During this stage, you take the ability to create mental images, sounds, and feelings learned in the stage of *mental operations,* combine this with the practical, hands-on experience gained during *concrete operations,* and learn how to apply this knowledge in ways that will help you expand your own life.

With a foundation of security and the knowledge that you know how to survive in the world, you begin to distance yourself from your immediate family. This is the time for you to explore – in depth – the feelings, motives, thoughts, and activities of those in the wider world around you, those outside the cocoon of family.

As in the earlier stage of *mental operations*, you copy the important people in your life, but now you will copy from friends, schoolmates, teachers, shop owners, ministers, actors, singers, sports stars, dancers, people in business, science, or in the news, and a host of other models.

You observe and copy the way these heroes and heroines behave, talk, interact, what they wear or drive, and their entire lifestyle. You run into your personal limits and fears, and have to decide for yourself how you feel when you copy others, and whether or not you like the results.

Slowly you become aware of the subtle nuances of what you are trying to copy. Slowly you discover that what you observe on the surface does not always produce the imagined feelings or practical results. What looks like a glamorous or exciting life can feel empty and alone...and this leads to paying closer attention to feelings and the people and situations that trigger them.

Gradually, you begin to understand some of the reasons why these heroes and heroines do what they do, what motivates as well as limits them, and what interests drive their work forward. In doing so, you will come to a deeper understanding of the fact that each individual has a unique set of gifts, talents, limits, motives, hopes, and fears.

You begin talking to a wider circle of adults and are amazed to discover some of their reasons for choosing a particular career, a life partner, a special school or trade, or how they got beyond a particular obstacle. You'll try some of these paths, integrating successful ideas, and abandoning tactics that fail.

This may lead you to consider work that looks quiet and boring from the outside, but can become a fascinating journey of discovery once you pass a certain threshold of interest.

You learn how to make difficult choices, work your way out of compromising mistakes, and ride out discouraging situations. Slowly your goals, dreams, and planning become more realistic and display better timing. If you are allowed to observe and experience a wide swath of life, you come to discover what you value, and you develop a set of ethics and moral guidelines that rest on a broad, strong base that is good for you and good for the world.

As *formal operations* conclude, you find you have grown and developed well, continuously widening your familiarity with both objects and people. You have developed the ability to create and sustain mental images, sounds, and processes in your mind. You are reasonably good at identifying feelings and in gaining additional experience in building, assembling, growing, reproducing, reshaping, and rearranging the objects and processes that exist in the world. You have gathered a basic framework of motives, values, ethics, meanings, and probable outcomes to be used in setting up your own independent life, and now you move further into the external world to express your own choices. You are ready to create a life for yourself through learning, working in, and contributing to the wide, wide world outside the family and the home. ∝

23 ∞
Arrested Development

> *"All kids are gifted,*
> *some just open their packages*
> *earlier than others.".*
>
> Michael Carr

BEFORE WE GO ON TO THE LATER STAGES OF DEVELOPMENT, LET'S GO back to take a quick look at what happens if these early stages are not successfully completed.

Going back to birth, you enter this reality and the *sensorimotor* stage of development. Like every newborn, from the moment of birth, you begin to experience the sights, sounds, tastes, touch, smells, feelings, and other sensory inputs that flow through our reality. Perceptual stimuli are everywhere, however, your needs are *not* well attended to and you spend much of your time feeling uncomfortable and distracted by attempts to get basic needs met. The reality you experience is too wet, thirsty, hot, cold, hungry, or characterized by rough handling. You are not free to notice the many little touches, sounds, sights, or movements going on around you be-cause you are busy crying. Since nothing is familiar and you are not feel-ing secure, you report your discomfort loudly regardless of time, place, or the rules of society, creating further tensions in the family you belong to.

During the *sensorimotor* stage, encoding of the brain and develop-ment of neural networks proceeds at a furious pace. Every sight and sound, every touch and smell you encounter provides data for your brain about how the reality is structured. If you are not allowed to crawl and walk freely…if your explorations are interfered with and you are not allowed to touch anything except for a few dull repetitive toys…the encoding of brain cells will slow drastically, as will the development of neural networks that are so crucial for decision-making later in life. Whole areas of your brain will not mature or function well.

If you experience neglect, insecurity, or fear on a regular basis, your central nervous system will become habituated to producing neurotransmitters, chemicals, and hormones that bring about insecurity, fear, tension, and anger. You will live in a state of constant stress.

When these two things occur – poor encoding of brain cells, and a predisposition to tension and stress – learning will be difficult for you. To learn means to encounter change, and since your own needs for change, for something to be different, were not addressed as an infant, you are not able to be comfortable with the change implied by learning something new. We would label you as learning disabled, maybe severely learning disabled, perhaps even retarded, and in the future, you could be forced to return to this level of extremely subjective learning by crawling around among objects if you are to 'learn how to learn' anything at all.

Whether or not you successfully complete the stage of *sensorimotor* development, your physical growth and development continues and by the age of two, you will enter the stage of *mental operations*.

This is the stage when you focus on recreating in your mind all the people, places, and things that make up your world. Indeed, in order for your world to stabilize, you must learn to recreate it mentally.

This is the stage in which the development of storage banks of sights, sounds, sequences of events, and feelings are essential, for you will work with these for the rest of your life.

If this stage is interfered with and not successfully completed, you will be unable to create mental images (spatial intelligence) which may leave you insensitive to the many moods of people and situations. This is because you cannot distinguish subtle differences in the spatial patterns involving unique arrangements of eyes, nose, brows, and mouth. Visual cues have no message for you because you have not created an internal image bank. Thus, you remain oblivious to the visual signals given off when people are hurried, worried, angry, curious, frightened, or preoccupied and inattentive.

If the data bank of sounds in your mind is deficient, you will be unable to detect subtle changes in tone, pitch, rhythm, emotional, or loud/ soft qualities. When a sound from the environment has died away, you will not be able to reproduce it correctly. This leads to speech difficulties and an inability to sing. When someone sounds angry, you may respond inappropriately, if at all, because you do not have a repertoire of tones, loud/soft volumes, and words with basic emotional meanings attached to them. You will be unable to clap your hands rhythmically, to dance in time with music, or to modulate your own voice to communicate what you are feeling. You may end up always whining or talking too loudly or in too demanding a tone because you are unaware of how you sound.

The success of *mental operations* is essential because any inability to reproduce and creatively rearrange the images, sounds, and feelings of your mental data banks will eventually leave you less able to cope with the highly symbolic reality we humans have developed.

With a limited bank of images, sounds, and sensations, you may be unable to imagine the consequences or assess the effects of your own words and actions on friends, family, and schoolmates. Thus, you will behave inappropriately. In addition, because we normally make subtle decisions about feeling based on what we see, hear, smell, etc., you may be missing an entire range of feeling states, something we label as emotionally disabled. If you are already learning disabled, the addition of emotional disability is devastating. When something is out of sight or out of earshot, it is also out of mind. You cannot re-create it using mental operations and reality remains unstable and unpredictable and so does your behavior.

It may take so much mental energy for you to cope with reality that you become prone to depression and mental illness. This would be further complicated by the tendency of your body/mind system to produce neurotransmitters and chemicals that sustain tension and stress.

In the end, if *mental operations* are not successfully completed, development of the brain and the central nervous system is seriously delayed or even permanently handicapped. You will be left with fewer options and lower creativity because the image banks that hold the symbols of reality are partially empty, and those that you have are not well-connected in complex networks.

Regardless of whether you have developed smoothly or not, when you reach the age of seven, you will enter the stage of *concrete operations.* This is the stage of hands-on learning, practical experience, and a deeper exploration of the rules and boundaries of reality.

In this stage, you will test things out in real time, discovering for yourself what works and doesn't work. A cake may bake nicely at 350° but burn miserably at 450°. An imaginary fort may seem simple, but there are all sorts of techniques for building one successfully. The corner store may be only a few blocks away, but getting there successfully requires spatial skills that allow you to recognize landmarks when the layout is reversed and you are on your way home. If you are already basically uncomfortable in the reality, playing games with friends on a hot day involving quite a bit of sweat may increase your level of discomfort to the point that you refuse to play and become overweight.

If you are criticized or laughed at, expected to take on adult re-sponsibilities, or subjected to additional stress, fear, or physical, mental, or emotional abuse, you may shut down and refuse to explore the reality in a hands-on way at all.

When *concrete operations* are interrupted or not completed, you lose the opportunity to experiment with the objects, sounds, and process-es that fill your world. Without the hands-on experience of this personal testing, you will not be secure, either with yourself or within your reality because the goal of this stage has everything to do with anchoring your ability to survive on your own in the world.

Without the time and freedom to explore reality and test things out for yourself, you will have nothing new to offer to the reality later on. You will not be involved nor will you care about the general condition of people, objects, or processes, thus, you will not make an effort to make the world a better place. You will be narrow and unrealistic and will have nothing of your true self to give to anyone because you have not developed enough of the inner self to give anything away. Usually you will 'take someone else's word for it,' and will be forced to depend on others for many things, including the truth.

At worst, you may never realize that every object is subject to differing processes and relationships, or that every individual has different skills, boundaries, capacities and perceptions. You will be ripe for the 'one size fits all' mentality, and when confronted with unique situations, you will use the same solution for every problem. When the solution does not work, you will not understand why and will conclude that reality does not make sense. For you, everything will remain arbitrary and inconsistent simply because you do not trust yourself to observe or try new things, and you will not have the confidence or experience to back yourself up in any sort of trial-and-error situation.

Without trust in yourself, your insecurity, fear, and confusion in-crease as you grow older. The world is not a safe place and you need some-one to take care of you. You have lost your sense of inner authority and become dependent on peers, a spouse, the corporation, the state, or big in-stitutions. Without a sense of inner authority, your most common response to problems in the world becomes, "Someone should do something…"

When *concrete operations* are not successfully completed, you may withdraw from any true involvement with the real world. You may live in books, TV, alcohol, drugs, or your imagination. You may lack common sense, or be oblivious to the most basic and practical demands of living. If you spend a great deal of time playing with a single object, process, or area of study, you may end up with a highly-developed skill or interest in that one area, yet be unable to transfer what you know to other areas. Often you will be unable to cope with many concurrent problems and demands from other spheres.

If both *mental operations* AND *concrete operations* have been interrupted, you will be left with no inner life of the imagination and no outer experience of reality testing. You may fail to comprehend anything outside of what is happening in-the-moment or the immediate environment. This can result in a paralyzing inability to cope with change or transition of even the smallest kind, and thus personal growth and development comes to a halt or slows drastically. You become ultra-conservative and cling to fundamentalist rules.

Despite your failure to successfully complete the first three stages of development, you will enter the teen years and begin grappling with the abstract reasoning processes of *formal operations.*

In this stage of development, your goal should be to move into the wider world to find heroes and heroines, explore lifestyles different from what you have so far experienced, and begin to identify your own path to power, wisdom, and grace. This is when you must begin taking responsibility for yourself, forming relationships with friends, and dreaming of what you will become. However, if the earlier stages have not been completed successfully, it will be increasingly difficult for you to navigate this stage.

If *formal operations* are cut short or not allowed to proceed, you will not develop the in-depth understanding of people and events leading to the ability to set up and maintain a successful, independent life on your own. You will tend to idolize cultural symbols of success and choose heroes or heroines that are destructive or represent an unrealistic shortcut to power, fame, and fortune.

If you never learn to honestly evaluate the people or events in your life and assess their relevance to yourself or your dreams, you may get caught up in relationships that are negative and disparaging. You will not engage in activities that fulfill your deepest desires because you have never learned to recognize your gifts and talents. Without the practice of imagining what you want, going after it, then assessing whether the reality matches the image, you will lead an unexamined life. If you do admit that something is not right, you may be unable to identify what must change. Is it the image or the way you are going about achieving it that must change?

Because you are unable to use abstract reasoning, you will not be able to imagine a set of activities leading to a goal with an outcome that feels right for you. Neither will you have the confidence to try new things and allow yourself to make mistakes because you will find it too expensive in terms of time, energy, and money.

As a young adult, you will cease creative activity and settle for the structures, solutions, and routines of others, whether they are good for you or not. You do not understand why something can look good yet feel bad, and you do not understand why you feel like either you, or life, are not enough.

If *formal operations* are not successfully completed, you do not have enough patience or strength of mind to pursue the things you truly value. You will not have a firm set of ethics to guide your life toward what is good for you and others. As you go through the motions of living, things begin to lose their meaning and you find you do not understand either yourself or others, therefore you do not challenge the conventions of society that may be unworkable for yourself or others. You spend your whole life merely trying to get by and sometimes get ahead. ෨

24 ଔ
Advanced Stages of Development

*"There is no heavier burden than
a great potential."*

Charlie Brown

PREPARING TO TAKE A DEEP LOOK AT THE LATER STAGES OF DEVEL opment, I suddenly stalled. Something in me knew that I was going to see something about my own life that would serve as a warning about my future. Days went by while I argued with myself. How could I presume to know anything about theories of human development? What about all the possible theories that might exist somewhere in books, magazines, or dissertations sitting in dusty libraries, theories that I knew nothing about and might contradict or shortchange with my limited knowledge. What if I ended up sounding foolish?

Surely not everyone carried the general perception that human development was completed somewhere in our teens. In fact, I told myself, most people probably didn't give it even half a thought.

Until my bouts with kundalini, I considered myself to be like most people and assumed I was all grown up. Hadn't I proved that by getting a job and moving into my first apartment? Now it was obvious that growing up included development that went far beyond my former assumptions.

As I struggled with myself over whether I should say anything about human development, it brought up another issue, that of my work in this world. I was avoiding going further with my own personal development because I didn't want to deal with my own future.

Years earlier, during the visits of the little men in brown robes, I saw a good portion of my future and my work, and had somehow managed to ignore what I knew. It wasn't that I forgot what they showed me or that I deliberately buried it, or even that I was unwilling to do what they asked. It was just that thinking about it brought waves of anxiety and other emotions that were difficult to deal with, so I ended up skirting the subject, then making half-hearted attempts to get started, then going back to doing nothing. Now I was afraid that assembling what I knew about human development would force me to deal with what I had learned from the little men in brown robes. Lost in anxiety, I remained stalled.

Then one day, without warning, my reality shifted and split open as if I were back in the early, uncontrolled days of awakening kundalini. I entered a period of living in multiple times. For more than a month I found myself in my adult past, which was split at least three ways – the way that it actually unfolded, and two other ways that could have been.

Following this period of reliving my past, I returned briefly to the present, which then opened and ran parallel with two additional possible futures. Each of these paths had a unique outcome.

One path seemed to be the result of doing nothing. The other was the result of taking up that path and living it fully. The third was disastrous. As these parallel lives unfolded, I experienced myself as approximately one year older for each day that went by. Without warning or feeling ready, I was caught in an avalanche of emotions, problems, and challenges of the two lives. To my great distress, the effects of the physical, mental, and emotional stresses in the two additional lifetimes overflowed constantly into my daily reality and I aged rapidly.

To cope with the tumult of three lives and keep up a plausibly normal front, I found it necessary to let go of my ordinary self constantly. Every other day I would come to crisis, disintegrate, then quickly reform and reintegrate as I tried to rise to the demands of my 'ordinary' life. This forced me to rely more and more on inner silence to gain some semblance of sanity and balance.

During this time, I was tired and felt increasingly fragile. There were days my bones ached, and looking in the mirror ranged from upsetting to terrifying as I watched myself age. At times, the woman I saw there barely even resembled the face and body I was used to.

Gradually, I began to see that the two additional lives were showing me the results of full development versus arrested development. I moved from stage to stage all the way to and through my own choice of deaths. When the period ended, I felt I had already seen and lived my whole life in triplicate. Finally, I began to write again, picking up where *formal operations* left off and trying to capture the essence of what I had learned as each unique stage of life unfolded.

❧

By the time you complete *formal operations* somewhere between the ages of nineteen and twenty-one and begin to launch yourself into the world, you have been undergoing the transformation to an adult body for at least several years. Your body has been manufacturing hormones that bring sexual maturation, and drawn to the opposite sex, you fall in love.

Pushed by hormones and a desire to experience all that life offers, you enter a sexual relationship. This triggers the spontaneous awakening of kundalini that expands your consciousness, propelling you into the great Void, home of the *I Am*. In this experience, your entire central nervous system is suddenly connected to Source, your brain is 're-wired,' and there is an increase in the range of frequencies across which your consciousness can perceive.

When this occurs, you have entered the fifth stage of development, that of *natural intelligence*.

Upon entering this stage, your inner knowing is activated and begins a subtle transformation of both body and mind. Consciousness – if not fully awakened – becomes at least less limited, bringing gifts such as intuition, and sometimes clairvoyance and clairaudience. The senses become acute to a fault, and you are increasingly awake to life and all of its nuances at every level. Later, when you look back with clarity, you will say that this was when you truly fell in love for the first time... and that you fell in love with everything.

In the early stages of *natural intelligence* your heart is open, alive, and overflowing. The world buzzes with electricity and excitement. You seem to know what your new lover is thinking, feeling, and doing every moment, whether you are together or apart.

In fact, you know what everyone is thinking, feeling, and doing every moment because some heretofore unacknowledged force plucks images, sounds, and feelings out of your brain's data banks and arranges them in ways that show you what people are thinking and feeling. It is as if you have developed an entirely new set of senses and this allows you to perceive a much wider and deeper range of information, all of which keenly impact your attitudes, decisions, sense of who you are, and what you do with your life.

Throughout this stage, *natural intelligence* works to unfold the concrete aspects of your life that will help you to evolve further. Spontaneous visions and the famed 'still, small voice' spring from the intelligent field that our reality is embedded in and attempt to guide your career choices, relationships, and lifestyle. You will discover that your passion, the thing you love to do, is your gift to the world, and when difficulties occur, you plumb their depths, drawing much more wisdom from them than others might get.

Sometimes these visions and your inner voice occur in response to the myriad thoughts and questions that pass through you as you respond to the world about you. At times it may seem that something very mysterious – a spirit guide, disembodied personality, or even a devil – has suddenly become a factor in your relationship with both yourself and the world, but it is merely an open, awakened consciousness presenting information that you are curious about and that is not available via the physical senses. Allowing curiosity to guide you, you explore the intelligent visions and voices coming from within in the same way that you once explored the physical objects around you when you were an infant in the *sensorimotor* stage.

Uncertain, you turn the things you see and hear around and around in your mind while paying close attention to gut feelings as well as any sudden, shifting physical sensations. You take note of the startlingly clear dreams that occur while trying to sleep, as well as the pictures that appear in your mind's eye during daydreams or moments of relaxation.

Before long, you discover that these visions and voices occur in response to what is going on in your everyday life. If you make a decision or take some action that will upset health, love, finances, or another aspect of life, there will be spontaneous warnings that run through your mind or a clear gut feeling that something is wrong. There may be a string of outrageously frustrating mishaps that prevent further movement along the wrong path.

If you continue along the path that is wrong for you, you may have vivid dreams filled with insight or hear your inner voice lecturing to you. You may find yourself out of the body, in a lucid dream, a vivid daydream, or an alternate present that is a real as your everyday reality. Whatever it is, you begin to understand that reality is not as you first thought. If you don't back away, you learn that your own choices and decisions are causing the disruptions, so you gather your strength and make new decisions.

Even though you may not immediately grasp all the implications of what is happening, you continuously try new ways of seeing, hearing, communication, and experience. Not only do you accept what works, you learn from it, and everything that you learn continues to fill you with increasing wonder and ever-greater awareness.

The world may occasionally light up with a golden glow. you may experience moments when you feel fluid, powerful, or even without solid boundaries. You may see an event take place before it physically happens, and may find yourself in two places at once. Relying on the trust that was developed in the earlier stage of *concrete operations*, you begin to watch and wait for this inner knowing to offer itself, a process that is generally referred to as the development of the sixth sense.

As the stage of *natural intelligence* unfolds, not only do you pay close attention to the images, sounds, and feelings that consciousness reveals about hidden aspects of reality, you develop some interest in learning more about what is happening and possible within consciousness. You make choices and act only when the information in your gut or in the visions and voices indicates that the choices will have good outcomes. You begin to go after information in order to find extra guidance in navigating reality, and your decisions are based on an uncanny recognition of the big picture as well as hidden details that come to you spontaneously. You become comfortable with the truth in all things, and freedom begins to anchor your entire life, which slowly orients itself in the direction of health, peace, love, and living your passion and purpose.

Gradually, you develop a clear and deliberate trust of your own knowing, and come to depend on your mind and its deep intuition. As you make choices that honor this innate *natural intelligence*, you will be guided along your path. If you are still young, uncommitted, and flexible, you will make the transition to a balanced life with a minimum of fuss. Your choices allow you to avoid a great deal of pain and sorrow, and to return to your path quickly when you discover you are off track.

All of this stretches your earlier perceptions of physical reality, removing old limits. The world is neither bound by nor determined solely by physical, mechanical, or chemical events. Something else is afoot! Because of the information, dreams, visions, and that inner voice, it is as if a whole new light is shining on the reality you have always known. The world takes on a new and different quality and offers new meaning and depth.

Although it requires some effort, you successfully navigate the stage of *natural intelligence* because it is as if a new dimension has been added to life, an inner dimension. As in all previous stages of development, you have discovered more of yourself while expanding the possibilities of the reality in which we all live. Since the original condition of mind *is* ecstasy and oneness, you will be inexorably drawn toward the joy that characterizes the *I Am* experience and communication with all that exists, resulting in a life that is joyful and full of interesting possibilities.

If the transformation to *natural intelligence* is allowed to continue and become integrated, there will be a basic shift in the way that you perceive and act. Thus, it is with an attitude of experimentation and curiosity about the further potentials of reality that you enter the next stage of development, that of *creative intelligence.*

ogg

Entry into *creative intelligence* moves you along the continuum of deepening exploration of your existence and the far-reaching possibilities of reality. Cycling once again from concrete development to abstract development, you move from the practical tasks of setting up relationships, career, and a home of your own, to thoughts about how to improve and expand your impact on the world. Exploring at a much deeper level of awareness, you ask yourself, 'What is possible with the people, products, events, and ideas that surround me?'

The experiences of knowing what others are feeling, thinking, or doing have shown you that communication between individuals is an ongoing telepathic channel that is always open, always on. Finding yourself in the past, the future, or some alternate present has changed your understanding of what time is. The experience of finding yourself out of the body or feeling so completely fluid that you have no physical boundaries has changed your assumptions about space.

The continuous flow of images that appear in mind in response to your choices and decisions have signaled not only a deep and constant communication between yourself and everything around you, it indicates that some part of you has your deepest welfare in mind. The power of your mind to create images, when combined with the power of the body to act, makes the potential of reality unlimited. The possibilities of space, the use of time, the sheer power of intent, will, and choice – all become tools of exploration during the development of *creative intelligence.*

The unnerving discovery that whatever you think or believe is what will generally happen, brings up the questions, "Did the experience happen because I saw it?" or "Did I see it because the experience was going to happen?"

Either way, armed with these intriguing questions you begin to probe the connections and relationships between the *internal* visions, voices, and knowings, and the *external* situations, events, and outcomes observed in the world.

You begin to experiment with the power of thought, attempting to discover what will happen when you deliberately create images of a desired reality. Repeatedly, you create and then sustain a particular thought or image and discover, in fact, that it *can* be created. You find that many situations within reality can be altered. You discover that holding a thought or image in an effort to change reality affects your own actions and level of energy as well as the outcome.

As the learning progresses, however, there are problems. Frequently you discover that you are unable to manifest reality in an immediate way. You gets results...but the timing is poor. The desired event occurs when you no longer have the time or interest in it. Too late, you discover that you have created a problem for yourself.

In other cases, you see something in the future that you don't like, and attempts to fix it create disaster. For instance, you see a serious physical attack on one of your children at school. You decide to take action. When talking to your child, you repeatedly suggest a change of schools until the child finally agrees. But horrors! It is in the *new* school that the child experiences the attack that you saw in the warning vision! You discover too late that you have created the very thing you were trying to avoid. All of your efforts and precautions ended up putting the child in the very place necessary for the attack to occur.

Thus, the critical questions, *Should I take action...What action should I take...and when should I take it?* become a pointed lesson in humility and the proper use of your great ability to see and hear many things. You realize each of us has important lessons along the path in life and it is not always appropriate to intervene.

You continue to play with everything that comes your way, trying to transform or at least affect them for the better when it seems right. Using your abilities to move about in time and space, to heal, and to communicate at many levels, you play with efforts to change family, friends, acquaintances, and strangers. You tinker with the circumstances you find yourself in, social events, the weather, other peoples' health, their actions, their attitudes, legal outcomes, commitments, perceptions, and a host of other factors in daily life. You discover, indeed, that you can create positive change in many situations. You can also increase the awareness of almost everyone you come in contact with.

But about the time you begin to accept the fact of your own ability to create helpful change within reality, you begin to feel tired and be overwhelmed with all the responsibilities of this self-imposed burden.

At the same time, you discover that many of your efforts bring only short-term change. As soon as you leave or are not available, people revert to their usual fears and destructive interactions.

You focus on attempts to bring family, friends, and those who are close to you into a state of greater awareness, to lead them toward self-acceptance, love, peace, and purpose. To some extent you succeed – but this then has a secondary effect on you. The more *they* awaken and the more insight *they* have – the more they challenge *you* to grow further. You are forced to examine all of the hidden areas in your life in which you revert to old habits based on being rigid, manipulative, fearful, ungenerous, angry, unforgiving, or caught in guilt. In order to keep one foot standing firmly in the pool of peace that you discovered during those transcendent moments of awakening to love, you teach yourself where you must change, what you must let go of.

If you are a wise learner, one by one you clean the nooks, closets, and attics of your personality, giving up the remaining shreds of fear, anger, and upset, exchanging each for new and deeper perceptions in quietness, clarity, and flexibility.

Instead of struggling with an overwhelming world to be changed, or a dangerous world to be tamed, you find it is *yourself* that must change; it is *your* mind that must be tamed. Rather than a pressing need for prediction and control, you need simply to allow your own knowing and to rest in your commitment to what is good, beautiful, and true.

For this to happen, you must maintain your inner quiet, and as you do so, you come to know ever more clearly what your life is about. Realizing that you must honor your purpose for being here, you begin to focus on completing your life's work and no longer make an effort to control external reality. You know all that is needed is to follow your path and reason for being. You are not here to play around with aimless change just to prove it can be done, you are here for a reason. You have a gift to give.

At last, you turn to the work you came here to do. As you do so, fatigue lessens; reality begins to flow smoothly and takes on the soft and gentle aura of tranquility. Finally, you are on your true path.

No longer hampered by resistance, distractions, cultural stiffness, guilt, anger, fear, or the need for attention, there is the emergence of an immeasurable, infinite fountain of love from inside you. You recognize yourself in everyone and everything, and find that through a flexible, peaceful love, you always have what you need, you know what you need to know, and your experience is one of continual pleasure in being of service.

At this time, your great ability to create and sustain change comes into its full use, along with the gifts of love, patience, peace, compassion, wisdom, insight, vision, and healing. Whether you are here to raise children or raise money, patch up bodies or patch leaky tires, keep a dying mother company or keep a company solvent, grow corn or quietly grow old, you do so with love, grace, and a natural ease.

You will be able to maintain health, joy, and peace while continuing to live out your purpose within the physical, mental, emotional and spiritual realms.

As you weave together the unique threads of awareness, energy, intelligence, and purpose that make up your Self and your reason for being, you realize that the voices you have heard or channeled for many years are really one voice – the voice of your more evolved Self. Those wise spirit guides and helpful-yet-disembodied personalities that once frightened and intrigued you turn out to be pieces of yourself from a future that you were growing into.

The visions that you dramatically thought were being 'shown' to you were really glimpses of your natural vision as seen with the eyes of this highly evolved Self. The knowledge of people, objects, processes, and feelings that you were privileged to see and understand were really being known and experienced through the as-yet-unintegrated body of your fully evolved Self. And the love, health, peace, patience, wisdom, compassion, and joy you managed to tap into were the basic characteristics of that already Realized Self.

Gradually, your whole perception of reality changes its base from that of trying to make life be what you once envisioned it to be, to accepting the creative drive to evolve within yourself. You begin to allow this self to express itself naturally. This brings peace and the end of all guilt. You are a natural, loving human and what you see and feel is natural for humans to feel. You come to the end of the constant difficulty of judging every little thing that occurs or threatens to occur. In fact, you are no longer caught up in judgment at all.

Reaching the point of your own last judgment releases a tremendous amount of personal energy and you are now free to put this energy into your work, accomplishing what you came here to do. You realize that everything unnatural is difficult and draining to keep going, and you tend to create and reinforce things with the innate ability to sustain themselves. You are interested in eternity and things that are natural.

As your *creative intelligence* is fully integrated, you and the world synthesize in a joyous, intense oneness of self and everything in the reality, and this becomes your constant experience.

With a deep and abiding grasp of the essential oneness of everything in the world, you enjoy and are renewed by the internal reality she live in – a little pool of peace from which love overflows. Anchored in this pool of peace, you enter the next stage of development, that of *abstract intelligence.*

◌

Upon entering *abstract intelligence,* you cycle around to a new level of practical, concrete experience within reality. Since the opening of your mind years ago in the initial kundalini experience, an expanded range of wave frequencies has been sustaining your body/mind system. Little by little it has altered you physically, mentally, emotionally, and spiritually.

Now in the stage of *abstract intelligence*, you find yourself exquisitely sensitive. This super-sensitivity to people, things, thoughts, and events forces you to perfect your inner quietness or be constantly assailed and upset by the chaotic activities, talk, and even thoughts and feelings telepathically communicated by everyone.

As your inner quiet deepens, the sensitivity increases. This increasing sensitivity calls for an even deeper quiet within. As the cycle of deepening silence intensifies, you begin to experience the side effects of this profound inner quiet. You find yourself entering a fluid state of awareness that ignores physical boundaries more and more frequently.

In these inter-penetrations of yourself with everything in the reality, you discover you can know and become other forms of matter at the very core of your being through intent and will. By shifting your basic frequencies, you can become a tree, or you can allow the tree to become you, with the qualities and characteristics of each becoming completely interchangeable. You can come to know a washing machine, a petunia, teacup, violin, or a cat as well as you know yourself. You find you can become one with many kinds of matter in ways that transcend ordinary cause-and-effect laws.

You begin to explore other dimensions, traveling through the universe of reality systems where you learn many things about the true nature of reality. As you continue to explore, you become comfortable with the fact that there are many realities, many beings, and many worlds. You meet other beings and have experiences that are not possible in our earth-based reality system. In fact, there are many versions of our earth-based reality systems, including one without any sickness, sorrow, accidents, anxiety, anger, anguish, or death. In some of those worlds there are people whose bodies are made of light and who experience only health, joy, peace, and extraordinary creativity.

Using your many abilities to communicate and to be in more than one place at a time, you visit favorite realities, develop relationships with other beings and intelligences, and joyously join advanced beings to help create new versions of your original world, all by using the energy of the great love that flows through you.

As your evolution continues, you realize that the supreme ecstasy found in the *I Am* state is moving to the foreground and expressing itself in and through your being. You realize that love is an actual force; it moves through mind/space creating the waves of energy that are the foundation of all worlds. Love is the force that condenses particles from the endless field of energy that we live in, and love is what draws those particles together to create the basic patterns of form that seed the physical world. Love is holding everything together in our mind/space reality, and you *are* this love.

Love is the great mystery of life. Where does it comes from? Why does it exist? How does it knowingly create the universe? Why does it bring such joy and bliss? How did we come to so seriously misunderstand what love is? These are the great questions and love is truly the greatest mystery, as well as one of the great wonders of the world.

Unhappiness, illness, accidents, and hurt are mistakes in thinking based in fear. The fear is backed by the incredible power of the mind and creates destructive interference in the flow of energies through the body. Yet within the great love flowing through all things there are frequencies that completely cancel out fear, sickness, pain, and death.

With great sadness, you recognize that the whole seething mass of humanity living upon the earth has succumbed to arrested development and believes in their own mistaken, misdirected thought. You become acutely aware of how we create and sustain our troubles, pain, and death using the great power of thought. We do so without knowing what we are doing. We do not understand that disease, accidents, and death can be erased by recreating the original frequencies, that created and maintained us. You begin to understand that if we want the power to make life better, we must take full responsibility for what we are creating.

As the exploration of other realities continues, you discover the meaning of what it is to transcend time. Some of these realities are based on a different range of frequencies and because your physical body shares in the effects of whatever frequencies you are tuned into, the effect of time spent in some of them occasionally adds years to your body overnight. At other times the opposite effect occurs and the aging process is dramatically reversed, dropping years from your body in what appear to be unexplainable ways.

As you move through the stage of *abstract intelligence*, your inner quiet continues to deepen, your sensitivity increases, and the reason you came here is accomplished. The work you have come to do is fulfilled with grace and power. You evolve into an eternal being, a being of light.

As this is completed, you find yourself at a crossroads. You can begin to withdraw from the reality you have lived in so long and so intensely, or you can extend your stay, playing and working for an indefinite length of time. If you stay, you can practice using your creative abilities while enjoying the people you care for, and sometimes encouraging them to find their own path and purpose.

Continuing to deepen your inner peace and quiet, you spread a sense of peace and love wherever you go. You teach others that in the physical world of space and time, truth is 'what *is*,' but in the world of eternal mind the only thing that really *is,* is the ecstasy of love and the awareness in the *I Am* state. The rest of it is all relative, a changing illusion formed of temporary structures made possible by the power of mind and the action of intelligent energy moving through patterns of all sorts, whether human, plant, animal, or planet.

Finally, there comes the day when you feel your time here is drawing to a close and you are ready to leave. You may or may not have other lifetimes to complete in the future, but you know that eventually you will begin the long journey of letting go of everything but the Light and the pure awareness of the *I Am* state.

As you get ready to leave the people you have so long been entwined with, you may announce to important family and friends that you will be leaving soon. You may begin to give away or otherwise take care of your few physical belongings. You may wish to visit those with whom you have been close and maybe even engage in some small ceremonial good-byes.

As the stage of *abstract intelligence* is completed, you will celebrate the fact that you have made full use of the body/mind system to discover and realize the potential of the Self. You have long transcended the usual boundaries of the reality and will spend more and more time in fluid awareness until you feel totally translucent. Maintaining the joy and power of your individual consciousness, you prepare to take the first step out of human existence toward full immersion in your body of Light. This requires patient acceptance of the lingering details of physical reality as you continue your private work of inner quiet and final transformation.

When the time is right, you step out of the body with full awareness and joy. As you leave, you have the option of taking the body with you, or you can leave it to disintegrate. You have no need of the physical self any longer, but you may like the shape, color, appearance, and characteristics of this body and use it as a temporary pattern for your new body of light.

Retaining the most important lessons of life, you will continue learning as you journey on. The lessons learned have changed you at the core and taught you that love and awareness are the only eternal conditions. The rest is up to us and what we are interested in experiencing. The goal of human existence is to enjoy the gift of life and continue evolution while learning to use the great power of mind and love to create in ways that continue the system of *Life*.

If you are so drawn at the time of leaving you could choose to enter and more fully investigate realities that you discovered or visited while still in the body. Free of the limitations of the body and the demands of relationships with other humans, you can experience whole new realms of potential and a changing variety of intelligences.

If other realms and forms of existence do not interest you, or if you intend to come back to Earth in another time frame, you may enter one of the cities of light to rest, study, and prepare for your return. These are beautiful places that many humans go to between the cycles of physical lives.

If you are not planning to return to physical existence on Earth, you may enter and explore other planes of existence that offer completely different experiences. Eventually you will return to the highly evolved world of the light people and prepare to leave all form behind forever. To do this you will join your Higher Self and reach back toward the particle state, then the state of energy, until you finally relax into the light of pure awareness and the bliss of the Absolute... only to eventually begin again in some distant time and place. ಚ

25 ∞
Development Tragedies

Mary had a little lamb
whose fleece was white as snow,
and everywhere that Mary went
her consciousness would go.

Penny Kelly

WHAT HAPPENS IF YOU DO NOT SUCCESSFULLY DEVELOP AND INTEGRATE all of the potentials and lessons in the later stages of human development?

If you grow up with deep internal stress that begins in the *sensorimotor* stage…if you do not have rich storage banks of imagery and sound that come from *mental operations*…if there is little trust in yourself and the security of knowing how to navigate and survive the practical challenges of living that were learned in *concrete operations*…and if there has not been the encouragement to explore your individual path of interests and passion in *formal operations*, it is much more challenging to awaken kundalini, however, it is not impossible. Obstacles to full human development can be found in any of the stages, but so can successes.

However, let's look at what happens for far too many people. Let's pretend that you enter your teen years with a heavy burden of negativity, including a deep sense of shame or fear regarding sexual experience. Let's say that this blocks you from further development. Let us also pretend that you never get interested in anything that becomes a passion, that you don't know how to interact openly and freely, and that you never become interested in the deeper side of consciousness, thus meditation or contemplation is totally foreign to you. If all of this is the case, it is doubtful that you will ever experience the entry into *natural intelligence* or be able to overcome arrested development. If this is the case, you will remain immersed in the traditions and rules of the way you were raised and will not take up the exploration of your body, your mind, or your life. You will never become conscious of the fact that mind and its pure awareness do not really recognize separation, and you will spend most of your life defending your separateness instead of developing your wholeness and oneness with all that exists. You will remain a child in an adult body.

However, let us say that even with a background of incomplete and negative development in earlier stages, you fall deeply in love and *natural intelligence* is awakened either partially or fully. There are several possible outcomes.

If you have a partial awakening and do not have the support and skills flowing from the earlier stages of development, you may fail to recognize the significance of what has happened simply because you are not accustomed to paying attention to what is going on within you. You may also have a partial awakening in which you realize something unusual has occurred, but then try to ignore or deny the changes, and fail to understand or take advantage of the gift that has been handed to you.

If you have developed a lifestyle and relationships that are based on conformity or fundamentalism, and then have even a partial awakening, the extraordinary clarity and knowing that comes with this awakening can be interpreted as frightening, even hallucinatory phenomena. You could have flash pains and sickish sensations. There can be numerous, relentless, irritating, and unexplainable obstacles that you struggle valiantly to deny, overcome, or resist, but these obstacles are cues that something is not right and that you are off-track with your development. If you are drowning in confusion and the spiritual emergency that sometimes characterizes this stage of development, you will fail to use the new sources of information coming from within that are available to you in practical ways.

It is also possible that you have a full awakening and end up with a full-blown psycho-spiritual emergency. In the worst of outcomes, if there was never any successful completion of *sensorimotor, mental operations, concrete operations,* or *formal operations,* then there is no safety and security in the world, you cannot maintain a permanent picture of reality by drawing from your image, feeling, and sound banks, you have not tested the practical aspects of reality enough to develop a sense of inner authority, and abstract reasoning to assess outcomes is not possible.

In this case, the entry into *natural intelligence* with its visions, voices, unusual lights, buzzing sounds, and strange sensations can be so disruptive that you are no longer able to function in our reality. You are labeled a psychotic, sometimes schizophrenic, and put in a hospital.

Sometimes you will remain sane but may begin at a fairly early age to painfully self-destruct because you never grasp the significance of the connections between mind and body. Self-destruction will be accomplished through the consistent choice of things that are harmful to yourself and others, and by failing to listen to your inner wisdom guiding you in other directions. There will be the acceptance of institutions, habits, careers, marital partners, friends, foods, personal routines, and thought processes that lead to constant health problems, depressions, unsatisfactory relationships, failed businesses, and neglect of the self. You may not allow yourself to feel the great love within you, and will never consider the possibility that you have a reason for being here.

In some cases, your visions and voices may be recognized as the development of a sixth sense, but without the development of wisdom and personal responsibility, you are only interested in displaying what you can do to impress others. Labeled as something out of the 'spirit world,' your intuitive gifts are dramatized or glorified and used to control others while bringing attention to yourself. These gifts and abilities are never recognized as parts of your more highly developed Self and you don't see that they are the means by which you can choose health, peace, love, success, and understanding regarding your purpose in life. Completely unaware of how and why you know hidden things, your intuition remains a novelty used to manipulate others.

More commonly, if the entry into *natural intelligence* comes when you are no longer young, you have heavy commitments, and are caught in complex routines and ruts involving spouses, children, and debts, you will be much less flexible and it may feel like life is falling apart. Often your current situation becomes the excuse for not making any changes and your life is characterized by constant inner conflict. If you are used to living with deep stress as your usual state, the challenges of an awakening are just more of the same and you may feel that life just gets more and more difficult, always bringing more stress.

In any of these situations, there may be an ever-present denial that you are feeling any pain, unhappiness, frustration, sorrow, or pressure to do anything differently. Over the years, the effort to repress and *not* feel these feelings and fears will lead to a lasting fatigue. The slow death of your dreams will result in bitterness, or a penetrating loneliness.

Without the successful completion of the very earliest stage, the *sensorimotor* stage, it is very difficult for you to explore and integrate yourself into the landscape of the entirely new reality presented by the full awakening of consciousness. Without successful *mental operations,* you have never learned to stabilize your reality. Without *concrete operations*, you have never been free to explore and experiment to see what works for you. And without *formal operations* you have never been able to compare your inner reality with outer reality.

Now, without *natural intelligence* you are unable to handle the initial expansion of consciousness that is necessary for you to reach for your full potential. In the end, the reality consumes you rather that renews you. Life becomes an existence to which you have not contributed from the depths of your heart; an existence in which you cannot or will not allow the expression of your inner self. You find life repetitive, boring, and have a constant need to be entertained. You are not really comfortable with yourself. You are a tragedy in the making, your development stalled at an even deeper level than before making life difficult as you enter next stage, that of *creative intelligence*.

 timer

As you age and life hardens into a routine, it becomes more difficult to move into the sixth stage of development, however, the unfolding often continues in a lopsided way. You may manage to move into the stage of *creative intelligence* if there has been even a very partial awakening earlier, but your use of consciousness and its power may be misused, often to your own detriment.

Creative intelligence calls for deep changes in both the self and your understanding of reality systems. You may have great difficulty managing the loss of boundaries that occur in this advanced stage without the stability offered in the successful conclusion of earlier stages.

At this stage, shortcomings and failures in the earlier stages become even more difficult to overlook and you will, as a matter of habit, overstep other's rights and boundaries, or allow them to run your life. Most often, you will not take responsibility for creating the life you want to live, and your explorations of how to use power will remain a continuous, effort-filled challenge that are mechanical and lack good timing. You never discover that efforts to change others require that you change yourself.

When peers challenge you to grow, you become angry and defensive and may try to manipulate them to maintain the illusion that nothing can challenge or change you or your position. You resist aging, and insist that you are not getting old and are still powerful. This illusion that nothing is changing, as well as the fears generated by such rigidity, gets in the way of your ability to address your ongoing evolution and development. Worse, when you do not tap the great well of love within yourself, it all seems somehow incomplete, boring, not enough.

When you are pressured more deeply to change by family and those close to you, you resist, make excuses, refuse to cooperate or adopt any humility, and ignore the disappointing outcomes in too many areas of your life. When things turn out badly as a result of your resistance, you try to cover your butt by making last-minute, radical interventions that create chaos and distract from what is going on under the surface. If someone sees through your ruse, you blame others, or ignore the reactions and re-percussions going on around you.

When there is a partial entry into *creative intelligence*, your efforts may go toward changing other people instead of yourself. If you have achieved some level of power, material success, and control in the world, this stage may cause you to get so caught up in the excitement and power of being able to impose your will that you fail to think about the true use-fulness of what you are creating. You do not examine the long-term results of your 'great idea' and ignore the outcomes that others will be forced to deal with if they get your way. You also ignore the feelings that you are creating and generally fail to assess a broad spectrum of future results.

Sometimes your attempts to create the life you want will proceed smoothly, but only outer appearances are attended to. You only want to look good. You may become rich and famous but seldom consider the good that you could create for others in the world. Using your intuition and imaging abilities you make cool, detached decisions that employ ev-erything from physical force to manipulation in seizing opportunities that will help establish a reality that directs power to yourself.

Sometimes this can be carried on for quite a time. You may even be good at what you do, or successful and influential in the world in which you move about, but it is all a game based on fear or anger, guilt or self-ishness, anger or a desire for control. The possible consequences of losing may drive you to do things you are not proud of or would not otherwise consider doing. Eventually, like all structures based on fear, anger, selfish-ness, or guilt, the reality will come crashing down destructively. A reality that simply grabs for power is not naturally self-sustaining.

If the lessons in the previous stage of *natural intelligence* have been only partially integrated, you may reach a pinnacle of success only to fall into the grip of a life-threatening illness. You discover too late that you failed to listen to the guidance of your inner voice or to pay attention to the little visions and sensations that indicated the need for correction or healing in your physical body.

Or, you may reach the peak of success and find that you don't really have a clear idea of what to do with the power now in your lap. You just wanted to get there and enjoy the position and prestige.

If you belatedly try to develop policies and structures that you hope will be acceptable, you find yourself running into power struggles and manipulation by others on an overwhelming scale.

You did not bother to take the time and trouble to find and enable others who shared your purpose and vision, thus you cannot build a sense of oneness and teamwork among those in the situation with you. You are unable to bring about any good or lasting effects because your team members have hidden agendas of their own.

The result is that you cannot trust them to help implement your last-minute plans, which are really just an attempt to make yourself look good and hang onto power. Unable to put into effect the changes you want, you discover that all you can do is hang on while those around you try to manipulate you out of the position. Even if you manage to hang on to your position and power, you find yourself entirely alone. Too late, you discover that the last-minute changes you are trying to create are merely a short-sighted effort to keep yourself in a position of control. Sometimes even the members of your own family seem like frightening, irritating strangers ready to upset or destroy your self-created bubble of illusion.

For you, reality remains something outside the self, a wild card that always gets in the way of life as you visualize it. For you there is no inner quiet, no synthesis of self, life, and purpose, and thus you remain in a state of potential that has been artificially expressed and is slowly disintegrating both inside and out.

cs

If you enter *abstract intelligence* in this condition, you find that the work you are doing is overwhelming, seems endless, and leaves you worn out, fatigued, and depressed.

Without the deepening inner quiet, you end up over-sensitive to what is happening around you and generally irritated by the world. You are frightened by the world's need for constant change, its seeming violence, and the desperate selfishness of people. You are getting tired, old, and feeble, and instead of perfecting peace and quiet *within*, you are crabby and insist on having peace and quiet *around* you.

Instead of employing the great power and wisdom that has been so long in the making, you see power everywhere around you but tell yourself you are powerless and outdated. Frustrated because you never allowed yourself to do what you loved or to give your particular gift to the world and feeling you are running out of time, you begin to withdraw from active participation in the world. As you do, the routine of your daily life becomes less and less attractive. Tired and discouraged, you want to forget the whole existence and, becoming less and less active, gradually you do.

First, you stop learning anything new and constantly resort to old information and things that worked in the past. Next, creativity withers. Then you begin to forget what you have already learned. Slowly you become uncertain about whether and how to respond to the people and events around you; finally, you are confused about where you are. Unable to move forward clearly, you get tangled in the unfocused operation of a brain that can no longer generate helpful, timely, and intelligent images, sounds, feelings, or actions.

At this point, you stop taking care of yourself. Succumbing to growing disability, sickness, uselessness, and approaching death, you spend less and less time focused in the immediate reality around you. The less time you spend in the world of your body, the less you take care of it and the worse its condition becomes.

Giving up in despair, you abandon the body in longer and longer bouts of senility. When you return your attention to it occasionally, you are frustrated and embarrassed by its slowly disintegrating condition. Instead of entering the luminous awareness of inner quiet, you settle for mindlessness and increasing helplessness. You will wait in fear and silence for death to appear and will wonder why you put out so much effort earlier in life if it was all to come to this wasteful end.

Since you have not developed your inner quiet, you has no opportunity to consciously and deliberately enter fluid states of awareness to explore the inner experience of people, plants, animals, and the things around you. Instead you are stuck in the disintegrating body and seek to escape from having to deal with everything. Thus, you are not able to enjoy the great power of *abstract intelligence.*

In your eleventh hour, tragically, you never discover your power to know or become one with anything, nor do you discover the true reality of living without sorrow, sickness, or painful death. You cannot explore other realities, and if you should drift into them, they frighten you. You do not experience either the shock or the delight of transcending time; rather you get lost in time and often end up reliving the past. And you do not discover your own powers of transformation, which allow you to step out of the body whenever you are ready.

Often, it is easier to develop some serious disease or dysfunction and this becomes your excuse for leaving. You do not want to stay because your body/mind system has degenerated into uselessness, and yet you do not want to go because something in you knows that you didn't accomplish what you came here to do, which was to give your gift and to evolve the self.

"But," you tell yourself, "it's not that I'm choosing to leave family and friends, the disease is what makes me go."

Instead of the conscious intention of preparing to leave, you wait to be forced out. Instead of a pleasant farewell ritual and gathering in a place of enjoyment, your farewell ritual takes place around a hospital bed where tubes, machines, and needles carry out the act of pretending you want to stay. Instead of discovering the inner experience of a machine, the machine mimics the experience of your life and its processes. Finally, the body shuts down, death arrives, your life is over. ०३

26 ‹ঙ
The Trials

"The world we see that seems so insane
may be the result of
not understanding the nature of reality."

Penny Kelly

WHEN MY EXISTENCE IN MULTIPLE TIME FRAMES CAME TO AN END AND I had written out what I learned, life was suddenly quiet. I felt a bit disoriented. The simple, single, ordinary reality that once seemed so reassuring was momentarily pale and unreal by comparison.

Even more disorienting, the powerful death experiences in them had changed something deep within me. Death was no longer something that seemed vague and far away. It was excruciatingly real, it was right there in front of me, it was circling all around me, in me, watching, waiting, smiling. With one eye now on the face of death, I tried to relax and enjoy my new insights, integrating the fine points and waiting for the next set of questions to send me exploring new depths of awareness. Instead, I found myself deeply divided, pensive, and caught in some dark place.

Overwhelmed by all that I had experienced over the past eleven years, I began to spend a considerable amount of time and energy trying to get back to being some kind of 'ordinary woman.'

Although I didn't yet recognize what was going on inside myself, I was embarking on a long period in which my mind would work feverishly to integrate everything I had experienced. The pieces were all there, I understood each one in detail, and I was fairly comfortable with them. I just didn't know what to do with any of the things I now knew. The kundalini experiences themselves, the travels out of the body, the efforts my mind made to present me with information, the long, powerful tutoring of the little men in brown robes...these were still just pieces. What was I supposed to do with the fact that sex was an electromagnetic event in the body, or my ability to track an individual through many lifetimes? And the understanding that we are all meant to evolve gradually over our lifetime into an advanced state of consciousness, often called Christ-consciousness, was only one of the big issues, and there were dozens of smaller and related issues.

Tangled in the processes of integration, I constantly overhauled my view of the world and reality, attempting to make all the things I had experienced fit together congruently.

This overhaul process was made infinitely more difficult by the fact that I was a product of my own time. I was born and grew up in an atmosphere in which everyone had succumbed to the belief that only science was real and only things that were scientifically proven could claim to exist and be valid. If it couldn't be empirically observed, controlled, and duplicated, it either didn't exist or didn't matter. Anything subjective was scientifically invalid.

The result of accepting this set of scientific beliefs about reality was that my entire Self as Experiencer was, at best, a terribly flawed participant and a questionable source of perception in an unreliable, unsubstantiated reality. At worst, I was reduced to nothingness, a slightly crazy observer whose experiences were meaningless. This set of beliefs was why I once thought I was going insane when I observed things others didn't see, hear, or feel. When my perception began to move through time and space in an uncontrollable manner, when I could neither duplicate the exact phenomena on demand, or explain the reason for this inability, I was certain all was lost and I had gone off the deep end. It hadn't occurred to me that my conclusions of coming insanity were based in my own scientific belief set and that the belief set was seriously inadequate or incomplete.

The result was that I tried to keep my psychic abilities well to the background and out of sight. As an educational consultant specializing in Accelerated and Brain-Compatible Teaching, I could talk freely about the brain, the mind, cycles of consciousness, frequencies of operation, and things of that sort. But outside of a small circle of family and friends, I was excruciatingly uncomfortable talking about experiences that involved past lives, time between lives, clairvoyance, or any of the other skills I had at my disposal. Only within my immediate family and a small group of students did I feel I could use some of my abilities. Yet even within this small circle there were clear limits to what I could share and discuss.

For months, with the constant activity of overhaul going on inside me, I found myself anxiously wanting to return to the mindset that would allow me to be an ordinary woman. In conflict with this desire was the fact that I hated to hide my psychic abilities, to pretend I didn't know things, to stall around the issues of my own life's work, or short circuit the truth. As time went on it became more and more difficult to return to this ordinary woman status.

I had just decided that I needed to address what I came here to do, which was simply to write, to teach people about the mind, to teach them how to heal themselves and how to develop themselves, when I found myself embroiled in what I eventually came to call a 'trial.' The trial was a physical, mental, emotional, and spiritual experience of extraordinary proportions that lasted for weeks.

Similar to my experience of living in multiple time frames, it began early one afternoon when I heard an alarm clock going off and observed myself getting out of bed somewhere, deciding what to wear and how to fix my hair, then getting in a car and going off to a courtroom.

Once there, lawyers, people, and paperwork consumed my time and energy. Several hours later after testimony and argument, court was adjourned for the day and I watched myself return home. Over the ensuing weeks, the trial proceeded through a series of witnesses and testimony, pro and con, until finally a verdict was reached and I was acquitted of charges surrounding the issue of abortion and allowed to continue teaching women how to practice a new kind of birth control using plants from nature.

I was relieved when it was over, but this trial was only the first in a long string of trials. Several months later I found myself involved in a new trial centered on charges of practicing medicine without a license. This second trial went on for several months and it had barely ended when a third trial began based on charges stemming from some kind of peace activities or demonstrations that I was accused of organizing. This trial seemed to drag on endlessly and when it was over, I was again greatly relieved.

In the spring of 1992, a fourth trial began based on possession of a controlled substance, which turned out to be an herb that had been declared illegal by the federal government so that the herb could be produced exclusively by a drug company. This turned out to be a very interesting trial, but in the fall it was followed by a fifth trial based on charges of slander and defamation brought by a large corporation. This one was long and nasty. A sixth trial the following year centered on helping people to die, was over quickly, but it was followed by a seventh based on charges of unpaid taxes and an argument over land.

Sometimes these court trials were merely irritating, sometimes the proceedings were quite interesting, but mostly they were long and grueling and I tried to just shut them off, to say 'no' and not participate. However, the moment I would drop my guard and start to relax, there it would be again, proceeding steadily, distracting me, interrupting my awareness with its activity, sometimes claiming my full attention. It was difficult to not show up for something that was going on inside of me, and thus I found myself frequently a hostage of my own mind until the trial was over.

cs

It was now 1994 and I had been wrestling with my mind, my consciousness and my perception for fully fourteen years when I unexpectedly came down with arthritis. It started in the ring finger of my right hand, and although I noticed it, I thought nothing of it and it soon went away.

A few months later it flared in my right elbow, and by autumn it was everywhere in my body – shoulders, hips, knees, fingers, toes, spine. My right arm was in a sling and at times I limped so badly I needed a cane or walking stick to help steady and support myself. I felt that my condition was partly the result of the stress I had been under for so many years, and I was convinced that if I could just get back to some kind of ordinary life, everything would get better.

Out of energy and wanting to stop both my educational consulting and my small classes in intuition, I struggled furiously with myself over the desire for a life in which I could just go back to being something I had long since forgotten how to be.

I wanted to enjoy my family, to stop taking care of people who were struggling to find themselves and their path, and to live without feeling the pressure of the world's fear, or its anguish and pain. I wanted to be able to run to town and pick up lettuce or ice cream without having to change my shoes or do my hair. I wanted to talk in the plain ways that expressed my farm-oriented roots, and to live in ways that I felt were sensible and healthy.

I wanted a reasonable schedule and I wanted the time to heal my arthritis. I wanted peace, privacy and quiet. But most of all, I wanted to go back to being an ordinary woman, one who worried about the house payment instead of what was going on in my mind or the world.

When a new trial began in early 1995, stemming from charges by the government that I was teaching insurrection, I felt that my entire reality was coming unglued. I complained frequently to both my husband and my daughters about wanting to be just an ordinary woman, so they knew I was struggling with this, but no one knew about the trials. Although I had once mentioned them briefly to Stan, another educational consultant, and even started to write about them, I eventually dropped the subject for fear that I would sound like some kind of female Walter Mitty, wrapped in one dramatic projection after another.

Now, at a time that I felt I could least afford the mental and emotional energy because I was busy detoxifying my body in order to heal the arthritis, I was back in that elusive courtroom. By the end of February I had all but collapsed from exhaustion and by the beginning of March, I had withdrawn from everything and everyone, spending day after day resting, alone in my bedroom.

My husband took me to Hot Springs, Arkansas, over Easter for a change of scene and several days of relaxing mineral baths and massage. But at the hotel I found myself constantly drawn in to another time frame. Now, besides my ordinary, everyday consciousness and that of the government trial for insurrection, I repeatedly found myself in the 1920's with Al Capone and a group of his buddies. They had gone to Hot Springs for a little vacation and I was pulled into the struggle between Capone and the woman he had taken along for company. She was an Italian girl from the Chicago area whose real name seemed to be Maria although she had renamed herself once or twice, trying to make herself appear more sophisticated and worldly. She had been Capone's girlfriend for some time but now he was beginning to tire of her. This prompted her to try to make him jealous, so she made love to one of his buddies while they were in Hot Springs. The result was that Capone dumped her, taking the train back to Chicago without her, leaving her stranded and without money. For a time, she stayed in Hot Springs, working as a prostitute to make money and contemplating suicide. Eventually she went back to Chicago and tried to rebuild her life but her family never accepted her back and she had become a drifter.

When I mentioned to my husband that I was having a hard time staying in the present and that I kept finding myself back in the 1920's with Al Capone, his gang, and their women, he startled me by saying that down the hall from our room and around a strangely angled corner was a door with a small brass plate on it engraved with the name *Al Capone*.

I thought he was joking, but when I left our room to go and look, there was the brass plate and Capone's name on it. Upon inquiring at the front desk, I was told that Capone had liked Hot Springs, that he always stayed in that particular suite, and that he frequently brought friends and cronies, usually renting the surrounding rooms to accommodate them. For the entire length of my stay in Hot Springs, I was seeing everything through Maria's eyes and feeling what she experienced. When I wasn't in the 1920's, I was at my own trial in a time and place that I did not recognize. I came home not much more rested or restored than when I left.

The trial finally ended in late April and in the weeks that followed I began to relax a little although I still refused to see or talk to anyone outside my immediate family.

Summer arrived and the difficulties associated with detoxifying my body in order to rebuild my inflamed and deteriorating joints began to ease. I also began to realize that if I was going to heal I had to rethink my entire life from what I ate to what I did for a living. Slowly I began to make serious changes and to address what I had come here to do.

By late summer, I had no more signs of arthritis and as the summer slid into fall and then an early winter, there were no new trials although I found myself anxiously expecting one to begin any moment. Over the winter, I continued the healing routines I had taken on, and as spring arrived, I began to think tentatively of things like teaching, writing, consulting, and gardening again.

Then one warm spring night, in what had become a rare moment of meditation, a familiar voice echoed through me. It was Edgar with his southern drawl, telling me that the trials that had been going on in my 'parallel life' were over and it was time for me to get on with my work here.

I was delighted by his visit, yet so shocked by his reference to a parallel life that I did not respond right away. I had heard the term long before, and even had brief moments more than a decade earlier when I experienced myself as a sick old man somewhere in China with a young, antagonistic wife. When I experienced the death of the old man, the experiences stopped and I hadn't given them further thought. In comparing the two, my experience of being the old Chinese man was pale alongside the trial experiences, which had been much more intense, more constant, more congruent, and had the quality of a lucid dream in which you knew you were dreaming but it was still quite real.

Edgar interrupted my thoughts to ask, "Do you think you are ready to get on with your work here? You know… in order to do this work you'll have to become an ordinary woman."

Momentarily, I was surprised, then exasperated. "I don't know, Edgar, I've tried to go back to that over and over…my mind doesn't seem to get the idea. And what do I do with all that I've learned?" I asked.

"You're trying to go back to being an *undeveloped* woman," he said, "move ahead to become an *ordinary* woman."

In a flash, it dawned on me that I *was* just an ordinary woman, that what I had become through my experience with kundalini was exactly what an ordinary woman was meant to become. For the first time in eons I remembered that awakening kundalini was not just a curse, a challenge, or a destiny, it was simply part of our inherent design.

We were meant to go from the limited perception and action we thought of as normal, to the developed perception and activity that allowed us to see, hear, travel, and act globally. We were meant to develop a whole new view of the workings of reality. In doing so, we would move comfortably from the experience of our reality as a place where things were limited to happening right now, at *this* moment and in *this* place, to an experience of reality that was unconfined in time and space.

We were meant to continue developing the body/mind until we understood that we were part of, and in communication with, everything that existed. If anything was happening at all, it was happening everywhere, including in us. If we performed some thought or action, its effect was felt everywhere, even across the universe.

Ours was a reality in which we were designed to evolve. We were not limited to the immediate environment for our entire life, or to action and perception only at this moment and in this place.

My abilities to see forward and backward in time continued to expand and refine themselves. There had been a mushrooming of my ability to communicate with other forms of energy regardless of whether they were people, animals, trees, plants, insects, elves, devas, the wind, the rain, the deceased, or the unborn. [8]

Why had we not developed our gifts of perception to the point of being able to perceive events happening elsewhere, to see across the entire spectrum of time, travel out of the body, or shift the frequency of

---

8 See *The Elves of Lily Hill Farm* for an account of my discovery of a group of elves living on our farm and their attempts to teach us to manage our vineyards and our lives much differently.

our physical system back into perfect health? The ability to see ahead into the future, to enjoy the continued relationship and communication of those who die and leave their bodies behind, to share knowledge and insight with plants and animals…all were such practical, important abilities. They were not the edge of insanity or the sign of the devil, they were the ordinary skills and abilities of an evolved human, and I was just an ordinary woman who had continued to evolve normally!

☙

Soon, important realizations began to click into place. The process that started while I was living in my two possible futures and then continued through the trials had gone on for five years.

From 1991 to 1995, I went through eight trials, each lasting anywhere from a couple of weeks to six months. As each trial came and went, I was acquitted because there were few arguments that would withstand my growing ability to explain the rules and workings of perception and consciousness. Like a master teacher, I had been able to get judges, prosecutors, and juries to listen to common sense and stretch the parameters of reality. I also transformed them in the process.

After each trial, I reached a new and deeper level of inner quiet. My sensitivity, verbal skills, and understanding would deepen. I would then think and act in alignment with what I learned. And each time I did so, I was hauled back into court for a new trial accusing me of breaking some other rule in society.

The trials forced me to think clearly about what I stood for. They brought a measure of experience and perspective that I could never have come by in the process of ordinary living. I continuously came to crisis, disintegrated, and quickly reformed my stance, which resulted in a depth and wisdom that went beyond my years.

As I went through each of these trials, I clarified the premise of inner authority, a concept I had learned from the little men in brown robes. The sad fact was that most humans had lost all sense of inner authority. They were free to decide how many credits they could handle in their college courses, which gas to put in their four-wheel drive cars, which low-fat foods to buy, or whether they would submit to chemotherapy or try to find an alternative.

But the real issues of true personal consequence, like whether or not they wanted to pay taxes, work, have an abortion, build homes wherever they wanted, clean up the water systems of their locale, change the government, or similar issues were off the table. In effect, those issues had been moved to the background because everyone was too busy making the money they needed to survive. We needed money to buy the basics of food and water, clothing, shelter, heat, electricity, and transportation.

All of the things that were given to us for free – land, air, food, and water – had been taken over by government. And all of the means of getting what we needed – clothing, shelter, heat, electricity and transportation – had been taken over by corporations. We were not encouraged to follow our passion or to work for ourselves any more. Businesses owned everything except the air we breathed. The same thing that had been done to American Indians had been done to us; we just hadn't realized it yet. We were left without any authority – either inner or outer. We no longer had the capacity to be self-sufficient and self-sustaining. Nor did we have any real power, which is simply the ability to *decide* and *do*. We ended up waiting for someone – anyone – to tell us it was okay to do anything!

Other things also became clear. The most obvious was that Mother Nature does not waste time and energy trying to make exact duplicates, only humans do. Neither does She need or offer proof that She or her perceptual phenomena exist; she simply *is* and you ignore her at your own risk. The two most basic rules of nature are diversity and change, and we were running against the development of our own nature by repeating things…the same things, day after day, the same schedules, the same ideas, the same habits, the same products, the same arguments, the same limiting beliefs.

In many ways, I was quite fortunate. My personal experience of reality was *not* just more of the same. The trials, and in fact all of my experiences in multiple times and other places, had come about because reality was truly a multi-dimensional affair, and normal human life was just a tiny slice of that reality.

We come here, get caught in relationships, jobs, and dramas, letting these things dominate our mind. We have brief tastes of multi- dimensionality in our dreams. We run into other capacities of consciousness when we use our imagination or experience psychic moments of precognition, synchronicity, or coincidence. However, we seldom deliberately develop our abilities! We almost never enter other dimensions and explore what is there. Instead we remain hypnotized by our immediate surroundings and spend all our time focused here, then ignorantly claim 'that's all there is.'

Another fact I suddenly grasped was that the human brain-mind was far more powerful and versatile than we ever suspected. I knew from my own experience that some inner place in the human being was entirely capable of producing events and experiences that were meant to help, to strengthen, to teach, heal, and balance life. Reality was far more complex than the thin trail of events we usually paid attention to and the trials were a perfect example of this.

As a result of my kundalini experiences, there had been an explosion of new perceptual abilities and a serious remaking of my views of reality. What once made sense in the world began to change drastically, and I found myself at serious odds with current thinking and the cultural milieu. Not knowing how to resolve this difficulty, I had attempted to go back to seeing the world the way I used to see it. I wanted to return to being like everyone else, to those things that I once thought constituted seeing and thinking as an ordinary woman.

But my mind had a mind of its own. Using its tremendous abilities to create, sustain, and attend to multiple layers of reality, it carried me into many realities, including that of 'the trials.' The trials were a result of my inner disputes with current, ordinary thinking. The trials were a part of my efforts to integrate my new way of seeing the world, and to settle the differences between my new perspective and the commonly held attitudes and ideas of other people. They were a test of my thinking, a way of clarifying and affirming that thinking. They were a way of strengthening my position, of bringing me greatly expanded experience. They were a way of anchoring my abilities until understanding and confidence grew into wisdom. And they were also the natural result of the fact that mind is the basis of everything and either has, or creates, what is needed for ongoing human development.

I realized that other people had this mechanism operating for them as well when they experienced vague daydreams, or got caught in worrying and asking, "What if…?" The only difference between my trials and the disturbing scenarios that flitted through their minds was the greatly expanded power of concentration and the ability to perceive over a wider band of frequency ranges that came as a result of kundalini.

One day I received a letter from a woman who lived in Fairfield, Iowa. She was a student of Maharishi Mahesh Yogi. She was reading an early version of *The Evolving Human* and my struggle to deal with kundalini. When Maharishi mentioned that kundalini was a dangerous development in anyone's life and that you needed a guru or a teacher to navigate the experience successfully, she showed him the book and told him that I was dealing with it on my own. His response was, "Only a Master makes it through kundalini alone. She was already a Master."

I found this thought very comforting. I *had* made it...and I made the journey alone. I thought back to the beginnings of kundalini and the fear that I was going off the deep end. It was now clear to me that my fears about the deep end had been right on target, except that insanity was not the result. Instead I found myself swimming among currents of consciousness and awareness that were far deeper, more powerful and convoluted than anything I had ever known. I came to understand how shallow and trivial my life had once been.

Before kundalini, I lived like a water spider, skimming over the surface, darting this way and that, wary, avoiding dangers, threats, or anything that got in my way, never looking below the surface, never examining the medium upon which I moved.

Now I was not only the water spider, I was also the water – both its surface and its depth. I was the bird that threatened to sweep down and pluck the water spider out of existence, I was the tall grass at the edge of the water, the breath of air that changed the nature of the water from liquid to ice, thus changing the seasons and the demands upon her. I was the cycle and motion of all these things...spider, water, bird, grass, air, movement that flowed this way and that, quiet now, active moments later, with thoughts, reasons, and habits unique to my being. ∞

27 ❧
Stillness

AS I WRITE THESE WORDS IT IS AN ORDINARY DAY EIGHTEEN YEARS after the first awakening of kundalini. The entire experience has rumbled to life from time to time over the past three and a half decades and I have been dealing with an awakened consciousness for longer than I was in the earlier, unawakened state. I no longer wrestle with the experience and the changes it has brought. I am grateful for them and for the understanding of reality systems that the changes have brought me.

I no longer ask myself why I had to understand what happened to me. It is the nature of each individual to come to grips with personal experience. The early drama of the kundalini experiences has faded, but the changes in my perception and experience of reality have been ongoing. I no longer have disturbing breaks in my stream of consciousness in which I constantly and unexpectedly see or hear myself or someone else in another time and place. Yet it is not that I have lost the ability to be clairvoyant, clairaudient, clairsentient, to be in two places at once, to be in one place at two different times, or many of the other gifts of perception that development of the body/mind system brings. It is just that the threads of these awarenesses are now neatly interwoven throughout my everyday life, forming a fabric of consciousness that is richly embroidered, many faceted and fascinating, not to mention useful.

Most of us have absolutely no idea of the scope of the reality we live in, or of the experiences and possibilities of the later stages of human development. Probably more than a few people will find these later stages difficult to grasp. Even so, a number of people suffering their way through a full awakening have made their way to my door and it has been gratifying to guide them through the process, offer explanations and insights, and hear the sudden intake of breath as they get it and murmur, "Ohhh! That's what's going on...!" Watching them flower is like a gift!

In my work, I have met many other people who have experienced an amazing array of the perceptions available in the more developed stages of human life and were at first frightened or disturbed, and who then became interested in a more well-rounded development.

The problem for most people is that they do not know that anyone else has had similar experiences. This isolation of perception along with ignorance of how or why certain perceptions occur leaves them at a standstill in terms of where to go with the whole development idea. It is possible to correct the flaws of earlier stages, and get around the obstacles of the stage they are in, but it takes some work and some time. Once they develop some confidence and a bit of understanding, once a more complete picture of the body/mind system and the nature of reality sinks in, they have a framework into which they can fit all of their experiences, their awarenesses, their perceptions, and their potential for further development.

૪

Since the time of my own awakening of kundalini, I have learned many things. It is clear to me that the reason 'psychic' phenomena occur is because everything in our physical reality is communicating at all times. Everything is alive. Everything communicates!

Mind is the awareness property of space, and space is the location aspect of mind. You are a location in space. Mind and space are two sides of one coin, and this is the Source of all things. You and I are made of compressed mind/space!

Because of the extraordinary property of awareness that exists within mind/space, anything happening is communicated or known everywhere at once, and thus it is possible to be 'psychic' simply by tuning in to things that are happening in times and places other than what is right in front of your nose. The reason we don't tune in to these other times and places is because we are generally more interested in what is happening right where we are.

We are all meant to develop through successive stages that unfold our perception and our abilities, lifting us into the realm where love, health, joy, peace, and creative self-expression are our constant daily experience.

The entire body/mind system runs on electricity born from the waves of electromagnetic frequency fields that swirl through the universe. These fields fill our world with an abundance of realms and dimensions of life. The body, as one of those fields, is truly a work of art in terms of the patterns of light that maintain and move through it. The brain, that magnificent organ that runs the body, is the interface between the physical you that exists in the middle of your personal E-M field, and the thousands of other E-M fields you encounter in the course of an ordinary day.

Your eyes pick up light waves and interpret them. The ears pick up sound waves and do the same. Over all, your body/mind system is picking up subtle signals from waves carrying over two dozen kinds of information at any moment in time, and is capable of picking up and interpreting much more than it currently does, much more than we typically allow. But many of us have stopped developing and are going in circles. We don't know ourselves at all.

As with everything, you can get into perceptual ruts, and if development is arrested, end up stuck in them. When development is re-ignited, it often feels like you have been 'awakened' from a long sleep.

When I hear people talk about the new age or the shift of the ages, I know that whether or not the planet rolls over, stops spinning, is bombarded by asteroids, or plagued by earthquakes, there *is* a coming change in consciousness, and that alone is enough to cause serious upheaval in anyone's life. Planetary changes of a physical nature would certainly complicate things, but a re-awakening of the processes of human development is a whole lot to deal with in the first place.

As you awaken, you may realize at first that you don't feel very good. Health comes when you begin to ask, "Why? What can I do to correct this? What do I need to know and do?" Then, as you work to re-establish good health, your whole life comes under serious review. Literally, you are re-creating yourself.

Joy comes when you wake up and realize you're not very happy. Again you end up asking, "Why? What is happiness? Who has been defining this for me all these years?" As you work to establish joy, you end up face-to-face with all the fears of what others will think, what judgments or decisions they might make about you. Finally, you come to understand that what you think of yourself really matters...since it is you that has to live your life, not someone else.

Peace comes when you wake up and realize you're tired of conflict, chaos, or the confusion of trying to please everyone, to make them happy, usually so they will leave you alone long enough to do what you think will make you happy! You begin asking, "What am I doing here in this place, in this time? Why don't I take responsibility for myself and let others take responsibility for themselves?"

With each little awakening, the heart opens a bit further. You come to the point when you're seriously, irreversibly awake, and discover, perhaps, that you really do not like the work you are doing. You realize you have never been able to do or be what you always wanted to do or be because you felt you had to make a good living. When kundalini – which *is* consciousness – awakens, you simply must live your truth because to do otherwise creates total havoc in consciousness. Suddenly, you have to do what has meaning to you. You must follow your heart. You simply cannot continue to do what you've been doing for the reasons you've been doing it. You must pursue your passion because that is what you came here to do.

As the heart opens further, creative self-expression flowers and comes into full maturity. Your heart pushes you to do what makes sense to you rather than what makes sense to others in the world around you. This can create chaos in your life for a while; your life may come apart for a while as you re-build and re-structure your skills, your time, and your energy. But if you pursue your truth, you will be utterly glad you did.

Eventually, as human development picks up where it left off, your habits of consciousness shift. The people and things you pay attention to begin to diverge from what you used to attend to. Slowly you move to a whole new level of common sense that encompasses not just the practical aspects of your daily routine, but the balance of life involving others, your relationships, and the whole earth of people, plants, and animals.

Along the way you find that true spiritual development is not just some lofty, detached state of mind. It affects your practical, everyday life in the most profound of ways. The way you breathe, the way you eat, your sex life, the work you do, how you shop, how you talk to yourself and others, what you think about, what you notice in the world around you, what's important to you, how you take care of yourself, and many other aspects – all change.

Quite a few people who look back on the changes they went through in the throes of spiritual development will say something like,

"Phew! That was a lot of work." Or maybe, "Wow, how did I get through all that?"

When asked if they wish it had never happened, to a person they reply, "No way! I would never want to go back to the way I used to be."

When questioned further, the 'way they used to be' is often described as a time when they lived in anxiety, or vague, general unhappiness. Some refer to this as their private 'dark ages' or 'those gut-grinding days when I couldn't be who I really was.' Some talk about the days 'when everything was so uncertain and it seemed like I never knew why things happened the way they did or what was coming next.' Others talk about 'those old days when there was no peace of mind, no joy, and I never really saw what was happening around me, and never felt very good.' They look out on the widespread misery of thousands of people across the world and feel a sadness that so many are suffering, still.

We are *all* meant – via kundalini or otherwise – to evolve into our full potential. Most people have an intermittent and sometimes over-whelming desire for some kind of spiritual experience, some awareness or knowledge that provides an answer to what life is all about. We all want something that will quench the deep, unspoken longing for peace and satisfaction, for meaning and understanding, or joy and contentment. This is the quest, the grail, the search for something that lies hidden until kundalini triggers the unfolding of the whole self. It is the Spirit of our Whole Self, formerly unrecognized and unacknowledged, that is released and activated, and which then moves us toward our full potential. True spirituality is the development of the true spirit of your unique self.

Sometimes when I look back, I ask myself, "If I could go from absolutely no intuition to a reality-shattering array of psychic gifts that I did not even know existed, and if this could happen almost overnight, then are there any limits to personal evolution and self-development if we work at it in an ongoing, purposeful way?"

I don't think so, and thus I am forever playing with, studying, researching, and experimenting with consciousness and its possibilities in, out of, and for the body/mind system. I have a desire to 'work on myself' in ways that will facilitate an even further development of the gifts I now have. Adding to the excitement of this is the fact that my entire experience of reality is based on a clear sense that I am co-creating my reality from day to day, rather than falling into the helpless, hapless response patterns that many people make once they get into this world.

Still, after all this time, I feel I am only just beginning to appreciate the fact that I live in a different world from the one I used to inhabit. What I now consider to be an ordinary day I could not even have imagined eighteen years ago. This is not just because of my ability to see forward and backward in time and space, not just because of my ability to communicate with other forms of energy, but because I live in a little pool of peace and joy that nothing ever really disturbs. It is a place we are all meant to discover and inhabit during the journey through physical existence. ෴

Appendix A

ભ

Steps Toward an Evolving Self

THERE ARE MANY WAYS TO ACCELERATE THE EVOLUTION OF YOUR MIND and consciousness. The acceleration brought about by kundalini is only one path. For instance, you could begin to develop consciousness using the old and time-honored way of quieting the mind such as meditation. You could begin using affirmations and visualization, both of which are forms of creative prayer. You could begin cleansing the body via fasting, so it works better and thus offers clarity of consciousness; or practice solitude and sacrifice, both exercises in unselfishness, which will strengthen and bring you to whole new perceptions of reality.

You could dedicate a week, a month, or a year to the service of some worthy cause, which becomes a form of sensitivity- and behavior-training, and which will alter your reality in fundamental ways. Or you might search for models and teachers, putting yourself under their tutelage, being a ready student when the teacher appears; as well as many other possibilities.

Whether you experience a singular, explosive evolution, or carefully and deliberately accelerate the evolution of consciousness, you are inviting change into your life as you open to an acute level of awareness. The reason for this is that evolution opens the heart and once this has happened, it is difficult, perhaps even impossible, to reverse the process of advancing enlightenment that follows. Thus, sensitivity continues to expand and eventually you come to the understanding that we all communicate completely at the feeling level, and easily experience the physical conditions, emotions, thoughts and intentions that others have.

The biggest problem once you reach this point is dealing with the social conventions that have taught you to bridge the gap between yourself and others by ignoring these things. You have been taught to *not* notice, *not* respond, *not* say or do anything, and *not* care, and you will discover you have to work quite diligently to do this. It takes just as much time and energy to shut these awarenesses out, as it does to acknowledge them, perhaps more, because miscommunication is almost certain when you overlook what others are really experiencing.

As you become more sensitive and your awareness expands, you may spend a tremendous amount of time and effort learning *how* to acknowledge what you are aware of. If you did not grow up with adult models that demonstrated the everyday use of intuitive awareness and how to manage this information, you may stumble badly, invading others' boundaries, frightening them, or alienating them with your carelessness as you decide what information to acknowledge.

Once you get used to acknowledging what you know, you will discover you really don't know how to respond. You end up asking yourself, 'Should I take action... which words should I use... what tone of voice, hand motions, body language, and eye contact will best communicate without invading, manipulating, or embarrassing others?' Patience and a sense of right timing develop as you learn and integrate these things.

Evolution of your consciousness results in an increase of the effects of *natural intelligence*, and a pronounced gravitation toward peace, health, and practical balance. You may have difficulty supporting or being involved in activities that run counter to peace, health, or joy.

Whether your activities are something you want out of, or you are not involved in something and want to get involved, you will find that how you spend your time can change quite a bit. The result is an improved quality of life in all areas, but first there may be difficulty or argument as your old interests begin to pale and you move in new directions, sometimes leaving people behind rather than fight with them.

cs

Shaping Reality

To develop a better picture of how you create your reality, imagine you are standing in a huge white cloud. A cloud is basically a gathering of droplets of water. Now imagine that each one of these droplets holds some kind of activity or stimulus that you can turn your attention to and focus on.

In one droplet is a bed with you sleeping in it, in another is food. In another is a drive along the lake, and in still others you see yourself driving to work, making love, having a tooth pulled, daydreaming, taking a plane trip, arguing with a co-worker, dancing, or fishing. Each droplet is a 'center of interest' and together they create a whole world of possibilities. Imagine next that you could create any kind of reality with all sorts of experiences and events simply by connecting the droplets any way that suits your fancy. Your attention and where you put it is the means by which you connect these dots; therefore what you pay attention to becomes your reality.

If you gather up a few droplets and keep going back to put your attention on only those droplets, you will quickly become bored. Your awareness, as well as communication, will be seriously limited. In an effort to make life more interesting and tolerable, you may end up trying to distort what is happening with those few droplets in order to provide your self with a little change, but essentially your range of experience stays pitifully small. The biggest loss is that by staying focused on just those few droplets, you will be unaware of important experiences and information outside those drops that would increase both the power of your mind and the creative functions of consciousness.

However, if you go on to explore and connect thousands of droplets, then your reality will be much different and your awareness greatly expanded. By continually adding droplets and developing new definitions of meaning and relevance among them, reality becomes an ever-new experience and boredom is unknown. Your awareness continues to expand, increasing the power of your mind, your communication skills, and your grasp of the reality you are immersed in. You come to understand that *the reality of an individual is defined by his or her perceptual habits.* You also see that when it comes to perception, no one can point a finger at someone else and say "He did it to me!" The truth is, perception is something you do to yourself.

No one can force you to point your perception toward any particular center of interest. However, there are subtle rewards for many of our perceptual habits. The promise of money, food, power, influence, romance, sex, freedom, friendship, possessions, health, esteem, unique-ness, status – these are only a few of the rewards, not to mention the most powerful reward of all, that of being 'normal' and admitted as a bona fide member of the reality. If there is any tragedy to being human, it is that most of us are caught in unproductive habits of perception and undeveloped consciousness.

Paying Attention

If you want to develop your mind and consciousness, a good place to start is by paying attention to the details of your everyday consciousness. Begin to notice who or what you are giving your attention to, and ask yourself "How do I feel about the interaction (or information, or experience) that I have when I talk with that person (or think about that subject, or get involved in that activity)?"

If the interaction, information, or experience brings you or the other people involved anything other than joy, then there is work to be done to discover what sort of mis-creative thought is involved.

When you are at work, driving your car, talking to someone, or vacuuming the floor, ask yourself, "Am I where I want to be? Is my mind in the same place my body is? What kind of perception am I having? How does it make me feel?"

Assess how much time you spend on those kinds of perceptions and having those kinds of feelings. Is it a minute now and then? Is it half your day? Constantly? Every time you run into that particular friend? Each time you listen to certain music or engage in a specific activity? All the time?

Then, regardless of your reasons or excuses, ask yourself "Why does it feel that way, or why do I think these things? Why do I see it that way?" Don't bother asking, "Why does he (or she, or anyone other than yourself) see it that way?" Focus on *yourself* and your reasons for being or doing.

Look for answers both in you and around you. Is the feeling a habit? Is that how you were taught to think and feel about such situations? Is it self-pity? Is it the music on the radio influencing you? Is it the influence of a particular neighbor? A co-worker? Is it something about your job? Whatever it is, figure out how to change it if it doesn't bring joy.

Laws of Consciousness

Back when I first began to monitor my perception and give myself directions to 'see this' or 'do that,' I had only marginal success for a long time. It seemed that my mind would tease me with bits and pieces of information, but the full answer or experience was often just out of reach. Still, I continued to study my own mind, to track the threads of experience that I hoped would lead to the desired information or outcome. Then one day I asked myself why I was getting partial answers, bits and pieces. The answer that came from my own mind was to sit down with a pencil and paper and write down all the reasons that came to me.

And the 'reason' that came to me as I wrote was, *'The first law of mind is loyalty to the existing organization of the body/mind system.'* Once an individual body/mind has been created, once consciousness has been programmed and set in motion, from that point forward, loyalty to the individual is in effect and will prevail. Only when the pressure to change has built up sufficiently, or found a relatively non-threatening way to integrate the information and make the change, or suddenly makes good sense to you will you really be open to new ideas. If you see the effects of those ideas as frightening or destructive, you can remain blocked.

This loyalty is *very* protective of you as an individual. However, it can operate in ways that are troublesome. The troublesome side is that precious little information is admitted to consciousness if it threatens the beliefs, balance, or existence of the individual. The mind tends to protect and nurture an individual body/mind at all costs. Present patterns and habits of consciousness are maintained until, little by little, enough experience has accumulated to allow you to grab onto something whole and steady, even if it is not yet altogether comfortable and familiar, thus allowing the transition to be made with a minimum of pain or chaos.

Good examples of this are found in people who have witnessed some traumatic scene or suffered some shocking incident. Sometimes the scene of the trauma is completely erased. Sometimes even the day before and the day after are obliterated as well. Occasionally awareness of the entire individual history and personality are blocked, as in complete amnesia.

Nightmares are another good example of the mind's protective mechanism. When you are dreaming and you run into something too terrifying, you simply exit the dream by waking up and returning immediately to the realm of consciousness you inhabit in your daytime reality. People who faint when something shocking happens are abandoning their waking consciousness in an attempt to block awareness. And those involved in serious or fatal traffic accidents will often pop out of the body instantly, avoiding the pain and watching the efforts of those who try to revive them.

In contrast to blocking, when you are really ready to move on and develop further, your mind will be tireless in its efforts to introduce new experiences, perceptions, and people that will catalyze your development. You can ignore, resist, or poo-poo these perceptions and people in an effort to avoid dealing with such changes, but the mind knows better and never gives up.

The law of loyalty to the organism usually requires that change be introduced to you gradually, or at least with a little warning, much of which is accomplished during sleep consciousness. In the dream state you often practice dealing with something troublesome or terrifying and then, when the actual event occurs, you are somewhat prepared and well-rehearsed. When change and new ideas are introduced gradually, individual tolerances are seldom exceeded, the mind moves gently, almost imperceptibly, to integrate the new information, and the result is a slow continuous developmental process within the whole Self.

Because of the mind's protection of the individual organism and its consciousness, our reality ends up being self-reinforcing. Most of it is made up of the habits of perception and the rest arises out of the habits of behavior that follow the perceptions. We think the same things in the same ways over and over, and then we see and hear and do the same things over and over. Inertia prevails until something or someone comes along and affects our perception in ways that push us to change.

Over the years of teaching intuitive development I have been asked again and again what are the simple, everyday things that can be done to develop consciousness in the body/mind. There are several things that can be done quite easily. In fact, they are deceptively easy in that they require so little effort for such a huge gain.

Keep in mind as you take up any of these that the first steps taken to return you to joyful equilibrium and balance upon the earth quite often upset the balance that you think you have created. So be patient if things come apart.

First...

Pay attention to what is going on in and around the body at the same time you are paying attention to what is going on in the mind.

The body and mind are two intimately connected feedback systems representing both sides of you as an objective-subjective individual. A friend once told me that she went to the bank one day to draw $5,000 out of her savings account at her husband's insistence. He had found a business deal that he was sure was a good investment. When it was time to sign for the money her whole body began to shake and sweat profusely. Her knees refused to hold her up, she began to be irritated with herself for feeling faint; and even after taking a brief break and getting a drink of water, it was only with extreme effort that she was able to get her name written in a legible fashion and leave with the money.

This turned out to be a wonderful example of body and mind trying to tell her something. Mind, which reaches into any place and time, already knew the outcome of this 'investment' and tried to get a message across via the body. Only when it was too late did she discover that he had not invested the money in the profitable business deal he had told her about. Eventually, this caused such a strain that the marriage fell apart and she was out one husband and one savings account. Although this is one of the more dramatic examples, even with very little practice you will find that paying attention to both body and mind at the same time results in a high degree of awareness which is basic to developing any kind of skill.

In another practical and more common example, let's say you recognize the momentary flash of a particular kind of discomfort. This is your own body's signal for the onset of a cold and flu, and the first moment you begin to feel less well, you begin making changes in your schedule and daily routine.

Seeking to get back to feeling good, energetic, and in balance, you immediately stop eating, increase fluids, soak yourself in a tub of hot water, go to bed early, and perhaps take a day off to rest. If this is done soon enough there will be only a couple of sneezes, an occasional cough and relatively dry eyes and nose. You may still feel tired and have a cold, but the symptoms will be almost non-existent, a phenomena that will hold true for many other physical problems as well.

If you are *not* sensitive to what is happening in your body/mind and you ignore or don't notice that something is taking hold of you, whether it is a cold, a poorly informed financial investor, or a cheating mate, you will generally end up suffering much more than if you had paid attention to the small signals that your mind tried to make you aware of in the beginning.

If you are in the habit of trusting only the material objects in your life, the things you can permanently see, hear, and touch, then it will be a major transition to begin working with something that at first seems as evanescent and wispy as the mind. It is also likely that you have been brought up to either ignore your body, or think of it as something unreliable and fickle. Trust is the first step toward development of full consciousness, the use of natural intelligence, and all the related psychic skills.

As you begin to watch what is happening in the body, and what is going on in the mind at the same time, you will eventually come to see that there is no separation between them, and you will begin to trust that each is an accurate reflection of the other.

When they contradict one another, you have a problem to clear. It could be that you have been taught something that isn't true, you may have a bias or prejudice to eliminate, you could be caught in fears, or something as simple as wanting things to be the way you want them to be regardless of what this means for others. Whatever it is, when you have cleared the problem there will be a return to congruency between body and mind. This congruency is essential if you are going to develop your consciousness, for only as you learn to trust your body will you also learn to trust your mind.

The old saying, 'Charity begins at home' could well be modified here to read 'Consciousness begins at home, in your own body/mind.' Later on, when you begin to do the more deliberate work that requires full use of your expanded abilities, you will not only have two ways of receiving information, you will have two ways of checking that information, one through the body and one through the mind.

Second...

The ability to form a good question and the freedom to ask that question are very important factors in your development.

As soon as you ask a question, your intuitive mind will immediately set to work to orient your attention toward those areas and activities that will lead you to the answer. Whether you ask the question of someone else, they ask a question of you, or you ask a specific question of your self, the mind immediately makes a full effort to produce the information sought. Ideas will drift through your mind, you will notice things you never noticed before, and your attention will shift in subtle ways.

If you ask a question and remain blank, you are often blocking. Perhaps you are not ready to know yet. Perhaps the answer would be too destructive to the present situation or life conditions, and fear of that destruction keeps you from facing what consciousness would like to present to you. Maybe the question is too broad. Or perhaps your life experiences have been too narrow to permit a reasonable answer, one that you will recognize and understand. Sometimes the question is irrelevant and you really have no use for the answer.

Keep in mind as you ask questions that it is important to be clear and simple. If you ask a question or give yourself directions that sound something like, "Please show me some information about my career," and a few moment later your mind is filled with images about a gangster who went to jail for extortion, what does this really tell you about your career? You asked for 'some information,' but how do you apply the information that came to you? 'Some information' could apply in many directions.

Of course, it is possible that consciousness has presented you with a perfect reflection of your life's work, but more than likely you would now have generated more questions than answers. Does the answer reflect how you feel you are treated? Does it say something about how insensitive you are to others? Does it tell you what's coming in your future? Does it refer to the past? Does it reflect what you secretly think about the company you work for, or does it express what a hidden part of you feels should be the reward for your work? Does it tell you that if you don't make a change you will end up doing something illegal or dishonest and then have to suffer the consequences? Does it tell you that you feel trapped in work that you do not feel is worth doing?

Because you didn't really ask a specific question, you will have great difficulty recognizing a helpful answer and would most likely dismiss the whole answer as a bunch of gobbledy-gook. To be specific, the question might have been framed as, "Show me the future of my career," or "What do I need to know about my boss, Mrs. Smith?" Or "What is the best way to get a raise?"

The best way to set about forming a specific question is to first acknowledge what you already think, feel, and know about the situation you want clarified. Do not dismiss what you know and feel as if it is not valid and the only thing that is valuable is some strange, outlandish psychic message dredged up by some unfamiliar mechanism of consciousness!

Most 'psychic' questions and their answers simply reinforce the truth of what you already know and feel. The real power of asking a good question comes when you are just checking, just asking for clarification about something you think you already know and feel, and the resulting images that appear in your mind indicate something counter to what you think you know. This is often the first clue that there are hidden forces and factors working, the outcome may not be what was hoped for, and thus you should begin to examine the situation in greater detail.

Again, survey all that you know, and carefully decide specifically what else you would like insight into or information about. Then make your question or directions as specific as possible. For example, if you are a businessman who is just about to sign a contract, you might ask, "Once this contract is signed and implemented, how am I feeling about the contract six months from now?" Or perhaps you want to know, "What financial (or staff, or buildings, or tooling) impact will I be experiencing three (or six, or twelve) months from now?"

If you are a teacher and are having trouble with a particular student named Sue, you might sit quietly then ask, "Show me exactly what I must do to connect with Sue."

If you are a doctor or medical person and a patient named Albert is not responding to the treatment you are giving him, clear everything else from your mind then ask, "What does Albert need right now in order to begin healing?" When the ideas and images begin to come to you, it is essential that you write them down, trust yourself, and carry them out.

Another tip when forming questions is to ask one question at a time. Do not ask several unrelated questions at one time, or when an answer comes in, you may not know which question to apply the answer to. And when you're just beginning, keep a written record of each question and its answer.

Third

It is essential to be able to recognize, organize, and understand the symbolic information contained in 'frames of reference.'

From morning to night every day of your life, you move your attention among visual, auditory, kinesthetic, olfactory, gustatory, or other sensory information coming at you from the surrounding environment. You constantly experience a variety of input, and to each thing you perceive, you attach a meaning such as good, bad, interesting, dull, sweet, scary, worrisome, friendly, unfair, etc. Each set of perceptions, with its attached meaning(s), is called a *frame of reference*. Your mind is filled with perceptions, all of which have been classified in some way. Many have multiple, even contradictory meanings – depending on context, and each frame of reference is symbolic of the people, places, and events you have experienced on your journey through life.

Each frame of reference occurs within a unique context, and this context flavors and modifies the frame of reference, adding to the meaning you have already given it. For example, you probably have memories of your first love, and maybe a popular song at that time became 'your song' for a while. If just this small example, there are several frames of reference: one is the name of the person you loved, another is the face or personality of that lover, another is the special song you shared. Each of these frames of reference is linked or networked to one another in your brain/mind. They are also linked to a host of other frames that were formed during that same time – the first kiss, a favorite restaurant, the way you danced together, special moments, the issues you argued about, the pain of breaking up.

Your frames of reference form a unique personal history and a symbolic library of the way you have experienced and interpreted reality. They are, for you, symbols of experience to which you have attached all sorts of thoughts and feelings, and these frames of reference are nicely stored in the image banks, sound banks, and sensation banks of your brain. These are the same image, sound, and feeling banks you have been building since birth.

As you study and work with frames of reference you will discover that every single object, perception, action, and person in your entire reality has been cataloged and assigned a meaning. Even those things that you never gave a thought to before have their attached meanings. For instance, water is the symbol of emotion, as well as life itself, windows are a symbol of new perspective as well as 'seeing the light.' An elephant is the symbol of great wisdom, while an ostrich is the symbol of someone that refuses to see what is right in front of him. Depending on how you look at things, a cup of coffee could be either good or bad, homosexuality could be either natural or a curse, a dog could be either a great companion, a symbol of natural instinct, or a symbol of lower life, and finding a lover could be either something anticipated or something forbidden.

In spite of the fact that every human being catalogs reality and assigns meaning from his or her unique point of view, there is an amazing uniformity of meaning in symbolic imagery across all cultures. One of the great discoveries of Carl Jung was that the symbolism of dreams and the development of psychic visions were amazingly similar around the world, regardless of age, background, culture or belief!

The value of learning to recognize and use frames of reference is that, because of your own fears and filtering system, much early psychic information comes to you in the form of symbols found in a string of frames of reference. If you cannot recognize and interpret the information and meaning in these symbolic frames of reference, you will misunderstand the coded message your mind is presenting to you.

Worse, you may think that it did not present a message at all. And in the later stages of your development, even after you are not afraid of direct knowing, the ability to use and understand symbolic information is critical when you are looking for information in a subject or field of study whose language and imagery are unfamiliar to you, perhaps medicine or economics. At times like this your brain/mind will present information in the form of symbols that 'look like... sound like... feel like... or remind you of...' and you will have to interpret and then extrapolate the information that comes to you.

The best way to become skilled in recognizing and interpreting frames of reference is to get a spiral notebook, then keep a written, dated record of your dreams and begin to study them. They are packed full of frames of reference and symbols that are unique to you. If you do this, you will learn more about yourself and the reality you live in than you can even imagine at this point.

Fourth...

You will need to develop a working understanding of time, what it is, and how your sense of time is created.

As you work to develop your consciousness, it is very important that you understand the nature of time; otherwise you will be hampered by your own belief system that is most likely based on the notion that you can only see backwards in time.

Picture yourself in a universe full of wave frequencies moving in every conceivable direction. Some of these wave frequencies carry information that happened in our physical reality six thousand years ago, some carry information that happened two weeks ago, and some carry information that is happening right now. In addition, some carry information that will not happen in physical reality for five months or ten years, and many carry information that will not happen in our physical reality at all.

Because Absolute Space is almost empty of matter, it is considered a vacuum, and motion continues without interruption when in a vacuum. Each frequency wave carries information, and will continue moving through space without interference, effectively forever. These frequencies make the illusion of time possible. As you stand in the middle of this frequency soup, you simply cannot put your attention on everything at once, so you focus on one place and time by tuning your brain waves to perceive what is happening there.

When you shift the focus of your brain waves to another spot, and then another, and another, the result is a sense of passing time due to the movement of perception from one piece of information to the next. Everything within our reality is formed from frequency waves that occur within a fairly narrow band of the frequency spectrum, and expanding your ability to shift and tune your brainwaves to a wider range of frequencies is not only the key to an expanded consciousness, it is the secret to moving around in 'time.'

To move around in time, you must be able to momentarily quiet your mind. To quiet the mind you must stop thinking, worrying, planning, hurrying. This is why meditation is so valuable. It teaches you to quiet the mind when you need to.

One of my favorite paths to inner quiet is to breathe deeply while I turn my attention inward to the center of myself and imagine I am looking at a large, clean whiteboard. You can use whatever method works for you, but once you are quiet, you give yourself directions to tune into some other person, place, time, event, etc. Immediately, sometimes even before you have finished giving the specific direction, the brain begins its usual business of forming pictures, sounds, and sensations related to whatever you gave yourself directions to see or know. In fact, when you have given yourself directions or asked a question of any kind, be ready to hear the answer instantly! If you sit there and expect answers to come slowly floating past on a banner drawn by a dirigible in the sky, you will have already missed the message. The brain quickly fills individual awareness with an avalanche of information and you will find that an important part of development is teaching yourself to be ready for the incoming information.

In other situations, let's say when an odd picture flashes through your mind, when you hear a voice talking in your head, when you get a funny feeling that runs counter to the way you would normally expect to feel about a situation – Stop, Look and Listen! When you're under pressure to make a decision, and you get the feeling that you just have to close your eyes and back off a minute or two – do it! Take the time to pay attention to and listen to yourself. By letting your mind take over for a moment and feed you information from the past, the future, or the hidden background, you will discover a magic truth – that a part of you is tuned in to a far broader range of knowledge and information than you think, and that unknown Self is truly wishing to work with you.

Fifth…

Develop the ability to shift your brainwave frequencies at will and to move among beta, high beta, alpha, theta, and delta frequencies.

The various electromagnetic frequencies at which your brain operates determine what kind of conscious awareness you will have. The range of frequencies that your brain moves through every day are:

High beta (roughly 30-40 cycles per second)

Beta (roughly 12-30 cps)

Alpha (from about 8-12 cps)

Theta (from 4-8 cps)

Delta (from 0-4 cps).

These frequencies constitute the normal range of human brain operation.

The two important facts to be aware of here are that your perception changes as your brainwave frequency increases or decreases. So if you can learn to shift your brainwave frequency, you will be able to alter your consciousness and also have access to a much broader range of information.

Each frequency is not only connected to a much broader range of harmonic frequencies outside the normal channels of perception, each is also particularly good for accessing certain times and kinds of information. Although any frequency can be used to access any time and place, I have found that high beta is especially good for accessing the future, while beta is most useful in the present and for completing practical tasks. Alpha is good for light creativity, for healing, and for moving across reality to access parallel realities and the past. Theta is excellent for moving out of the body, for deep creativity, for deep healing and restructuring of the personality, for viewing past lives, and for re-experiencing any part of the past.

In delta your everyday conscious awareness is basically not available. This very low frequency is known as 'slow wave' sleep and is used mostly for quieting the body during synthesis of the delicate molecular chains and structures that are necessary for cellular repair, replacement of essential nutrients, and replenishment of brain chemicals.

A favorite example of how your perception changes as your frequency changes can be found in the following situations. Let's say you are sitting at the table with your three-year-old and he spills a glass of milk which splashes across the surface of the table and over the edge onto your leg. In high beta, which is a very energetic, sometimes 'hyper' frequency, your response would often be to gasp in startled horror, jump up frantically, and yell at the child while running frantically to get a dishcloth, possibly knocking over other things on your way.

In beta, you would be more likely to simply run for the dishcloth, intent on wiping up the milk before it goes any further. In alpha it is likely you would have a quick premonition that the glass was in a poor spot, and when it went over you might say calmly, "I knew that was going to happen," while you walk over to get the dishcloth and return to wipe up the milk.

In theta, you would probably sit there in your chair and stare at the milk running down your leg, noticing how it feels and wondering how far it will run once it hits the floor; while in delta you would not know that the milk was spilled at all; your consciousness would be elsewhere.

Each brainwave state not only changes your perception about what is happening at the moment, it changes what you notice about that moment, your inner judgment of the event, and your external or behavioral response as well.

Learning to shift your brainwave frequencies not only changes your experience of the reality you are currently in, it opens the door to other realities and moving about within them. If you do not have the guts to explore your present reality in great detail, you will not have the strength to explore any other realities. The whole business will simply be too frightening.

At first you may have to go through an entire relaxation exercise to get to the various levels of consciousness. But after a while, you will find that you have developed a high degree of flexibility and can simply blink your eyes and be in alpha, or close them and move beyond high beta.

To get some idea of these different levels of brainwave activity, sit on the sofa or at your desk in the middle of the day with your eyes open. Notice the room around you, the TV or the telephone, and be aware that you are most likely in beta with attention directed toward the external world.

Now close your eyes. For a minute or two you may remain in beta, but then your brainwaves will begin to slow down. You will begin to notice every little sound around you. These sounds will seem to be unnaturally loud, and this is a signal that your brainwaves are slowing still further. Sometimes there will be a click or series of clicks, but not always, and when you begin to be comfortable just listening to the symphony of sounds in the surrounding environment you are dropping through alpha.

Continue to sit there listening to the sounds and letting your mind wander. Sometime later your body may jerk, or you may notice that it begins to feel heavy, sometimes extraordinarily so. When it does, you are moving into theta. If it is the end of the day and you continue to sit there you will probably become extremely drowsy and want to go to sleep. If it is the beginning of the day and you are well rested, you may enter theta and see a small helpful vision which may appear much like a piece of a dream. You might also have a bright idea that will provide the solution to a recent problem. If you fall asleep for any length of time, you will eventually enter delta, the frequency in which the only consciousness is that which is inherent in your cellular form, which in your case is the human form and the basic thought that maintains your physical being.

Sixth ...

Affirm to yourself, over and over, that you are accelerating the evolution of your Self to its full potential.

We all talk to ourselves constantly. Most of what we tell ourselves is awful. Things like "I can't do that..." or "My mother would roll over in her grave if she knew that I..." or "That's too heavy (too much effort, too painful, too expensive, takes too long)," or "I wouldn't know where to begin..." are simply negative and unproductive reinforcements of the reality you currently live in.

One of the great gifts of developing your Self is the increasing freedom from the limitations of your present reality. Reality is a construct built by you, and reinforced by both yourself and others. It need not be so restrictive. Even if you never get to the point of exploring other realities or moving about in time, you can at least experience the tremendous expansion of the reality you were raised in by simply moving a few of the boundaries.

Get a notebook, or create a section at the back of your Dream Record, and begin to write down all the things you don't like about yourself, can't do, or are afraid to think about.

Once they are *all* written, as many as you can think of, turn to a fresh sheet of paper and begin transforming every single negative statement that you wrote, making it into a positive statement about yourself. Do not use negative words like *no* or *not* to create positive statements. For example, if you have a statement that goes something like "I hate my boss," don't change it to "I do *not* hate my boss." Leave out the negative '*not*' and instead create a statement that goes something like, "I appreciate the way my boss is pushing me to be smarter/more productive/stronger/ more aware of who I am." Or maybe, "I appreciate the strength of mind my boss has," perhaps, "I know there is a great boss for me somewhere."

When you have finished transposing all the negative statements into positives, read the entire list of positive statements out loud to yourself. Read them regularly for a while, perhaps once or twice a week for several months. Then stop reading them for two months. Then read them regularly again for another couple of months, adding or amending them as desired. Then stop again for two months. At the end of a year you will notice deep changes in your assessment of yourself.

There is another thing you can do along the same lines. At the same time you are transforming every single statement of fear or worry into something good, start another section and write down all the things you would love to experience within the expanded reality you know exists but haven't experienced yet.

For instance, if you would love to develop clairvoyance, or maybe the ability to see the electromagnetic field around people, you might write a statement that goes something like, "My vision sees into all times and places" or "My sensitivity to the electromagnetic aura around people is growing every day and becoming more obvious to my eyes," or "Every time I relax, I see the lights around people and things."

When you have written as many things as you can think of, your last statement, after all else has been covered, should be "*I Am* love." Read these out loud to yourself at the same time you are reading your positive statements. Stop for two months, then begin again, following the pattern described above.

Begin to watch for coincidences, for synchronicities, for moments of clairvoyance or precognition, or times when your sixth sense is operating. Since almost everyone is naturally kinesthetic, you may find yourself saying, "I just have a feeling…" (about something, or that something is going to happen). Write down every instance of expanded perception that occurs, along with the date and time. When you no longer have time to write all that is happening, you will know for sure that your mind is opening wider and wider.

There are many exercises that can be used to accelerate your development and those outlined here are only a start. If most of the above information is just 'words on paper' without clear meaning, if you have no idea of how or where to begin, then you would be best off with a good teacher who will create experiences that open your consciousness and teach you what you are capable of.

Do not fall into the trap of looking for a single teacher or guru that you can follow for the rest of your life. Instead I would encourage you to experience as many teachers as possible, for each one has something to teach you. The bad teachers will teach you to appreciate the good teachers, and the good teachers will move you into deeper awakening and understanding every time you get together. Eventually you will become familiar with the workings of non-local reality and for the most part you will become your own teacher. When this occurs you will know you have truly evolved a long, long way. ෬

Appendix B

ෆ

Analyzing Dreams
Helps You Understand
How You are Using Your Consciousness
To Create Reality

EVERY NIGHT WE GO TO SLEEP AND ENTER INTO THE WORLD OF dreams, but not everything that happens there is 'just a dream.' Much of it is experience that you enter into in realms and realities outside the frequency bands of space-time, and which your brain then tries, via the 'dream,' to translate this into images and symbols that can be understood by you, once you are awake. Using the millions of perceptions already stored in your brain, your mind pieces together a representation of what you experienced using the thoughts, feelings, sound of, and meanings attached to each symbol or frame of reference.

When you are in the sleep state and out of the body, you are in the world of non-local reality. Although you may try to follow the rules of space-time reality while dreaming, you are not bound by these rules. Since dreaming is the basic process of consciousness by which reality is created, our excursions into other dimensions are an effective way to speed up the development of consciousness. This is why it is important to pay close attention to what happens during your dream experiences - it tells you clearly exactly what you are doing with consciousness!

All individuals manage their consciousness and create their reality congruently in both the waking state and the sleep state. This means that your dream experiences will have just about the same problems, qualities of character, shortsightedness, successes, and accomplishments as your waking experiences. If you can make advances in any of these areas while you are dreaming, you will find that what you learn often transfers nicely to waking consciousness, and vice versa.

Once you learn to manage your dreams a little better, you will discover the added benefit of being able to practice all sorts of things while in the dream state with greatly increased creativity, less energy expended, no money spent, and relatively little interference from family, friends or your traditional ruts. What's more, it seems to add hours to your day, and creates a seamless reality.

To develop your skills in understanding frames of reference – which are the language of energy – and with dreaming as well, you must learn to remember your dreams and write them down. Do not try to tell yourself or anyone else that you never dream because this is absolutely not true. Everyone has dreams and it is natural to remember them. If you do not remember them and seldom have, this is simply an indication that you are somewhat lazy with your mind or deficient in several vitamins and trace minerals, especially Vitamin B-complex.

To reinforce and support the idea that you can remember dreams, put a notebook or clipboard, a pen, and a flashlight beside your bed. Then, every night sit down on the edge of the bed for a few minutes and tell yourself, "I will remember my dreams… It is easy for me to become aware of my dreams… I am clear and lucid during my sleep consciousness." Picture yourself waking just enough to make a few notes to trigger your memory in the morning, and then climb in for the night. When you wake in the night just after a dream, try to at least jot down answers to the basic questions Who? What? and Where? If you can write more, include When? Why? and How did I feel?

Besides noting the people and the actions that happen in your dreams, it is also very helpful to make notes about the overall mood of the dream. Sometimes there is a vague aura of anxiety, sometimes a wondrous awe, a sense of fear, feelings of boredom, those of foreboding or excitement. Also note how the scenes change. Are these changes chaotic and confusing, or do they seem to progress naturally, sensibly, and congruently? These are all very important indicators of how you feel, how you perceive reality, and about the background forces that tend to work on you and color both perception and action.

The frames of reference created in dream experiences are powerful additions to your reality. They are stored in the brain just as everyday physical experiences are. These experiences then become part of the image banks, sound banks and feeling states that were created way back when you were in the *mental operations* stage of your development and that undergo continual expansion and modification throughout life.

All frames of reference become part of the spatial and chronological networks of your perception; things learned while in the dream state become useful skills in everyday life, and things understood during dreaming become helpful perspectives when in the waking state.

Your mind has wide access to all the information and experience found in the space-time continuum, and nowhere is this more apparent than in the sleep state. The following dream and its analysis will give you an idea of how to approach the study of dreams and begin to understand the information your mind is trying to share with you. This dream is taken from my Dream Record and offered me the information that the relationship I was basing my whole future on was going to come to an end. If I had known enough to understand what dreams were for, and how to learn from them, I might have been able to save myself almost two years of frustration and heartbreak.

> Date: Tuesday, Feb. 5, 1980
>
> Directions: None given
>
> Type: Cartoon Dream
>
> "There were two small bears, brown ones, living near my Grandma's house in a large game preserve. One was dressed as a male. He wore blue jeans and a checked shirt. The other was a female. She wore a cotton print shirtwaist dress. They could talk and think and acted just like people.
>
> "He, the male, got outside the game preserve one day. I'm not sure if he was lost or just really unwilling to find the way back in. He met or found the female who was also outside the preserve. He complained a lot about everything. He was hungry and he was frightened and needed help, or protection, or to be taken home, and a list of other things.
>
> "The little female bear just listened and smoked her cigarettes, was cool, calm, and unmoved by his inactivity or efforts to take care of himself. But she never left him. Once he begged her for something, either a cigarette or a cinnamon stick, and she was about to share it when he said something. She slowly and deliberately, without taking her eyes off him, put it back in the pocket of her dress and continued to watch him silently.

"He continued to complain and whine. Occasionally a tall, dark-haired man named Ahab would go hunting with a gun and one day he and a companion saw the two bears. The tall man, Ahab, aimed his gun at them but I don't think he ever pulled the trigger. It seems like the shorter companion intervened or somehow they (the bears) were transported back into the game preserve.

"The sense of this place was fantastic with miles and miles of green forests and fields, rivers and mists, bushes and many vines, all like virgin land and all protected and surrounded by a high fence. The female stayed near the male but refused to listen to his complaints and he got weaker and weaker.

"One day she looked inside a tent-like covering he was sleeping in and he was nothing but bones, just a skeleton, yet she was not upset or sad. She knew that he had chosen and also that he was alive.

"Then she was in the house, now as a person, with her sister, Pam, and her daughter, Nell. I'm not sure but either they were coloring or doing some art activity. I vaguely recall taking something out of a box and then later cutting a round hole in the ceiling. Some copper, either a pole or a pipe or something was being worked with or used. Woke when the alarm went off."

Now let's take the above dream apart and examine each frame of reference as an experience designed to inform and prepare me for better functioning within my daily reality, which in this case involved both my present and my future.

There were two small bears	=	Two grouchy people who are still small, not grown up yet; also refers to two people who may just be able to 'bear' staying together, they are only putting up with one another.
brown ones	=	Not bright and cheerful, brown is often thought of as a muddy color, dull and drab. Brown is also the color of business, so they may be in business together.

living near Grandma's house	=	Grandma is my symbol for old-fashioned values and commitments. The bears did not have old-fashioned values or commitments, although these values were 'near,' or in their background.
in a large game preserve.	=	The game here refers to the mating or marital game, and also refers to the games people play, along with the possibility that the relationship is only a game, not real.
One was dressed as a male.	=	The man playing the role of husband.
He wore blue jeans and a checked shirt.	=	The jeans are work clothes implying labor and sweat. The checked shirt symbolizes indecision and checkered ideas, not solid ideas.
The other was a female.	=	The woman playing the role of wife, indicating that the relationship is similar to a marital situation.
She wore a cotton print shirtwaist dress.	=	Simple, cheap clothing indicating that she may be selling herself cheaply; the shirt-'waist' dress symbolizes dressing oneself in something that is 'wasteful.'
They could talk and think and acted just like people.	=	This phrase speaks for itself but suggests that the 'realness' of each was hidden behind a facade. It also indicates that they thought they were thinking and acting like any other people would think and act.
He, the male, got outside the game preserve one day.	=	The man playing the husband role stopped playing the game, a serious development in any relationship.
I'm not sure if he was lost or just unwilling to find the way back in.	=	It was unclear why he stopped feeling the way he used to feel but several factors may have been instrumental in this.

He met or found the female who was also outside the preserve	=	The one filling the wife role is also not making much effort in the relationship, or may have stopped believing that it can last. This also implies that he may have 'found' or learned that she was unwilling to play his version of the mating game; perhaps she wanted to be more real.
He complained a lot about everything.	=	Gives a clue as to what the nature of his communication is and the fact that he is dissatisfied about a lot of things.
He was hungry… frightened… needed help… protection… or to be taken home and a list of other things.	=	Indicates that he was a man who wanted something but may have been afraid to go after it alone. He wanted help, probably from the female, and expected to be protected from failure. Or, he was staying with the female because he wanted someone to take care of his house, meals, and other details of living.
The little female bear smoked her cigarettes, was cool, calm, and	=	Smoking cigarettes is the symbol for burning money, letting it go up in smoke without care or concern for the waste involved. Smoking is also an indication of deep anger, as in a smoking hot anger.
unmoved by his inactivity or lack of effort to take care of himself.	=	She did not try to make him put more effort into the relationship, nor did she point out the things he might have done to succeed.
But she never left him.	=	She did not give up on the relationship either.
Once he begged her for something, either a cigarette or a cinnamon stick	=	He asked her for money or to do something that involved more waste of money. The cinnamon stick symbolizes doing something 'sinful' which means to go *against yourself* in either thought or action.

and she was about to share it when he said something.	=	She at first agreed with him and then he said something that she either didn't trust or perhaps it wasn't honest or right; something that bothered her deeply causes her to pause in her willingness to share the burdens.
She slowly and deliberately, without taking her eyes off him, put it back in the pocket of her dress and continued to watch him silently.	=	Whatever he said caused her to back off, to withdraw from him and to watch him carefully, without leaving or giving up on the relationship. She continues to watch, perhaps hoping things will change for the better.
He continued to complain and whine.	=	He was still not willing or able to communicate effectively.
Occasionally a tall, dark-haired man named Ahab would go hunting with a gun	=	Refers to the driven side of the man as having the character of Captain Ahab. Indicates that he wanted to be in charge, to go out in the business world and make a big splash, catch a big fish, make a whale of a lot of money.
and one day he and a companion saw the two bears.	=	"He and a companion" indicates that there were at least two sides to the man: the business side of him which was characterized as an Ahab, and another side of him. They take a good look at the relationship from another, perhaps more realistic perspective.
The tall man aimed his gun but I don't think he ever pulled the trigger. It seems like the shorter companion intervened	=	The man decided to end the relationship but either did not or could not. The shorter side of him, the side with 'short'comings, the side that was smaller and immature was afraid to say anything.
or somehow they (the bears) were transported back into the game preserve	=	The situation is somehow glossed over and the two bears decide to try again, to renew the relationship.

The sense of this place was fantastic	=	Their illusions about the relationship convinced them that everything was wonderful, fantastic.
miles and miles of green forests,	=	When you are in the forest you cannot see the horizon or what is coming at you. They couldn't see the forest for the trees. The color green indicates both new growth and lack of experience; being green.
fields, rivers and mists,	=	Fields are places both where serious games are played and where things grow; rivers symbolize both constantly changing emotion and the currents of life and experience; mists mean foggy vision.
bushes and vines,	=	Bushes often symbolize a low growth rate, or under-growth and immaturity; and vines symbolize clinging to someone or something.
all like virgin land	=	virgin land symbolizes an area or situation you are not familiar with and have no experience in handling.
protected and surrounded by a high fence.	=	The fence symbolizes that they have returned to an exclusive relationship, that each is off limits to the opposite sex. A fence is also a barrier to letting in knowledge.
The female stayed near the male but refused to listen to his complaints	=	They stayed together but he continued to complain, and expected her to fix things. Also indicates that she refused to hear the seriousness of what he was communicating, or was unable to understand what he wanted.
and he got weaker and weaker.	=	His love and affection grew less and less; his resolve to maintain an exclusive relationship with her weakened.

One day she looked inside a tent-like covering he was sleeping in	=	A 'tent' symbolizes temporary housing, he is only 'camping out' in the house they live and sleep in.
and he was nothing but bones, just a skeleton	=	The heart and soul of the relationship is gone and only the structure of their life remains, a bare-bones structure with no meat, no blood, or life.
yet she was not upset or sad.	=	A clue that this is all going to work out for the best.
She knew that he had chosen and also that he was alive.	=	A clue that his decision is a good one for him and for his own growth and development in his life.
Then she was in the house, now as a person	=	The miserable period of being a bear is over, also a hint that she stays in the house and he moves.
with her sister, Pam, and her daughter, Nell.	=	Two new sides or perspectives of herself come to the foreground: her sister Pam (who lives in Alaska) indicating that she lives in a 'cold state' and her daughter, Nell, a young, immature female.
They were coloring or doing some art activity.	=	The whole painful experience is coloring her life and her activity, she is having to re-create her life anew.
I vaguely recall taking something out of a box	=	Something boxed-in has been set free indicating that the real woman is emerging.
and later we were cutting a round hole in the ceiling.	=	The ceiling is the symbol for the head or mind, it also indicates an ability to move up in life, an expansion of upper limits.
Some copper, either a pole or some pipe was being worked on	=	Copper pipe is used for plumbing, indicating that she is plumbing the depths of her soul. Symbolizes trying to bring new water (new feeling, emotion) into her life but she is seriously 'pole'-arized for or against something and much work must be done. ∞

Sometimes dreams and their frames of reference are not really dreams in the sense we usually think of with lots of hazy, unexplainable scene changes. Instead, they can be simple direct messages that we hear clearly just as we are waking up. After I started to practice dreaming with conscious efforts to manage, direct, and understand them, I began to get information and feedback that was fairly clear, interesting, and sometimes humorous. The following is an example:

> Date: Friday, 11:41 p.m.
>
> Directions: Have a dream telling me whether it is worth it or not to continue working on my Handbook (for psychic development).
>
> Woke hearing only the phrase: "Handbook... a positive idiosyncrasy" in a voice that sounded exactly like that of the *Star Wars* character R2D2.

Although the basic message here is positive, the fact that it was given in the voice of a robot hints that my writing was very stiff and mechanical. The fact that the messenger's voice was one from *Star Wars* indicates that I am struggling with the issue of 'stardom.' I wanted to write, and naturally I wanted this writing to be good, but I didn't want to attract attention to myself as a psychic. I didn't want to be known as a psychic because at that time, I still thought it was just too weird. Therefore, I was trying to make my writing sound scholarly and ponderous and to avoid anything that sounded 'New Age-y.'

When I finally gave the manuscript to several people to read and comment on, I found they thought it was indeed too stiff, too scholarly, and lacked the flow, the understanding, and vibrant feeling I felt about the entire subject. Then someone I respected pointed out that the things I was doing regularly with consciousness and the experiences I was sharing were so far out on the edge, there was no way it was not going to sound like New Age stuff to 99% of humanity. I finally had to say, "It is what it is," and relax a little.

Whether you are interpreting frames of reference from a dream, a brief vision, something that you saw during a private or guided meditation, or as the results of visualization, the process is the same. Write down what you saw, then take it apart, frame by frame.

If you get stuck trying to figure out what something means, read the frame several times in several different ways. Pay attention to the *sound* of the words. The same sound can have many meanings. For example, if you meet someone named 'Mary,' remember that the sound "mare-ee" can refer to being merry, to a side of you that wants to be married, to some kind of union, a partnership or a coming together, or to an actual person named Mary, perhaps a friend, a sister, or co-worker who has certain personal attitudes or characteristics that apply to the situation.

If you are still stuck, just ask yourself, "What does the symbolism of Mary mean?" and go rummaging through all the different ways you could look at the entire frame. If nothing comes to you right away, just let the question hang there in your mind while you go about your work. The answer will come to you later with an 'Aha!' (or maybe an 'Uh-oh!').

As you learn to work with frames of reference you will be surprised at all the different ways your mind has cataloged the experiences you've had. And you will be astounded at the thousands of fine meanings you have attached to all the ordinary things that appear in reality as well as how these meanings change according to context.

For an eye-opening experience, try putting together a written description of some event in your life, using as much detail as possible. For example, describe an event from your childhood, or your wedding and honeymoon, your graduation, a hated job or a beloved career, the birth of your child, or even the course of events of just today from the time you woke up to the time you ate supper. Then take it apart frame by frame and study it. You will learn much about yourself and about perception. ⁊

Appendix C

cs

Elementary Telepathy

THE FOLLOWING PAGES ARE INCLUDED SIMPLY AS EXAMPLES OF THE great ability of mind to reach into any space-time frame and gather information or experience.

In this first set of experiments shown, Jon, the transmitter, had absolutely no training in exercises of this sort, but he readily agreed to try and turned out to be good at it.

Date: January 22, 1981
Time set for transmission: 11:30 to 11:35 a.m.
What was picked up: "Something black… shiny… spinning…"

My drawing:

Actual Object as drawn by Jon:

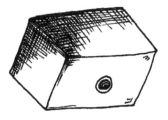

My Comments: "Nothing much came through between 11:30 and 11:35 a.m. except a bunch of female chatter and conversation. Maybe our watches were not synchronized because right before the specified time, about 11:25, when I was relaxing and getting ready, the above picture shown as *My drawing* came through. I was not able to determine what it was."

Jon's Comments: "The object was a small, rectangular piece of steel that I just finish tapping a hole in."

Date: January 23, 1981
Time set for transmission: 11:30 - 11:35 a.m.
What was picked up: "Something dark... or gray... long... thin."

My drawing:

My Comments: none

Jon's Comments: "The object was a black, felt-tip pen.

Date: January 31, 1981
Time set for transmission: 11:30 - 11:35 a.m.
What was picked up: "Many corners... oblong... lightweight... lettering or numbers connected with the object... something you put *in* to other things... boxy... feel a sense of pulling through my neck and shoulders."

My drawing:

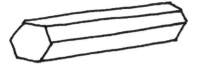

My comments: none
Jon's comments: "The object was a ¼" Allen wrench."

Date: March 25, 1981
Time set for transmission: 11:30 - 11:35 a.m.
What was picked up: "Rectangle... rectangular object... gray color... maybe blue or blue-gray... has lines on it... can look into it or down through it... hollow... supporting..."

My drawing:

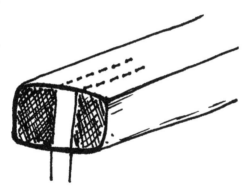

My comments: "I had a hard time picking up anything at first but after a while I had the impression maybe Jon was not sending the transmission as planned and that I was receiving anyway by going inside him and looking through his eyes, seeing whatever he was seeing at that time! Later that day when we met I asked him what he had transmitted to me and he apologized and said he forgot. So I showed him what I had picked up anyway. He got all excited and told me he had worked all day with tubular steel that he was fitting to a fixture as table legs."

Jon's comments: none

Date: March 26, 1981
Time set for transmission: 11:30 - 11:35 a.m.
What was picked up: "Heavy for it size... cone... cone-shaped object... like a pyramid."

My drawing:

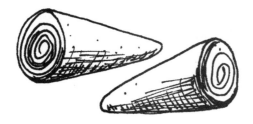

Jon's drawing:

My comments: none
Jon's comments: "The object was a triangular-shaped piece of steel.

Appendix D

ℭ𝔖

Ongoing Exercises in Telepathy

THESE EXERCISES IN TELEPATHY WERE CONDUCTED AS PART OF ONE OF my ongoing teaching programs focused on developing and using intuition. Each of the three women involved had been in the development program which I was conducting for approximately six months. These exercises deal specifically with the sending of impressions from one mind to another while the object being "sent" was held in the hands and concentrated upon by the sender.

Each woman was asked to take a turn transmitting four objects to another woman who was the 'receiver.' The time allowed for the transmission of each object was five minutes. Both sender and receiver were in the same room. The receiver's back was to the sender who was seated on the other side of the room. The rest of the group was also present to observe. The receiver's impressions were reported aloud during each transmission and recorded as follows...

Series 1

Sender: Esther

Receiver: Donna (Donna's favorite sense channel is visual)

Object #1: a ripe tomato

Donna: "It is something that has bumps on it... it's bumpy... Is it round?... It is orange in color... I have a sort of sweet, acid-y taste in my mouth, is it an orange?... it is soft... is it a peach?... the color is red... is it a tomato?"

(Note: It is important to state here that although each of the women asked questions aloud during the time they were receiving, these questions were actually directed toward their inner Self. Each of the women has worked to develop an internal mechanism for recognizing simple *yes* and *no* answers that come from inside of them, without confirmation or support from anyone or anything external. All observers are instructed to keep very quiet and to make no sounds or movements that might distract the receiver, and there is a rule of absolute silence among them during the transmission. The only talk allowed is an occasional question from myself that pushes them to be more specific, that confirms a correct reception, or that signals when the transmission time is up.)

Object #2: a Phillips-head screwdriver, about 6" long, with a wooden handle, with one black and one red stripe around the handle.

Donna - "It is long and thin... there is silver... is there black?... it is cold and hard... is it a knife?... I see the color of wood... (When asked how long she thought the object was, she said "It feels about 6 or 7 inches")... is there a star connected with it?... a triangle... something triangular..."

Object #3: a brown kneesock

Donna - "Is it big?... it is long... it feels soft, very soft... is it brown?... I feel a tightness in my foot... is it a shoe?... it is big at one end and smaller at the other... it feels tight on my leg... is it a sock?"

Object #4: a gold, plastic comb, about 7" long

Donna - "I'm picking up something that's warm... it is flat... is it yellow?... is it something that has a handle?... it feels like it has two parts, a top part with a smaller handle... is it brown?... is it plastic?

ℂℨ

Series 2

Sender: Cori

Receiver: Esther (Esther's favorite sense channel is kinesthetic)

Object #1: a cream-colored, dried squash gourd

Esther - "It is light in weight... it's like it's bigger at one end and then goes in... it's bigger at one end and smaller... it's a light color, maybe yellow... is it some kind of food?... is it round?... is it squash?"

Object #2: red, cotton pincushion full of multi-colored, glass-head pins

Esther - "I feel it has something to do with the head... is it something to do with the head... is it a hat?... (long silence) I just see dots of red and green and blue... is it a hat? I don't pick up anything... I have a feeling around my heart... (When asked to describe the feeling she said 'I feel like I'm being stabbed, I have a prickly feeling in my fingers.')"

Object #3: a school photo of a young girl

Esther - "I feel it's something big..." (During most of the rest of the transmission she seemed to flounder around and be unable to pick up anything clearly.)

Object #4: an iced-tea spoon with a long, slim, silver handle

Esther - "It is cold... it is something to eat... it is white or silver in color... is it oblong or oval?... is it an egg?..." (When directed to find a part of the body that may have a relationship to this object she said, 'My stomach... it has something to do with food or medicine or something like that.')

଼

Series 3

Sender: Donna

Receiver: (Cori uses a combination of visual and kinesthetic sensing)

Object #1: a red, felt-tipped pen

Cori - "It is round... it seems to be light in weight... it has something to do with the hands... do you use it on your hands?... is it a ring?... it is long and thin... (after a long silence and moving of the hands) Is it a pen?"

Object #2: a metal, gold-colored, screw-on band used on a Mason jar when canning

Cori - "Is it big?... is it plastic?... it appears to be round... is it metal?... it has something to do with my head... is it an earring?... is it brown?..."

Object #3: a small, 9-volt, red, rectangular flashlight battery

Cori - "It is something that is flat... is it something that I would lay across my lap?... (after seeming disoriented) it has something to do with something across my lap... I feel something behind my right eye... behind both my eyes... it is a pulling... and I see sparkles... it is yellow or white in color... it is very bright..."

Object #4: an oval pocket mirror in a plastic, tortoise-shell frame

Cori - "It is something thin... and it feels warm... is it paper?... it has brown on it... is it plastic?... is it round?... it is round... it makes me feel that it's something I don't like to do... I don't get anything now... is it wood?..."

ଔ

The Stages of Human Evolution and Development

Stage	Age	Perception	Successful	Unsuccessful
Sensorimotor	Birth-2 yrs.	Concrete/ Explores Objects	Brain cells well encoded for our space-time reality and the physical world. Learning accumulates; is linked to pleasure. Is secure enough to explore separation. Learning is exciting	Brain cells encoded poorly or in spotty manner. Learning slowed; is linked to stress and insecurity. Fears and avoids separation. Learning is difficult
Mental Operations	2-6 yrs.	Abstract/ Plays, copies	Creates image, sound, & feeling banks. Develops imagination. Develops language & communication skills. Aware of nuances, shades of meaning. Creates preliminary information networks	Development of CNS slowed, delayed. Few images stored = poor spatial skills. Few sounds stored = poor language skills. Few feelings stored = difficult to connect & communicate. Poor neural networks; poor memory & perception
Concrete Operations	6-12 yrs.	Concrete/ Practical survival experience	Experiments using objects & imagination. Has security, can survive in the outside world. Discovers principle of "transfer". Gets organized, confident, self-esteem. Copes with a variety of situations	Limited to original "baby" perceptions. Limited ability to survive on his/her own. No common sense, single solution for everything. Confused by change, world is inconsistent. Cannot cope with more than one demand at a time

Stage	Age	Perception	Successful	Unsuccessful
Formal Operations	12-21 yrs.	Abstract/ Expands life, work, sex	Effort to create his/her own structures & routines Attempts complex activities/outcomes Makes plans for the future Assesses results before taking action Copies successful people & learns from them	Settles for structures, routines, solutions of others Little understanding of how the world works Tries to get by and hopefully get ahead Acts impulsively without assessing results Idolizes one poor role model after another
Concrete Intelligence	21-35 yrs.	Concrete/ Practical structures for living	Is passionate and sensitive Awakens kundalini, discovers intuitive feedback Spiritual development begins Oriented to joy, peace and health Experiments with new ideas from Self Trust and excitement	Is temperamental and selfish Represses kundalini, or if awakened has hallucinations, hears voices, tries to impress others Spiritual development aborted Oriented to pain, self-destruction, death Does what others expect Bitterness, fear, and loneliness
Formal Intelligence	35-50 yrs.	Abstract/ Explores mind	New connections between Self and reality Experiments with thought & manifestation Tames the self, releases remaining fear Invests energy in self-sustaining things Practices inner stillness	Reality gets in the way of wants & needs Life is boring, not enough, blames others Tries to keep up a good front Invests energy in getting power for the self Feels harassed, tormented, anxious, confused
Abstract Intelligence	50 & up	Concrete/ Truth	Deep sensitivity and inner joy Experiments with fluid awareness Experiments with self-transformation Experiences expansion of boundaries Discovers worlds of oneness, joy, health	Deep disappointment, reality becomes unattractive Feels tired, old, and often discouraged Sickness and disability occur Forgets individual identity Abandons body in frightening death

Glossary

CS

I HAVE DEFINED A GROUP OF VERY BASIC TERMS HERE THAT MIGHT BE useful in several ways. First, if you are interested in studying the mind, intelligence, perception, cognition, consciousness, and the abilities inherent in the human being, it is highly likely that you are going to end up running into these terms. If you do not have at least a basic idea of the definition of each, you can end up wrapping these important human skills in ignorance or misinterpretation. When this happens, you will become less effective in your communication as well as your analysis of news, activities, writings, and reports that originate from people and cultures where these kinds of abilities are considered normal and useful.

Second, there is a lot of misunderstanding among the general public about the whole subject of consciousness. Some of these terms have become part of popular culture but are not really understood at all. Some have been dismissed as occult nonsense because the scientific world has been unable to come up with an approach for studying these subjects. In fact, paranormal subjects are classified as paranormal simply because the scientific establishment has been unable to find a way to study these phenomena in such a way that the experimental methods can be controlled and their results can be duplicated by others!

Unfortunately, using this approach will probably go nowhere. These subjects are far too dynamic to be reduced to statistical studies and meaningless attempts to repeatedly influence cards or number generators. As pointed out earlier, Mother Nature does not waste time on duplications; her rule is individuality, diversity, and change.

It is my belief at this time that the only way significant study and statistical results will ever emerge is if a large number of people begin to develop themselves, then share their explorations, results, and observations with one another. In this way, two important benefits occur. The first is that as a solid body of knowledge comes together, it will be framed in the

298   *The Evolving Human*

words and understandings of our time and place, making it accessible to many of us that live in this time and place. The second is that it returns science to its proper place among the ordinary citizens and removes it from the few elite who use it to control others.

Alpha - a term that denotes both a specific brain-wave frequency and kind of perception. In alpha, your brain wave frequency will range from approximately 8 to 12 cycles per second. Perception is a combination of internal and external attention. Alpha is sometimes known as the *daydream state,* and is also called the *level of body regulation,* simply because you must be in alpha to focus your attention at least partially on your internal self if you want to learn to regulate things like blood pressure, heart rate, headaches, epilepsy, etc.

Astral body - sometimes called the *double,* the *light body,* or the *etheric double,* the astral body is part of the human energy system. It is composed of various densities of light and is like a rounded or oval, translucent version of the physical body.

Astral light - in a more technical vein, this refers to light coming from the stars. In a general sense it is often used to refer to the light around the body or to any light that isn't coming from a light bulb and isn't easily explained. Depending on the wavelength or spectral composition, it will be of differing colors.

Astral matter - concerning the word *astral* the dictionary says "… of, pertaining to, coming from, or like the stars; starry." In general, the term *astral matter* is used to refer to finer, less dense types of matter that exist in the universe.

Astral projection - a state of separation between the body and the consciousness. This occurs frequently but usually only for brief periods during the day. At night it occurs for longer periods of time during sleep. When the body is run down, ill, or injured, there is often more separation than usual because it is uncomfortable to stay centered in the body. This term is often used interchangeably with astral travel but the two are not the same. Astral projection is simply stepping outside the body but often staying near it.

Astral world - a term used to refer to most any dimension other than our own reality. It usually denotes a realm or field of conditions where time as we know it does not apply, or where there are other types of beings.

Astral travel - travel of the consciousness without the limitations of the body, time, or space. When you step out of the body you are 'projecting' but when you leave the body to visit your sister on the other side of the continent or enter other realms, you are 'traveling.'

Aura - the electromagnetic field around the body. The Russians call it *bio-plasma*, Mesmer called it *animal magnetism*, Paracelsus called it *vital force*, Karl von Reichenbach called it *od*, and the term used by Jack Schwarz is *bio-luminesence*. When we see part of the electromagnetic field around the earth we call it the 'Northern Lights.'

Beta - another term that denotes both a brain-wave frequency and a kind of perception. When you are in beta your brain waves will be between approximately 12 and 30 cycles per second, and your perception will be focused mainly on the external environment. Beta is a level of considerable physical action and energy.

Bi-location - this is the name given to the experience of being in two places at once, although sometimes it is used to refer to out of the body experiences or astral travel.

Channeled writing - sometimes called *automatic writing*, channeled writing usually refers to writing in which there is no conscious intent to write about a given subject. In general, channeled writing often comes from the more evolved parts of the Self whether they are integrated yet or not. The writer sits down, begins to write, and what ends up being written may range from something totally unfamiliar, to a wonderful synthesis of some kind, to a solution for a bothersome personal problem, to powerful poetry, plays and other insightful material.

Clairaudience - the ability to hear beyond the range of the physical ears. This is a faculty of extra-sensory perception in which sounds are formed in the mind and presented to consciousness for interpretation and meaning. In laboratory research, the meaning of clairaudience is defined as 'paranormal auditory perception of sounds beyond the range of the normal senses.' Clairaudience is often blended with clairvoyance and people with this faculty can often give details of names of both people and places. Musicians and mediums are often clairaudient.

Clairgustance - this is the ability to taste and experience the effects of something without putting it in the mouth or on the tongue. This is a most ancient faculty and was used by our ancestors to avoid poisonous plants, and to find effective plants for healing specific illnesses. It is still used by many animals for finding plant substances they need to maintain health.

Clairnasence - the ability to smell beyond the range of the physical nose. This is another very old faculty of perception and is often displayed in the ability to smell things that haven't happened yet or that happened in a present place but in a past time. Clairnasence was used by our ancestors to find both water and food, and when combined with clairsentience or clairvoyance, is useful for avoiding storms and finding one's way safely when traveling.

Clairsentience - the ability to form kinesthetic impressions of people, objects, etc. beyond the range of the physical hands or skin. This faculty is often described as the ability to feel or sense the conditions of people, places, plants, animals or things without knowing them, touching them, having been there, read, or been told about the conditions surrounding them. This is considered to be the oldest and the most common of all psychic gifts, almost everyone has a little of this.

Clairvoyance - the ability to see beyond the range of the physical eyes. It is a faculty of extra-sensory perception in which images are formed in the mind and presented to consciousness for interpretation and meaning. In laboratory research, the meaning of clairvoyance is defined as 'paranormal visual perception of objects beyond the range of the normal senses.' Artists and writers are often clairvoyant.

Communication - any act that acknowledges oneness or involves an exchange of energy such as speaking, looking, hearing, feeling, knowing, touch, arguing, ignoring, understanding, etc.

Consciousness - generally speaking, consciousness is considered a mystery, but is usually defined as the ability to be aware of your self as a thinking being, to feel and to know what you are doing and why. More technically, it is an awareness of Self-And-Something-Happening-To-Self.

Delta - a term that refers to both a brain-wave frequency and a kind of perception. When you are in delta your brain waves will be roughly between 0 and 4 cycles per second. In delta, individual consciousness seems to be temporarily turned off and there is no perception of either an internal or external nature. Delta is the level of consciousness used by the body to rebuild and repair itself.

Dharma - this term is less well known than its companion, karma, but dharma (the *h* is silent) is thought of in several ways. On the one hand it denotes a state of tolerance that simply accepts *what is*. In other traditions, dharma refers to the period of time *after* you have recognized how you are creating your own troubles, but *before* you are entirely free from the effects already created. In other words, you must live with the results of what you have chosen, wait for things to work out or to pass, and then make new choices.

Dream - a dream is most often thought of as the experiences, thoughts, and activities that you experience during the sleep state. Although you may not remember your dreams, they are important events and usually offer a chance to visit other realms and dimensions of existence.

Frames of reference - this is a bit or piece of perceived reality that answers the questions Who? What? When? Where? Why? and How?

Future - generally thought of as the events and experiences that have not yet happened in physical reality.

Grace - a greatly misunderstood term usually used to refer to vague concepts like benevolence or holiness. Grace is really the western counterpart of the eastern term *kundalini*. References to the *manifestation of grace* are similar to the expression *awakening of kundalini*. Both refer to a great expansion of consciousness and the processes of enlightenment.

Healing - to be made whole and complete, to be comfortable with all of the Self and its aspects.

Intuition - is defined as knowing or knowledge that comes from inside the self rather than through logic or by reason of external events.

Karma - originally an eastern term that referred to the effects or results of our actions, especially when those effects bring suffering or some kind of 'payback.' Karma might more easily be thought of as 'cause and effects' or 'choices and their results. When you have done something that has a poor effect, or you constantly make choices that bring you unhappy results, you are said to be 'caught in karma.'

Kundalini - an electromagnetic event within the body/mind system in which there is an acceleration of electrical current that moves through the body generating a sexual experience that culminates in the brain and that alters the basic operating frequencies of the human being.

Meditation - is the practice of quieting the mind for a variety of reasons. Sometimes it is for health, since lowering your brain wave frequency tends to refresh and renew you, and other times it may be for relief from anxiety and to trigger the relaxation response. Meditation is also used to clear the mind as a preparation for doing psychic work, for moving out of the body, to enhance your control over brain wave states, and to assist in your own development and evolution.

Mind - the awareness property of absolute space whose natural condition is stillness and bliss. In the individual, the conscious mind is a personal collection of thoughts, perceptions, worries, ideas, actions, knowledge, observations, interpretations, and meanings, etc.

Out of body - sometimes called an OBE or OOBE, this is the experience of the conscious self when separate from, or out of the body, while still retaining sensory perception and many linear processing capabilities.

Other Self - also known as the *astral body*, the other self is the part of your being that is capable of leaving the physical body for various tasks; it is the part of you that sees, hears, feels, and knows many things outside the range of the physical body. This is the part of you that visits other realms, and in some cultures, it is powerful enough to take the physical body with it on some of these trips.

Parallel life - is a life experience that goes on at the same time as your present life but in another place, perhaps in a slightly different time frame, or another dimension. Awareness of the parallel life can be such that you end up switching back and forth between them, or they may both run at the same time with one dominating, and the other seeming to be a bit more vague or dreamy.

Past life - this can refer to the childhood of your present life, but usually it refers to lifetimes and experiences that you have had in other time frames in a more distant past. If you have had unresolved issues, traumatic experiences, great love, serious diseases, or the development of unusual gifts and talents in other lifetimes, you will frequently carry the effects of these forward into other lives for one reason or another.

Precognition - this is the name given to instances where you suddenly know something that is going to happen in the future. Sometimes referred to as the '6th sense' or 'having a moment of ESP,' precognition is usually based on a combination of faculties such as clairvoyance and clairsentience, or clairaudience and clairsentience.

PSI – a slang term used to refer to psychic abilities, psychic energies, etc.

Psychic - usually a person who uses or displays psychic abilities. Can also refer to the faculty of being psychic or the extended senses that exist in the body/mind system. In terms of information, intuitive information is knowledge or information that simply comes to you spon-taneously; psychic information is that knowledge or information that you go after in order to be aware, make a decision, get insight, and so on.

Psychometry - a method of paranormal perception discovered by Dr. J. B. Buchanan in 1842 whereby an object, when held by a sensitive person, produces various sensations that convey the nature and history of the object. Psychometry is based on clairsentience and is often highly augmented by clairvoyance and other psychic abilities.

Reality - generally thought of as the world around you, human reality is actually a cooperative construct of our minds that emerges from – yet also helps create – physical experience, cultural experience, and the experience of the individual mind. There are many forms of reality available in many dimensions, but the effort required to maintain existence as a human leaves little time and energy to explore these other realities.

Telepathy - a faculty of extra-sensory perception that allows information, ideas, feelings, etc. to be exchanged between two or more people who, for one reason or another, are not using the more common means of communication such as voice, eyes, touch. Telepathy takes place most often between lovers, between parent and child, or between siblings. It is also common among any combination of human beings, plants and animals.

Theta - a term that refers to both a brain-wave frequency and a kind of perception. When your brain waves are between 4 and 8 cycles per second, you are in theta. Theta is mainly a form of perception in which your attention is focused internally and you are minimally able to respond actively to the external environment. It is sometimes called the state of Perfect Learning, and can be used to help restructure the personality and restore healthy, balanced perception and action.

Time - as we know it, time is simply a mental structure used to divide up the day and the night. But here it refers to the frequencies of long-wave energy that move through space creating intervals. Within these intervals are freestanding fields of activity and form. Time is derived from the rate of the frequencies moving through a given area of space. Time can be thought of as a matrix of frequency waves that maintain physical matter in a particular state, or as a factor in the space-time continuum that by nature of its frequency, defines a given place. By shifting your brain-waves to a particular frequency, you can enter another time and/or place to observe what is happening there. Also, the shifting of attention from place to place gives us our sense of passing time.

Transmodal perception - is described as an occasion when something that would normally be *seen and appreciated visually* is instead perceived with a different sense channel such as hearing, taste, or smell. Sometimes called *cross modal* perception or *synesthesia*, instances such as tasting a sunrise or a mountain, seeing a melody, distinctly feeling a color or smelling a sound are examples of this kind of experience. ❀

Index

R

radio for a mind 53
Raoul 80
reading
  becomes impossible 57
  copying Edgar Cayce 64
reality
  as self-reinforcing 262
  becomes transparent 157
  caught between two worlds 85
  definition of 259
  disappears 22, 72
  no longer able to discern what's real 78
  overlaid with undulating shapes, colors 77
  perception, dreams, reality interchangeable 80
  pink place 76
  realms of the \ 76
red-winged blackbird
  appears at spider's death 56
  first appears 30
religious dogma 170
Rob, the neighbor
  lends book 44
  meeting 43
  takes us to a lecture 87
Roger Sperry 152
Royal Oak, MI. 132
rumbling sound 21, 72, 74, 83

S

science 240
seeing
  auras 95
  a white glove 90
  daughter as geometric form 75
  ghost-like shapes 92
  giant rabbits 79
  lights in factory 40
  little men in brown robes 79
  overlaid shapes and colors 76
  pink elephants 79
  sheet of newspaper 90
  tropical jungles 79
  ugly faces, tormented bodies 52
self-esteem 208
self-incineration 121
senility 237

sensation (feeling states) 206
sensorimotor stage 203
service 257
sexual experiences
  add to confusion 71
  and human evolution 179
  and religious attitudes 178
  become spontaneous 72
  becoming fluid 72
  craving 73
  healing effect of 177
  in air over Ben 68
  raped 83
  rivers of luminescence 147
shopping for year's worth of food 124, 126
short-term memory traces 152
sixth sense 221
sleep
  constant consciousness in spite of 53
  no longer happens 57
  poor sleep begins 43
  problem worsens 53
smell, increased sensitivity of 160
social conventions 257
solitude 257
sound of the words 284
sound/tonation banks 276
space 186
spatial patterns, recognizing 210
Special Theory of Relativity 151
spider, conversation with 54
spine, energy moving up 154
spirit guide 220
stages of human development
  abstract intelligence 226
  chart 295
  concrete operations 206
  creative intelligence 222
  formal operations 208
  mental operations 204
Star Wars character R2D2 284
St. Hildegard 170
St. John of the Cross 170, 171
Story Of Attitudes and Emotions 102
St. Paul 170
St. Theresa of Avila 168
students 134
subjectivity 240
suspended animation 76

www.PennyKelly.com

Penny Kelly is a writer, teacher, author, publisher, researcher, consultant, and Naturopathic physician. She is the owner and director of Lily Hill Farm in southwest Michigan where she teaches courses in *Developing Intuition and the Gift of Consciousness, Getting Well Again Naturally,* and *Organic Gardening.*

She was an engineer for Chrysler Corporation in Detroit, MI and left in 1979 to study the brain, consciousness, intelligence, intuition, perception, and cognition. This led to her work with schools and corporations as an educational consultant specializing in Accelerated and Brain-Compatible Teaching and Learning Techniques.

Penny raised grapes for Welch Foods for more than a dozen years and has been deeply involved in Community Gardening in Kalamazoo and Battle Creek, MI through grants from the Kellogg Foundation. She maintains an international counseling and coaching practice, travels widely to speak and teach, and raises organic vegetables, chicken, and beef.

Penny holds a degree in Humanistic Studies from Wayne State University and a degree in Naturopathic Medicine from Clayton College of Natural Health. She is the mother of four children, has co-written or edited 23 books with others, and has written seven books of her own. Penny lives and writes in Lawton, Michigan.

Lightning Source UK Ltd.
Milton Keynes UK
UKHW04f0618250718
326252UK00001B/117/P